Luvin a Young Ratchet City Boss

Luvin a Young Ratchet City Boss

By

Renessa D Jackson

Table of Contents

COPYRIGHT

COPYRIGHT© 2024 Luvin a Young Ratchet City Boss by Renessa D. Jackson. Unless otherwise indicated, all materials on these pages are copyrighted by Allure Productions LLC. All rights reserved. No part of these pages, either text or image may be used for any purpose other than personal use. Therefore, reproduction, modification, in any form or by any means, electronic, mechanical or otherwise, for reasons other than personal use, is strictly prohibited without prior written permission from the publisher and writer, except brief quotes used in reviews. This is a work of fiction. Any references or similarities to actual events, real people, living or dead, or to the real locals intend to give the novel a sense of reality. Any similarity in other names, characters, places, and incidents are entirely coincidental.

TABLE OF CONTENTS

PROLOGUE

On February 2, 1995, I, Raylexia Gavion, was born prematurely, weighing just 1 lb 9 oz. My mother, Raynell Gavion, was a party girl extraordinaire at 15, and my father, Jaylard Jacoby, was a 21-year-old absent parent. If not for my grandmother, Etta Faye Sizzlyn-Gavion, I wouldn't be alive today. My mom was, and still is, no mom at all. She left me and my brother, Rodereck, with Grandma Etta after we were born.

Money was always tight for Grandma Etta, so we ate whatever was available. She used to say, *"If it runs across that backyard or can be caught in the lake, we're gonna eat it if I catch it."* Our meals consisted of beans, greens, rice, fish, frogs, snakes, rabbits, turtles, and anything else she could catch or grow. *"A free meal is the best when money is low,"* she'd remind us.

Grandma Etta maintained a year-round garden filled with every vegetable, herb, and fruit you could imagine. She sold most of her produce at a vegetable stand to ensure we had clothes and shoes, supplementing the money our uncles sent every month to help cover the bills.

Our years with Grandma Etta were filled with fun and excitement. We had countless adventures in the backyard, climbing trees for fruit, picking vegetables, and helping Grandma Etta clean fish after our trips to the lake. She taught me how to prepare basic meals and how to be cautious around hot grease. Every day after school, I learned new recipes and helped her cook our dinner.

We lived carefree; our biggest worry being getting through the school day to see what adventure Grandma Etta had planned next.

I remember a conversation I had with Grandma Etta vividly.

"Raylexia, I won't always be here to take care of you and your brother. Remember, as long as you have each other, you're not alone. After I'm gone, the responsibility of taking care of him will fall on you until he is old enough to help.

Can you do it, Raylexia? Can you look out for your brother and make sure he's good after I'm gone?" Grandma Etta asked me one day while we sat by the lake cleaning fish.

"I will take good care of Rodereck, Grandma Etta. He is my best friend. I will make sure he's okay," I assured her, and she seemed to relax.

That turned out to be the first of many similar conversations concerning my responsibility for Rodereck. Yet, in my mind, Grandma Etta would always be there.

Royal, Ronlee, Rayvion, and Richmond are our uncles, each serving in the military and all a bit crazy in their own way. Uncle Royal is in the Navy and claims he can move things with his mind. Uncles Ronlee and Rayvion are in the Army, and Uncle Richmond is in the Marines. We didn't see them much while living with Grandma Etta, as they were stationed on different bases and often away on tours. However, they sent money every month to help with the household expenses.

Grandma Etta left our grandpa Jacob years ago because he wouldn't let her be free. He moved her to Detroit, Michigan, expecting her to change and become submissive. She couldn't live under his iron thumb and closed way of thinking, so she left him. He expected her to come back after a couple of years, refusing to support her in the meantime. Too bad he had to find out the hard way that Grandma Etta was a hustler. She left his ass and never looked back.

Rodereck and I never knew what bad times were or that anything was missing in our lives until Grandma Etta passed away while fishing for our next meal. I was only eight, and Rodereck was four. We spent hours at the hospital until Uncle Richmond came to get us. It took him four days to find our mom, but she refused to take us in. To say he was upset is an understatement. He had to call in all his brothers from active duty for the funeral. Uncle Rayvion couldn't make it back in time because he was stationed overseas. By the time he got home, they had already buried Grandma Etta in the family plot.

Grandpa Jacob returned for the funeral, devastated, as he had hoped to win her back one day. Her death showed him that time waits for no one. Unfortunately, the uncles didn't even have time to grieve because they were busy figuring out what to do with Rod and me. Their frustration was palpable.

"This is some straight bullshit," Uncle Rayvion muttered, pacing back and forth in the living room, seething with anger. *"I told you guys a long time ago; Momma should have made that girl take care of her own damn kids. Now look at us, stressing about how to find her and make her take her fuckin' kids. I'm still upset that I didn't even get a chance to properly mourn her or attend her funeral. Yet here I am, trying to make a grown-ass woman take in her own fuckin' kids,"* he ranted, not caring that Rodereck and I were sitting right there.

Uncle Richmond sighed. *"Nigga, did you forget that Mom took those children after they were born because Raynell kept leaving Raylexia in a box under the bed? Raynell is the worst mother in the world, but we don't have a choice right now. We're all stationed too far away to really help with these kids. I'm just afraid of what's going to happen to them living with her."*

"That's my fear as well," Uncle Ronlee chimed in, looking from brother to brother. *"We simply don't have anyone here who can take care of them, and those deadbeat dads she had them with either can't or won't step up. Bricks is in jail, and when I asked Jaylard if he could take Raylexia, he almost made me whip his ass. He said his wife doesn't know about her, and it would cause problems. I told him he should be in jail with his pedophile ass."*

"You guys act like Raynell can't take care of them when we all know the issue is that she won't. That girl doesn't give a damn about those kids; she never has. Mom once told me she goes up to six months without visiting them," Uncle Royal said in a defeated tone. *"We just have to get her over here and let her know she has to take her kids. We can figure something different out later."*

They all agreed and went to find our mom. It took them all their remaining leave time, but when they finally did, Mom didn't argue. To the shock of her brothers, she agreed to take us in.

Talk about going from heaven to hell. We couldn't believe how bad things were living with Mom. There were no more hot meals three times a day or anyone to put us to bed. At the age of eight, I became our sole caregiver. We mostly ate sandwiches because the food Mom bought didn't include anything Grandma Etta had taught me to cook. I made sure we bathed, got to school, and cleaned up the rooms because Mom was still in party mode. Nothing and no one was stopping her flow.

Mrs. Bee, who lived next to Mom in a boarding house on Christian Street, started coming over with food for us to eat. She made sure things were clean and got us to the bus for school when Mom left for days or even weeks at a time. She began helping us after hearing Mom beating me and Rodereck one night when she came home, claiming the rooms were dirty after being gone for weeks.

Mrs. Bee taught me how to wash and dry dishes and tidy up the rooms. She said if there were no dishes in the sink and everything was put away, Mom couldn't claim the space was dirty. She also showed me how to stretch our food by separating the meat and bread for sandwiches, how to ride the city bus to get to the grocery store, and where to pay the light, gas, and water bills. She warned me not to let anyone else in when Mom was gone, as it was dangerous, and people could hurt us.

My uncles met Mrs. Bee, exchanged contact information, and started sending her money to take care of Rod and me when she told them Mom wasn't paying the bills or providing for our basic needs. Mrs. Bee became our lifeline until she passed away two years later. Then we moved into the Jackson Heights Projects.

The first six months living in the projects with Mom were wild. She had about four different men in and out, each serving a different purpose. None of them lasted long or could claim any rights because she was always on the lookout for bigger and better things. She liked to drink, so Jobe brought her two cases of beer every week. She smoked weed, so Frank, the neighborhood dealer, dropped off half a pound every time he re-upped. David brought her groceries since he worked at the food market. Sammy even slid $100 under the door every week, whether she was home or not.

The crazy part was that they all knew about each other. They would be sick when she cut them off, but they never tired of her bullshit; it was always the other way around.

What am I talking about? My mom is that timeless beauty that never changes, no matter how old she gets. With an outgoing personality that captivates and holds a guy's attention, she stands at 5'5" with deep dimples, long, jet-black curly hair, an hourglass figure, and honey brown eyes. Her skin shifts from milk chocolate in the winter to dark chocolate in the summer. Mom doesn't look a day over sixteen and can easily pass for my big sister.

When I was twelve and Rodereck was eight, Mom had our sister Reign. For almost four years, we were happy. Her dad, Raquon, was a low-level street hustler who stayed with us and took care of us like we were all his kids. He cooked, cleaned, washed our clothes, and got us off to school. He even adjusted his hustle schedule to be there for Reign while I was at school, making his money at night.

That all changed a few weeks after I turned sixteen when Mom came home and tried to put Raquon out.

Mom walked in the house at 6 p.m. with a new man. *"Where is Raquon, Raylexia?"* she asked.

"He usually stays out until about 5 a.m., a couple of hours before it's time for us to go to school," I replied, without pausing from fixing Reign's hair for school the next day. Rodereck, Reign, and I had already eaten dinner and were cleaning the apartment, preparing for bed. Rod paid Mom no mind and went to clean the bathrooms. She didn't acknowledge him, so he didn't acknowledge her. She didn't even acknowledge Reign, who was the baby. I guess she wouldn't have said anything to me if she didn't need to know where Raquon was.

Mom went into her bedroom and started packing Raquon's things in trash bags. I could not believe my eyes, but more than that, I felt a sense of dread about what would become of us after he was gone. In the four years he had been living with us and taking care of us, we had barely laid eyes on our mother. She came home once every three to five months for a day or so and then was off again to only God knows where. I prayed that mom would stop this foolishness before Raquon came home, because she had another guy here and I had no idea how he would react. Their relationship was strange to me; it seemed that there were no feelings involved on either end. She stayed gone for extended periods, but when she came home, they had sex, and then she'd leave again.

Mom came into my room and woke me up at 5:20 a.m. *"Raquon is at the door and I need you to go open it."*

"Mom, he has a key," I reminded her, just in case she forgot. The next words out of her mouth shocked me completely out of my sleep.

"I changed the locks tonight. He can no longer stay here anymore," was her dry response, as if she wasn't sounding totally unreasonable. If anyone shouldn't be able to stay here anymore, I would think it should be her.

I jumped up and ran down the two flights of stairs to open the door and let Raquon in. To say he was pissed was the understatement of the year. He came in cursing and breathing hard as hell.

"Why the hell is my key not working?" he demanded as he rushed through the door, taking the steps two at a time to get to the living room entrance. He looked like a linebacker as his 6'5" frame filled the doorway. I wanted no part of the raging energy coming off him.

"Raquon, Mom came in and changed the locks," I told him, spooked out of my mind. Mom stayed doing stupid shit and then putting me in the middle of her mess.

"Why the hell would she do that?" he griped. *"She doesn't pay no fuckin' bills here. She can barely say she lives here. If the lease wasn't in her name, these people wouldn't even know who she is,"* he continued until he made it to the living room.

"What the fuck? Who the fuck are you, and why are you in my home, homie?" Raquon snapped with extreme bass in his voice.

"I came here with the lady," the guy said, looking over at my mom sitting on the edge of the sofa. Still, he never gave his name.

"What the fuck is really good, Raynell? Your ass has been gone for months, and now you wanna pop up with company in the middle of the night like you still live here? That's not gonna work. You and your friend can get the fuck out," Raquon said with a bland look on his face.

Mom finally found her voice. *"I'm back now, and I want you gone."*

Raquon let out a slight chuckle and looked her dead in the eyes. *"You must be smoking something more than weed if you think I'm about to leave my home so you can move the next nigga in and play house. I pay the bills, make sure these kids are straight, and get them off to school. You haven't been home to check on them in nearly five months. Did you think they survived on air? Raylexia just turned sixteen, Rodereck is twelve, and Reign is three. Who was supposed to take care of them if I left?"*

"Let me tell your retarded ass, nobody. They have no one else. Your brothers drop in here and there, but they live in different states. You put all that

responsibility on Raylexia like she isn't a child herself, but guess what? She is. Even if she could take care of them like she does when you're gone, what did you expect them to eat? How was she supposed to pay the bills? You get food stamps every month and don't even come this way to feed these kids. You pay no bills, so this apartment would have been gone. I don't know what you told player over there, but y'all gotta get the fuck out."

Dude looked over at Mom, and for the first time since they got here, I saw disgust on his face. *"Sorry, cuz. I had no idea this was what was going on. I assumed she was single and had no kids. We've been kicking it for months, and she never mentioned anything about them. My name is Heston, and I apologize for coming into your home this way. You are a better man than me because I would be ready to kill a bitch for less,"* he said to Raquon.

With that, he left the house without a backward glance.

Mom had the nerve to yell, *"If you could protect me, that would be fine, but you can't. You just ran off the one person who could. I'm not saying you can't hold your own, but you're not strong enough to protect me. Heston is, and y'all just ruined any chance I had with him. Y'all always mess up everything for me. If I didn't have y'all, I would be free to do me. Why do I have to worry about y'all? I had you; that should be enough."* She ranted.

Something came over Raquon, and he looked demented. It was the first time I had ever seen him so upset. Leaning down over Mom, he said, *"Look, Raynell, I have no idea what you're talking about, and I don't care to know. I'm not leaving, and you can't make me leave. You don't live here anyway, so continue doing what you've been doing. I got the kids covered. And start making those guys strap up if you don't want any more kids. It's not their fault they're here. It's yours."*

Mom became completely hysterical, yelling at Raquon to get out, claiming we ruined her life. Then she told him he was just a convenient babysitter until she finished with her other men. That was the last straw—he lost it and knocked her out. The neighbors called the police because of the yelling so early in the morning.

When they ran Raquon's name through the system, they found he had warrants. He didn't even attempt to put up a fight and went to jail with a smile on his face.

CHAPTER ONE Raylexia
Gavion

March 8, 2011

The day I knew things had come to an end in my relationship was when my boyfriend of ten months hit me for the first time. We were in the middle of a heated argument after I found out he'd been messing around with other girls. Zylar Crewens—eighteen, standing at 6' even with slightly bowed legs, a peanut butter complexion, a muscular build, gunmetal gray eyes, and inky black curls usually braided tight to the back. One fine-ass nigga, and rich to boot. The problem? He knows it, and girls are all over him day and night, boosting his already overinflated ego.

I refuse to be one of many, and he knows this too. For weeks, I'd felt something was off, but couldn't put my finger on it. Our time together is limited—his street obligations, my responsibility to my siblings. He has access to other girls; I have access to other guys. He's taken care of all my financial needs since Raquon left, and I appreciate that. But cheating? That's a deal-breaker. I'm not in love with him, but I care. I gave him something I can never get back, and I hoped he'd cherish it. If what I heard is true about him cheating, we're done.

I walked up to Zylar's house a couple hours after school. The first time I came here, I got a glimpse of how the elite live. This house is absolutely beautiful, and Mrs. Della did an amazing job decorating it. Those were my thoughts as I swung by the kitchen to say hi to his mom. Zylar had given me a key to use the side door, so I wouldn't bother his mother when I visited. It was hella convenient and saved me from having to explain my random visit times. With no parental guidance of my own, I try to show his mother the same respect Grandma Etta taught me.

"Hi, Mrs. Della. How are you today? It smells amazing up in here! What are you cooking?" I asked, the aroma making my stomach growl. I hadn't eaten since rushing over after school, and the smell of food was mouth-watering.

"Girl, slow down," Mrs. Della laughed. *"I'm doing alright. Just missing Z, so I decided to cook for him. I'm making collard greens, cornbread, candied yams, and oxtails smothered in herb gravy with a side of rice. Are you planning to join us for dinner?"*

Her warm invitation made me feel welcome, as always. I can't remember the last time my own mom cooked for me and my siblings. We mostly lived on sandwiches until I learned to grocery shop and cook from Grandma Etta and Raquon.

"I just might, Mrs. Della. Let me check in with Zylar and I'll let you know," I said, making my way from the kitchen to Zylar's room on the other side of the house.

As I approached his room, I heard Zylar on the phone. I stopped in the hallway, listening intently, hoping for the answers I needed. My heart sank as I overheard his conversation. He was clearly talking to another girl, and from what I could gather, she was more than just a friend.

"What in the hell am I, then?"

The reason I did this pop-up visit was because of the comments from girls in my neighborhood, bragging about being with a new nigga named Zy with deep pockets, driving a blue Mustang. Zy isn't a common nickname, and the blue Mustang was too much of a coincidence to ignore. I had to know if there was any truth to the rumors.

I refused to let Zylar make me look like a fool, so I continued listening, needing all the facts before I made my exit from his life.

"Chandra, I want to see your fine ass tomorrow around 8 p.m. If you come over then, I should be done handling business for Zaylar, and I'll be able to take care of you. My girl barely has time to take care of my needs, so I need you to come take the edge off," Zylar said, making my stomach churn.

"Nigga, you got me fucked up. How do we go from fuckin' around for over a year and a half to you having a fuckin' girlfriend that ain't me? You're quick to hit me up when you want your dick sucked or to hang out at the club, but we're just friends? Now you're claiming this other hoe like I ain't been here all this time," Chandra shot back, her voice heated.

"Aye, watch yo' muthafuckin' mouth. Don't call her out her name no got damn mo'. I already told you, you ain't my bitch, so I don't have to explain shit to you. If you don't want to handle my needs, I'll move on to the next. I don't have time to argue with a bitch that ain't mine," Zylar spoke coldly.

"Zy, you got me fucked up if you think you can just handle me any kind of way. I refuse to let another bitch take my spot, and I put that on everything. What are you gonna do if I tell her about us? Huh? Is she gonna be okay knowing you never stopped fuckin' with me after y'all started y'all's so-called relationship? Is she gonna be cool knowing everybody in your circle thinks I'm your bitch?" Chandra ranted, her voice rising with each word.

"I wish the fuck you would even attempt to approach my girl. I'll break your fuckin' neck. You know your place and you serve the purpose you signed up for. If you see me and my girl out anywhere, you better act like you don't know who the fuck I am. If you ever get bold enough to approach me while I'm with her, I will fuckin' have you murked. Play with it if you want to," Zylar threatened, his voice dripping with menace.

"I can't believe you're trying to handle me like this after I've been down for you all this time, Zy. What makes her so special that you would treat me this way?" Chandra's voice wavered, close to tears.

"She's my everything and I love her. Shit, if she could spend more time with me and enjoyed doing more of the things I like, I wouldn't be entertaining any of you other hoes," Zylar groused before laughing like the shit he just said was the funniest thing in the world.

"Really? So, all this time, I meant nothing to you? You didn't care about me at all?" she asked, her voice filled with hurt.

"Maannn, come on with this bullshit," Zylar snapped. *"I've been working my ass off to prove to Zaylar I can handle more responsibility. Being with you on some relationship-type shit was never part of the plan. I enjoy kicking it with you, and you've always played your position well. Now that I have a girl, things have changed. If Zaylar promotes me and puts me in charge of my own spot, I'll be able to make some things shake for my crew. I don't know how you confused our casual relationship with something serious, but you need to get your mind right. I don't have any plans on making you my girl, and I never have,"* Zylar said, indifferent.

"We've been fuckin' around for a year and a half, and you know I'm all about making that paper first. Spending time with you here and there was fun, but I never saw you as girlfriend material. You like to hang out and party more than I do, and you ghetto as fuck. What do I look like wifin' up a bitch that don't know how to carry herself like a queen in public?"

"I'm already trying to figure out how to make Zaylar let me oversee the older crew at the spot. I don't have time to deal with this bullshit you have going on. You ain't my bitch, so remember your place or get replaced. It's as simple as that. What you won't do, the next bitch will." Zylar's words confirmed he was messing around with more than just her.

"Nigga, you got me fucked all the way up if you think it's gonna be that easy to replace me. I'm gonna make you regret treating me this way. Believe that" she snapped back.

"Aye, I don't have time for this bullshit, bruh. I done told you what type of time I'm on. Are you coming by the spot or not? I got enough going on trying to solidify my spot with Zaylar. He's worried about me taking over because of some past issues with dad's old crew. But most of the loyal niggas have known me all my life and respect my hustle."

"They know what I'm capable of in these streets and that my word is bond. I just hope Zaylar makes the right choice soon because I'm tired of making these crumbs. I have a lot of new responsibilities that's been draining my pockets. You fuckin' with me about unnecessary shit is just adding to my stress. Things between us have always been simple. Now you're trying to complicate shit," he griped.

After hearing that, I started to make my exit. There was nothing else I needed to hear. The rumors circulating around the hood were true. Zylar is out here spending his time with other bitches. I don't have the time nor the energy to compete with other girls over a nigga that's supposed to be mine, so I decided to bow out gracefully and let them have him. This nigga had the nerve to try and play me, but like everything else in my life, I'll get over it.

Tomorrow is a new day, and as long as God allows me to wake up, there's a chance that things will get better. First, Raquon went to jail, leaving us with no support. Now, Zy decides to show his true colors. I guess I should have remembered what me and Rodereck found out when Grandma Etta passed: We are all we got (W-A-A-W-G).

I didn't bother going in to say a thing. I just turned and made my way out of his side door. As I stepped into his mom's front yard, Zylar came running around the corner of the house.

"Ray, why are you leaving? You just got here?" he called, using the nickname he was fond of.

"No, muthafucka, I was here standing outside your bedroom door listening to you make plans to meet up with some girl named Chandra," I said, my voice steady. *"Before we started this relationship, I told you my home life was complicated, and I basically took care of my siblings. You said you understood and were down to ride it out with me. Now you're making plans to be with other girls. I can understand it, though. You're young and want a girl you can spend more time with than I have. If I were your woman as you claim, there would be no need for you to entertain other girls regardless of our situation. You would only want to spend time with me, as I do with you. But since you are, and have been since we got together, it means I'm not the girl for you. You cheating on me proves that. So, from now on, I'ma do me, and you can continue doing you. There's no need for us to continue being in a relationship that's fake. I promise you don't have to worry about me draining your pockets anymore."*

I refused to let him hear the hurt in my voice as I spoke, turning to leave.

"Raylexia, what the fuck does 'you'll do you' mean? You're my girl, and I refuse to see you with anybody else. I'll kill your ass first. Chandra is just a friend that I kick it with from time to time. I love you. No, I'm in love with you, but your situation is just a lot to handle for anyone. Shit, we can't go to the dances or even to a movie, and when we do go out, you have to take all your mother's kids. We are 16 and 18 years old, not 35."

"There is literally nothing in this world I wouldn't give you if I could, because I want to see you happy, but I'm human, and I want to have fun too. Not always be cooped up in your mom's apartment or hanging out in my room. It's like I have this beautiful girlfriend with an outgoing personality that no one else gets to see. Shit, K-O is my closest friend, and he's only seen you a handful of times in passing. I don't want Chandra, but she's cool to kick it with when you're not around. So, in a sense, she's taking up your slack. I can't lose you over this bullshit, so we'll just have to work it out."

Zylar's words made me look at him like he'd lost his damn mind.

"I'll do me, and you can do you means exactly that. You've got real life and bullshit mixed up if you think we're working anything out. And what the fuck do you mean, taking up my slack? I don't have no muthafuckin' slack, nigga. We don't have a goddamn thing to work out. I'm done with your cheating ass. You cheated on me, and from the conversation I overheard, I must be the side bitch because she's been around for the last year and a half. You even feel comfortable enough with her to discuss your hustle, and she knows about the spot you work out of. That's more than just kicking it with this girl. You're in a whole relationship with her. I don't have the energy or time to stress over you cheating on me. My time is valuable, and I refuse to waste any more of it dealing with your cheating ass."

"My home life is hard enough just trying to survive. You were the one that claimed that I was yours and you were mine. I never asked you for any of that shit. I just wanted to experience sexual relations, and you are the only person who has ever made me feel anything. So, I think it's best if we end things now. You've already proven to me that you're not loyal. It doesn't matter that no one has seen me. If I'm supposed to be your girl, no one else has any business getting any of your time. She's coming to the spot to see you tomorrow, so I know you and this bitch are fuckin'. Would it be okay for me to go out and fuck another nigga?" I asked, my face devoid of humor.

Out of nowhere, I felt a blow to my face, and it was on. Zy had me fucked up if he thought he could hit me and get away with it. We traded blow for blow until K-O pulled into the driveway, jumped out, and left the car running to break up the fight.

"What the fuck is wrong with you, nigga?" K-O yelled, struggling to get Zy under control. *"Why would you be fighting her like she's a nigga? You're dead ass wrong for that."*

Ignoring both of them, I searched Mrs. Della's front yard for anything I could use as a weapon. I spotted a small ceramic flower pot, picked it up, and headed back over to where Zylar and K-O were still arguing. They were so caught up in their argument that neither one of them saw me coming until it was too late.

"Did you see how she fights? She was hitting me hella hard. Shit, it took everything in me to pull my punches, cause she swings like she thinks she can whip my ass. Ain't no pussy in me, so I had to correct that shit. The fuck you

thought," Zylar shouted at K-O, breathing hard and shaking as he struggled to get himself back under control.

"She hits and swings like a nigga, so I was trying not to snap and break her fuckin' neck. Then she just said some fucked-up shit to me. I don't play that disrespectful bullshit. She needs to understand I am the man in this relationship. She may be upset about me talking and fucking with Chandra, but that don't mean she can just talk to me any kind of way. I will break her fuckin' jaw behind the disrespectful shit she has coming out her mouth," he continued, sounding crazy as hell.

I eased closer to them with the pot in my hand and smashed it over Zylar's head. Then I started punching him repeatedly in the face.

"AHHHH!" he yelled out trying to block my blows. *"What the fuck?"* he exclaimed as K-O grabbed me off of him and struggled to move me away from him.

"Take that, you bitch-ass nigga," I shouted. *"You think you can hit me and get away with it? I'll KILL you out here, nigga."* I spat as K-O picked me up off my feet, whispering for me to calm down as he moved me farther away from Zylar.

K-O sighed and looked me over. My right eye was swollen, and my lip was busted. Zy didn't have a scratch on him, but he was covered in dirt, and I bet he felt me.

"Ray, are you okay?" K-O asked, but I didn't bother with a reply. I just turned to walk away after he put me down and released me from his hold.

Zy blocked my path covered in dirt from the flowerpot. *"I meant what the fuck I said, Raylexia. You are mine, and there are no outs with us. We're in this until the casket drops, and I mean that shit. I understand you feel some type of way about me still fooling around with Chandra. I will stop fuckin' around with her, but you're mine, and I refuse to let you go. You'll just have to get over it. I'll give you some time to cool off and come see you next week."*

"Make sure you think about what I've said. You belong to me. Don't test me on this. I know you're not used to dealing with a guy since I'm your first, but we have needs, and you're not always available when I call. I may have gone about this the wrong way, but shit, this is new to me too. You're the first girl I've ever made my girlfriend, so we'll have to learn this shit together." Zylar spoke like

his word was law, expecting me to just accept it and go with the flow like we didn't just finish trying to kill each other out here.

"Nigga, you sound crazy as hell. Like you can really stand here and dictate to me how we move forward from here. I have been faithful to you, and you showed me that I put my trust in the wrong nigga. I am done with you, and I can show you better than I can tell you. Nigga, fuck you," I said, turning to head home.

AFTER MAKING IT HOME from Zy's mom's house, I was exhausted. I quickly made my way into the apartment and headed straight for the bathroom downstairs. I closed the bathroom door and took off my clothes, eager for a long, hot bath to soak my bruises. I had no idea what I planned to do now that Zylar and I were done. He had been giving me a couple thousand dollars over the past few weeks to cover the bills Raquon used to pay. But now, with him out of the picture, I have no idea what I'm gonna do. I still have plenty of money saved up to tide me over for the time being, but after that's gone. *What am I supposed to do?*

I wouldn't be worried if I hadn't cut my ties with Daylon on the count of my relationship with Zylar because he always made sure to give us odd jobs to do to earn some quick cash. Now that I think back to the last time I saw Daylon. What the hell was that reaction I had to him after the game? It was so intense that it scared the shit out of me. I thought what I experienced with Zylar was naughty but nice, almost sweet, in comparison to my reaction to Daylon. That was more carnal and somewhat wickedly nasty. I never felt so much pleasure and then so empty in my life. That's another reason I have been keeping my distance from him when I know he's home on leave. I always thought of him as a friend, brother, or cousin. These new complicated urges I have directed at him make me feel shameful. *Should I feel this way when he is so much older? Isn't it wrong to feel this way?* Fed up with my wayward thoughts. I splashed water on my face and regrouped. All is not lost, even if the future feels daunting.

After washing off, I pulled the stopper to let the dirty water drain, then turned on the shower for a quick rinse. I dried off and dressed in a t-shirt and jean shorts. It was time to pick up my siblings from Winkie's. She knew I had gone to see Zylar, since she was with me when those hoes started talking about messing around with him. Come to think of it, she was with me when we first met as well.

Just thinking back to that day ten months ago made me smile. I had the time of my life cutting up with my friends.

CHAPTER TWO Raylexia
Gavion

10 *Months Prior*
May 15, 2010

Winkie and I had just finished doing our laundry at the laundromat and were headed back to our apartment building when I spotted the finest brother I had ever seen. Just looking at him made my pulse quicken. I had never felt this way about a guy before, so it took me by surprise. His muscles flexed under his V-neck gray Polo shirt, showcasing two iced-out dog tags hanging around his neck on a Cuban link chain. His bowed legs, clad in dark gray Gucci jeans, made powerful strides through our complex. I wasn't familiar with him, so I knew he was not from around here.

Taking in his appearance, I decided to be bold and ask for his number. Walking up to him and his friend with Winkie by my side, I asked, "Hey, my name is Raylexia. What's your name, and can I get your number to call you sometime?" To my relief my voice was steady despite the butterflies in my stomach.

It was a bold move on my part, but I knew I looked good in my denim acid-washed cut-off booty shorts, a black tank top, and black flip-flops. Nothing special, but because the boys around here ask me out all the time, and I am my mother's daughter, I have no hang-ups about my looks. I have what you call a slim-thick frame, standing at 5'5" with A-cup breasts, wide hips, and thick thighs. My hair is light silver and hangs down to the center of my back, with deep violet, almost amethyst eyes, and I have a rich chocolate skin tone that's blemish-free.

I could tell I caught him off guard because he almost tripped when he came to a complete stop in front of me. Then he did a double-take and smiled, showing stacked teeth on both sides of his mouth. His peanut butter complexion slightly glistened in the sun, making me feel things in my private area that I never experienced before. My stomach was doing flips, and my panties were soaked. Giggling up at him, I decided right then to let him be my first.

He smiled back, looking me up and down. "Sure thing, Ms. Sexy, you can have my number. My name is Zylar. Make sure you call me," he said smoothly. He called out his number, and Winkie quickly took out her Razor to store it for me.

"Oh, I will. You just make sure you answer," I told him, smiling wide.

"Bye, my future shortie," he said, grinning from ear to ear as he continued on his way.

"Girl, I can't believe you really asked that fine ass nigga for his number. That nigga looks good as hell, and his fine-ass friend is hella cute as well," Winkie said, still watching his friend as they walked off. "I wouldn't mind havin' a go at him. He can definitely get it." She gushed. "You hit the jackpot."

I chuckled at her as I, too, watched Mr. Zylar until he was out of view. "Winkie, I had to holla at him. There's something about him that makes my heart race and my stomach feel funny. He made my panties wet, and you know I've never experienced that before. I have a tingling sensation down below, and I feel the urge to squeeze my legs shut to make it stop. Shit, I was beginning to think there was something wrong with me. I've never really been interested in any of the guys around here, and you know that. Just seeing him has me feeling all types of things. What will happen if he touches me?" I asked Winkie, trying to understand what was going on with my body.

"Raylexia, you probably don't see the niggas around here that way because you've either beat the shit out of most of them in a fight or whipped them in every sport we play. It's hard to be attracted to a guy you can take in a fight. So, it's only natural not to want to give them your body. This new nigga just has that unknown it factor you're attracted to. Hell, who knows. He might just be your one," Winkie told me as we walked the rest of the way to our apartment building.

We were on our way home to get ready for the basketball tournament being hosted by the Belvins Brothers at the SPAR. Daylon and his brothers started hosting these tournaments the summer after I turned 12 years old. My girls and I always placed in the competition, so we knew we were going to win at least the $100 prize.

Since we all lived in the same building in the Jackson Heights Projects, we decided to get dressed at Winkie's place. Her mom agreed to keep Reign for me, and I was taking Rodereck with me so he could chill with his friends. "Here's her bag, Ms. Sandra. She already ate, but I put a snack in there for later just in case she wants something to eat," I told Ms. Sandra as she gave me a blank stare.

"Girl, if you don't get your ass on about your business. Me, Reign, and Tonya are going to be just fine. We don't need your snacks, cause we're going to eat whatever I cook," Ms. Sandra said, sounding offended by my mention of the snack.

"Sorry, Ms. Sandra. It's just a force of habit. I'm used to making sure she has what she needs no matter where we go," I told her as I went back to Winkie's room, where all my girls were still getting dressed.

All of my girls are beautiful in their own right, and we never had to do much to show it off. Deanna was the first one to get dressed and ready to go in our team uniform. We still wore the first uniforms we got while playing in the Slam Championship hosted by the Belvins Brothers during our senior year of junior high. The uniforms were black and gray and even had our names on the back. Deanna's vanilla skin shining, she stands at 5'2" and is the shortest one of us. It makes her large breasts, thick thighs, and fat ass stick out even more on her small frame. Winkie's caramel skin glows as she switches by, heading to the bathroom. She is a slim, fine beauty with huge breasts and an ample bottom. At 5'7", she's the tallest one of us. Shamena's ebony skin shines, showcasing her beautiful smile. She is thick in all the right places, with a big wide ass that sits up high. Standing at 5'5" like me, her weight fits her frame well. Then there is Johnya, who has the most scandalous frame of all. She has large breasts, wide hips, a big bodacious ass, and thick thighs, all packed on a 5'4" honey-colored frame. She and Deanna always reminded me of the girls that star in music videos, with their big breasts and tiny waists. Personally, I don't see how they tote all that stuff around. It seems like hard work, not to mention the unwanted male attention they can't seem to shake.

"Raylexia, you better tie all that damn hair down, so you'll be able to see the ball," Deana joked as I walked by.

"I see you got jokes. I'm waiting on Shamena to braid it back. That way I can roll it up in a ball and forget it. You know if it's not secure, I'll be pinning it up all night," I told Deana while giving Johnya the stank face.

"Why the hell are you just sitting there looking crazy? We have to leave in less than twenty minutes," I asked Johnya, who looked like she wasn't even trying to get ready.

"Raylexia, don't start. I've been arguing with Tyrone, and I just wanna chill before the game. I promise I'll be ready. Just let me be for a while," Johnya said, sounding so sad. I just left her alone and went to let Shamena braid my hair. She really needs to leave that snake-ass nigga alone. Her mom already made her start taking the birth control shot after his snake-ass got her pregnant on purpose. He's older than her at 21 and has his own place. When they first had their son Tylan, he tried to get her to move in, but her parents weren't having it. So now, every time we have a game or anything to do, he acts a fool.

"Shamena, come on and braid me up so we can go do this. I can't wait to see who all is in the tournament this time. Last time, those girls gave us hell. If Johnya hits those threes back-to-back, we should be good," I said as she sat down and started braiding my hair.

"Bitch, when has Johnya not hit her threes back-to-back?" Shamena asked, laughing as she braided the first section of my hair.

Johnya is our shooting guard, and she usually dominates the court, but today she might be a little off since she got into it with Tyrone's snake ass.

"She's in there chilling before getting dressed cause she and Ty's snake ass are into it for some reason," I said dryly, knowing Shamena would quickly catch on to my meaning.

"You know like I know they're into it because she has something to do other than stay up in that damn apartment. I hate she let that rotten ass nigga trap her with my nephew, cause he's foul as hell. He can run the streets day and night robbing muthafuckers and doing God only knows what else, but anytime Johnya wants to do something, it's a problem. I'm so glad her parents wouldn't let her move in with his hoe ass. Ain't no telling what that bum ass nigga would be doing to our girl. I can tell she's ready to make that break, though. We just gotta be ready when the time comes," Shamena said, giving me a look that made me think she knew something I didn't.

Deana and Winkie walked in, fully dressed and ready to go. Winkie had her short pixie cut feathered to the side with the edges waved up. She made me wanna switch up my braided bun to match her fly.

"Damn, Winkie, that hair on point. I feel kinda jealous with you hoes all looking fly and I have these damn braids," I vented, feeling a bit salty.

"Girl, what the hell are you talking about? Your hair is on point. Shamena has that shit in a crazy high ponytail with thin and thick braids swirling around in a pattern. Go look with your hating ass," Winkie said, putting me on blast before heading for the door.

I got up to look at my hair, and sure enough, Shamena had hooked me up something proper with the braids that I thought would be basic. Not only was my hair laid, but Johnya, Shamena, and Deana were all rocking high ponytails with their edges laid to perfection. We looked more like we were going to a dance rather than a neighborhood basketball tournament. We gathered all our gear and made our way down to the parking lot. Johnya's dad, Mr. West, was taking us to the SPAR since he sponsors our team.

"Hi, Mr. West. Where is Mrs. Johnny Mae? Is she not coming to the games?" we all asked, our voices overlapping with excitement.

"She'll be there. Tylan needed to go potty, and she refused to leave without letting him get that one out of the way before putting him in a pull-up. Are you guys ready to go win this thing? Last time you lost because you had to substitute Alaya for Johnya. This time your full team is here. Let's go take this thing."

"We ready! Let's go." We all yelled back and loaded up in his Jeep.

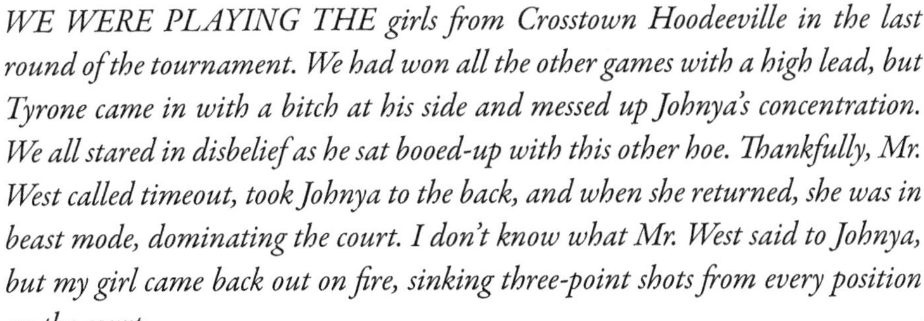

WE WERE PLAYING THE girls from Crosstown Hoodeeville in the last round of the tournament. We had won all the other games with a high lead, but Tyrone came in with a bitch at his side and messed up Johnya's concentration. We all stared in disbelief as he sat booed-up with this other hoe. Thankfully, Mr. West called timeout, took Johnya to the back, and when she returned, she was in beast mode, dominating the court. I don't know what Mr. West said to Johnya, but my girl came back out on fire, sinking three-point shots from every position on the court.

After that, we all stepped up our game. Deana, our small forward, has been driving to the goal, executing flawless lay-ups from the left side, hitting nothing but net. Winkie, our center, and Shamena, our power forward, have been getting rebound after rebound, passing the ball to me to drive down the court. In this game, I've been supporting my team by passing the ball to Johnya or attacking the goal from both sides. So far, Johnya and I are the top scorers, with Deana right behind us.

As a point guard, I can play all positions and help with defense when Shamena gets tired, as she tends to lose steam towards the end of the game. We had a 2-point lead with 10 seconds on the clock. I called for the ball and passed it outside to Johnya, who then proceeded to sink the perfect three from center court right at the buzzer.

We all went wild because we won $1,000 to split between the five of us with this win. Rodereck ran down onto the court to give me a hug, but what surprised me was when I saw Zylar approach me for a hug as well.

"Hi, Ray. You can ball, Ms. Sexy. Now we have to go get something to eat and celebrate your win. My treat," Zylar said, flashing the stacked teeth on the sides of his mouth. My body started up with the throbbing in my center, and my nipples started to poke out my shirt, making me wonder what this dude was doing to my body. Then my mind registered what he said.

"Sorry, Zylar. I have to go pick up my sister from my friend's mom, but you can come chill with me if you just want to hang out," I told him, wanting to spend more time with him.

"Sure thing, Ms. Sexy. Let me go tell K-O I'm following you back to your crib to chill. You sure you don't want me to get you something to eat to celebrate? Your team just won the whole tournament," he said, grinning widely.

"No, that's not necessary. We all went half on food and drinks to celebrate at my place. My girls and I always chill and unwind after the game at my apartment since my mom's never home. In fact, you can invite K-O to chill with us. It's normally just us girls, but you guys are welcome," I told him, noticing Rodereck mean-mugging him.

"Oh, come here, Rodereck." I pulled him over to introduce him to Zylar. "Zylar, this is my brother Rodereck. Rodereck, this is Zylar." They both gave each other a head nod, sizing each other up.

Not paying them any mind, I left with the girls and Mr. West to get our winnings. While Zylar left to get K-O and offered me and Rodereck a ride back to the apartments with him.

When we made it to DayVon to collect our money, I gave him a big hug. Releasing him from the hug I looked at him smiling. "You guys did good tonight. I thought y'all might not win there for a minute." DayVon joked.

"Ha, ha," I laughed. "I'm not going to lie. I was worried for a minute as well. Luckily, Mr. West was able to help Johnya snap back into shape." I grinned.

"Yeah, luckily," DayVon added grinning along with me.

He handed each of us $200 and we stood together with the organizers to take photos. Once done, I pulled DayVon to the side.

"How is Daylon doing? He hasn't been home in a while." I asked when we were out of earshot.

"He's okay. He should be home for the next tournament. I'll tell him you said hi." DayVon answered.

"Tell him I said to be safe as well. That's the most important. To stay safe." I clarified.

Daylon was like a big brother to me, and I don't know where me and my siblings would be now without his help. I met Daylon when I was 12 years old, just before he joined the Navy. He made sure me, and the girls could perform at all their events, and make money on the side. That is how I have been able to keep money in my pocket.

I left DayVon and told my girls that me and Rodereck would be riding back home with Zylar, and they were all smiling, even Johnya. I was expecting to see her all depressed because of what happened with Tyrone, but she seemed happier than usual.

Not bothering to hide my curiosity, I pulled her to the side. "Johnya, are you okay? You seem happy as hell, even though you just caught your boyfriend cheating."

Johnya's smile broke across her face, and it was blinding. My girl was happy. "Raylexia, my daddy just told me the best shit ever. I'm free of that snake-ass nigga. That nigga violated in the worst way; there is no coming back from that. I had a feeling his snake-ass was cheating because I stopped having sex with him right after I had Tylan. I just don't feel the same way about him that I used to. When I found out he got me pregnant on purpose, knowing I had dreams of going to the Air Force and college, things changed for me."

"Not to mention, we all just found out he's been setting niggas up to get robbed and then grinning back in their faces the next day. I can hardly stand to

be around him, much less have him touching my body. With this move he just made, I can move on without restrictions or worrying about him acting a fool. He broke up with me, so now I can put my plan into motion to let my parents keep my son when I apply for the military after we graduate," she said all in a rush, smiling hard as hell.

I gave my girl a hug, feeling her excitement and relief. Releasing the hug we all loaded up in the cars to head back to my place.

CHAPTER THREE Zylar
Crewens

When we arrived at Ray's apartment, she asked me and K-O to wait for a moment, saying she'd be right back. She and her girls all went to the apartment three doors down, where the one called Winkie unlocked the door. They went inside for about ten minutes and returned with duffle bags and backpacks. Ray also had a little girl, asleep in her arms.

Ray opened the door to let us in. I didn't know what I was expecting to find, but it wasn't this. For her to be living in the projects, her crib was laid the fuck out. They had a big screen TV in the corner housed in a wall unit that had to be 65 inches, and a Pioneer stereo system that had to cost a grip, all centered around a wraparound sectional. All the artwork and whatnots seemed to be of high quality.

"You guys can have a seat while I go put Reign to bed. I'll be back down in a minute or two," Ray said as she, her brother and her girls ran up the stairs.

I turned to see K-O staring at me with a what-the-fuck look. "I don't know, bruh. This is my first time coming over. You know I only met this girl earlier today," I explained, still puzzled by how they lived in the projects with such means. We continued talking about the game and how these girls could really ball until they all came back down wearing what I assumed was their sleepwear.

"Can I get you guys something to drink?" Raylexia asked as she approached what appeared to be a fully stocked bar, situated off in the corner leading to the kitchen.

"I'll have whatever you're having," I replied, figuring she'd probably bring me a beer.

"Okay. Coke it is then, and you? K-O, right? What can I get for you?" Ray asked, smiling brightly.

"*Wait, Ray. What do you mean, Coke? I'd prefer a beer if you have one,*" I spoke up quickly before she could open the can.

"*Oh, okay. You said whatever I'm having, so that would be a Coke. I don't drink alcohol, smoke weed or do recreational drugs. None of my friends do. So, in the future, tell me what you want. Don't assume,*" she responded, letting me know there's more to this girl than just a pretty face and a banging body.

"*So, beer it is. And K-O, what would you like?*" she asked again as she retrieved a Budweiser for me from a mini-fridge built into the backside of the bar.

"*A beer is fine with me, Raylexia,*" K-O finally answered after looking at me.

All the girls grabbed a variety of sodas and started talking about the highlights of the game. You could tell they were all close because they just said whatever with no filter, and no one took offense.

"*So, Zylar, where did you meet Raylexia?*" Deana, the short one, asked.

"*I met her earlier today in the center of these apartments,*" I answered, making Ray grin, her gorgeous smile lighting up her face.

"*No shit,*" the dark one called Shamena yelled, sounding incredulous. "*You live over here? I've never seen you before.*"

"*No, I live on the Southside. I was over here handling some business. That's how I learned about the games tonight,*" I answered, noticing K-O starting to talk to the one named Winkie. They had been giving each other the eye since we got here.

"*Y'all, let Raylexia talk to him and come help me with the snacks.*" The one named Johnya grabbed the other two and headed for the kitchen.

"*So, are you ready to talk?*" I asked Raylexia, noticing she hadn't said a word to me since I asked her for a beer. This girl had a crazy effect on my body, and it was taking everything I had to control myself. Never had I been in the presence of a female who made my palms sweat, mouth water, heart race, and dick throb by just being in her presence.

"*Sure, I'm ready to talk, but can I ask you a question first?*" Ray asked, suddenly looking serious.

"*Yes. You can ask me anything.*"

"*Okay, this may sound kind of odd, but why do you make my body react strangely? Since I met you today, whenever I'm around you or I see you, my heart starts to race. I get short of breath, my clit throbs, my stomach does flips, and my breasts ache. I don't understand any of this cause this has never happened to me before. Shit, if you ask my friends, they all thought I would be gay. If not for the fact that girls don't move me either, I would have been worried," Ray said all that with a straight face, waiting for me to answer. I almost choked on my next swallow of beer.*

"Are you telling me you've never had sex before?" I asked, trying to make sure I understood what she was telling me. Is she still a virgin?

"I've never had sex before, never kissed, and I have never wanted to until now with you. So why are you different? Why does it seem like I have no control over my body when it comes to you?" Ray asked, making my dick swell from half to a full raging hard-on. The look in her eyes told me she meant every word.

"Ray, if you were not attracted to anyone before, that just means you're mine and I'm yours. We were made for each other and just had to wait to meet. Sex for men is slightly different from women, so I have been with others, but after today you will be my one and only," I explained, letting her know that I am staking my claim, and from now on she belongs to me.

"So, you want to date me?" she asked, like she still had a choice.

"No, I'm your man, and you're my woman. As of today, you belong to me, and I belong to you. No more dating anyone for either of us." And I meant every word.

"I have never dated before. I told you; you are the first person to make me feel this way. So, I only want to be with you sexually. When can I have my first kiss? And sex? Will it hurt? Because my friend Johnya said it's painful." Ray voiced her wants clearly, and I could see the mix of curiosity and nervousness in her eyes. I knew I had to make it special for her.

"Yes, the first time will be painful, there's no way around that, but I promise to make it enjoyable for you. We can practice kissing whenever you want, and we can have sex when you're sure you're ready," I replied, letting her know that we will move at her pace.

"I want to kiss and have sex now. Don't the two go hand in hand?" Ray surprised me with her request. She has a house full of people, including my friend, and she wants to have sex.

"Ray, you have a house full of people, and you want to have sex now?" I asked, making sure she really wanted to lose her virginity with everyone around.

"Zylar, I tell my friends everything. So, they will know every detail from start to finish anyway. What difference will it make if they're here or not?" She asked, making my dick get even harder.

"Let's do it then. Where to?" I asked, standing up and reaching out to help her up from the sectional.

She took my hand and led me to a bedroom right off the living room. Which surprised me, I thought the door led to a closet. Once in the room next to the bed, I undressed her and then myself. She watched every move I made and trembled at each touch. Ray's breasts were small barely an A-cup, but her ass, hips, and thighs were evenly proportioned and thick.

I kissed every inch of her sexy chocolate body and taught her how to kiss without bumping our teeth. Our tongues wrestled for dominance in no time, and I discovered that Raylexia is a perfectionist.

"Open your legs for me, Ray. Let me see your pretty pink pussy," I said softly. Using both hands, I gently opened Ray's folds and kissed her tenderly, exploring with my tongue. Her body responded intensely shaking, with her juices leaking down her thighs. After a few minutes of licking and sucking on her clit, her whole body began to shake, and she climaxed squirting all over my face. The intensity of her response made me damn near burst from watching her cum. Trying to give her time to recover, I sat at the end of the bed and stroked my erection, watching her pant.

She looked over at me and smiled dreamily.

"You ready to try something new?" I asked.

She licked her lips, getting up from the bed and walking up in front of me. Getting down on her knees, she grabbed hold of my erection, squeezing softly.

"How? What do I do?"

"Get your mouth wet. Let your slob build up and run down and out. That's right, get it as wet as possible. Now wrap your lips around the head and pull your teeth back. Never let your teeth touch any part of my dick. That's right. Now take it as far down your throat as it can go. Breathe through your nose. Now suck hard and use your hands to massage all the areas you can't fit in your mouth. That's right, now bob your head up and down while sucking harder on the upstroke."

"That's right, remember to keep letting your slob flow out. The wetter, the better. Now reach down and lightly grip my balls. That's good. Keep it going just

like that. Ray, ooh shit! I'm about to bust. Do you want to swallow or spit it out?" I asked, giving her the choice.

Ray became more aggressive in her sucking, making my toes curl as I gasped for air. Then she pushed all the way down, swallowed around the head, and I came with a shout as she swallowed all my seeds. That shit took me by complete surprise. Ray had no business knowing how to do that, but I'm not complaining. That just means she's got good instincts when it comes to pleasing me.

Ray leaned back on her knees licking her lips, touching them with her fingers.

"Why do my lips and jaws hurt? They're tingling. Is this normal?" Ray asked, stroking my dick back to life. As she continued to caress me, I reached down to touch her tender folds.

"Damn, Ray, you're leaking everywhere, and your lips are hurting because this was your first-time sucking dick. You have to train those muscles, and it will hurt less as you get used to it," I explained, trying to insert one finger with no success.

"Ray, you're super tight. I need you to relax and let my fingers in." I rubbed her clit while inserting one finger. The harder I rubbed her clit, the wetter she got. I moved my finger in and out, adding a second finger on the return until she took three fingers, and I felt her barrier. Taking her titty in my mouth and suckling one and then the other, she started to ride my fingers, letting me know she was ready.

I reached for my pants and retrieved a condom, sheathing my dick. "Ray, come here. You're ready now that you're this wet and can take three of my fingers. Remember, it will hurt at first, but it will start to feel better once you get used to my size. I'll go slow so I won't hurt you. Are you ready?"

"Yes! Now! Hurry! Zylar, it's hot. I need you inside." Ray trembled moving restlessly on the bed.

I placed my dick at her entrance and slowly began to enter. When I reached her barrier, I backed out and then pushed forward, giving her all nine inches. Ray let out a small gasp and clenched the sheets. I paused to let her adjust to my size, but then Ray began to move her hips, and her pussy gave me a biting sensation on the tip of my dickhead. That sensation made me move with the quickness.

I was slamming into Ray, and she made small gasping sounds while rolling her hips to meet mine. Each time I slammed in, she performed a roll that caused that biting sensation at the tip of my dick. That felt so good it had me moaning like a bitch. Ray matched me stroke for stroke until I flipped us over and put her on top. She got into a squat position and bounced up and down hard on my dick, not slowing up at all. She was pounding so hard she made my back, legs, and toes flex. If I didn't just break her in, I'd swear she was no virgin.

"Ray, just like that. Take your dick, Sexy. Shit! Baby, I'm finna cum," I called out as I released my seed and damn near passed out. I could feel Ray shaking on top of me, letting me know she got hers too.

"That was amazing. I can't wait to do it again. How long will my pussy be sore? Will it hurt every time to start?" Ray asked question after question, not showing a bit of shyness after what we just did.

"You should soak in some hot Epsom salt water for about an hour to relieve the pain and soreness. You will never feel this pain again from sex. It only hurt this time because it was your first time. From now on, you should only feel pleasure when we have sex." I explained.

"That's good to know." She answered.

"You know you're mine, right? From here on out, you're my girl." I told her.

"Oh, so, you wanna be my man now? I thought you were joking." She asked me while smirking.

"Damn right. Give me your phone number so I can program it into my cell." I told her and pulled my cell from my jeans pocket.

"I'm not sure I want a man right now." She taunted.

"Don't play with me Raylexia. You fucked me. Now you are stuck with me. I'm your man and you're my woman. It's you and me from here on out." I told her. Now as serious as a heart attack.

She looked me in the eyes and bit her lip. I could tell she was thinking. So, I waited. She lifted up and off my dick to sat up against the headboard of the bed and looked off into space.

"What's going on? Talk to me." I probed.

She sighed and turned to face me, "my home life is a lot different from most other girls. I basically take care of my siblings because my mom is never home. I don't know if I'll have time enough to be in a real relationship with you. I'm just glad I got the chance to be with you. It was a beautiful experience. Being with you tonight is enough for me. I don't want to commit to something, and you later find me lacking. So, it's best we end it here." She explained.

"What? Hell no. We can do this. I have a car and will make the time. Shit, I'll come to see you. I'm not taking no for an answer. Now give me your phone number, and let's go take a shower. Then you can have a soak." I told her. I was determined to have her.

We got up after Raylexia gave me the number to their house phone, since she didn't have a cell. and went to the bathroom connected to the room to wash up.

Raylexia Gavion

*Z**ylar washed my body in the shower as I took a shower with him. He gently rubbed the towel over my tender folds igniting my passions once more. Dropping the towel, he pinned me up on the shower wall and licked and sucked my pearl until I orgasmed oozing and losing all my strength. Zylar let me down and sat me in the tub. He washed himself off, prepared me a hot bath to soak, and redressed in his clothes. He kissed me tenderly on the lips and left to get K-O to leave.*

I soaked in the tub until the water turned cool, washed off and got out. That water felt so good on my skin. Zylar wasn't lying; after soaking for an hour, I could barely feel any pain, just a hollow feeling inside like something was missing. I can't believe I had sex for the first time with Zylar on the first day we met. I was finally a woman, and I couldn't wait to share this experience with my girls. I'm no longer worried I may be Asexual. I finally discovered my sexuality, and his name is Zylar.

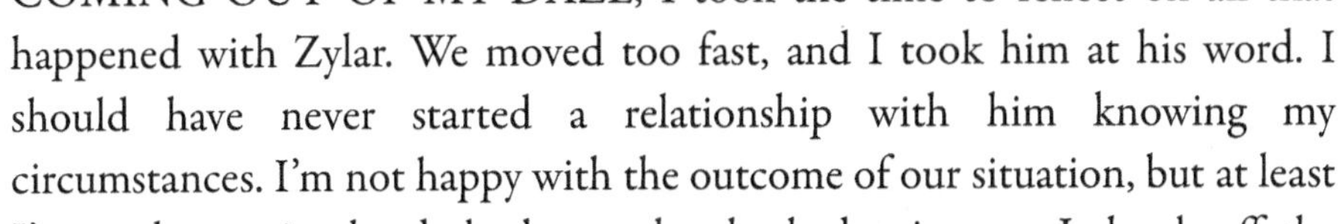

COMING OUT OF MY DAZE, I took the time to reflect on all that happened with Zylar. We moved too fast, and I took him at his word. I should have never started a relationship with him knowing my circumstances. I'm not happy with the outcome of our situation, but at least I'm no longer in the dark about what he had going on. I shook off the thoughts of Zylar. That was our final chapter. It's over now. Time to move on. I looked in the mirror and bowed my head.

I didn't even try to hide the black eye and busted lip I was sporting. I left out the door, walked three doors down and knocked on Winkie's door and got Rodereck and Reign. I could see that Winkie wanted to ask me questions, but she wouldn't dare to in front of her mom. We all made a promise to keep each other's secrets no matter what. It was keeping those secrets that allowed Tyrone's snake ass to take advantage of Johnya. Thankfully, she was able to drop his bitch ass and start preparing for her future.

CHAPTER FOUR Zylar
Crewens

March 8, 2011

"Fucckkkk!" I roared as I paced across the front lawn after Ray walked off. I had no intention of her finding out about Chandra or any of the other hoes I smashed from time to time. Shit, this is all new to me. I never had a girlfriend before, and there must be a learning curve somewhere in this shit. All the other hoes I've ever fucked with understood we're all just friends. Ray is the only exception. I better not ever catch her in another nigga's face. Just thinking about another nigga touching her has me hot.

Ray is not the most understanding girl. She warned me not to play with her emotions. She doesn't express her love for me openly, so with her, I have to feel her out and ask questions to know what she's feeling. Shit, I had no idea she would even be coming over today. She usually has to get her siblings after school, so this shit caught me by complete surprise.

K-O watched me like he didn't know what the hell was going on with me, and I couldn't blame him. I had never laid hands on a girl in my life, so this shit shocked me as well. Ray just has a way of making me lose control with no effort at all.

"What the fuck is going on wit'cha, my nigga? I'm not trying to get in your business, but when in the fuck did it become okay to hit a girl? I know she was tagging your ass good, but at the end of the day, she's still a female. We don't hit women, cuz. That shit you did was foul as fuck," K-O scolded me like I was five.

"I know that shit, nigga. I just snapped when she asked me that bullshit. If it was okay if she fucked another nigga, and my hand moved on its own. Before I even knew what was going on, we were trading blows. I have never fought a girl before, but to be real, I had to make a conscious effort not to break her fuckin'

neck for the way she was swinging back. For a couple of seconds, I thought she was a nigga. I had to really try hard to keep from hitting her too hard, bruh." I laughed, trying to shake off some of the anxiety I was feeling.

"Anyway, look, nigga. She caught me talking to Chandra on the phone and was spitting that shit about 'I can do me, and she'll do her.' I will kill that girl if she gives my pussy away to another nigga, and I mean that shit. I am the only muthafucker she's had and will ever have. I know I should have stopped messing with Chandra and them other hoes when we got together ten months ago, but Ray can barely do anything, bruh. I mean, I have never been able to spend the night at a chick's house before without being paranoid or worried about her parents walking in on us. Ray literally takes care of everything at home. Her mom be gone for months at a time. Shit, after her sister's father got locked up a couple of weeks ago, I have been buying food for the house and paying the bills. I give Ray $2000 a week to make sure she has what she needs." I ranted trying to get a handle on my emotions.

K-O looked at me shaking his head. Pissing me off.

"Look nigga. That lady literally never comes home. It's like those are Ray's kids. Ray is only 16, and she has never been to any school parties, dances, games—nothing. Shit, the only real activities we get to do are fuckin' or playing ball. Not to say I don't enjoy our time together, but shit, she's one of the most beautiful girls around here, and no one ever gets to see her but me. Ray doesn't like being around a lot of fake-ass people, so other than chillin' with her friends or you, she never really wants to go anywhere."

"I'm not used to a girl that's just cool hanging with me, having deep conversations and shit. I want to get out and party, but she's not having it 'cause she likes to stay home. That's why I was still dealing with the rest of them hoes. We like doing totally different things. Bruh, I mean, it's a lot of shit to deal with," I rambled on, trying to comprehend what the hell just happened.

"Damn, Zy. That's some wild shit, but what are you going to do about this situation though? Ray don't seem like the type to just do what you say. That girl damn near beat your ass in your own front yard," K-O chuckled like he said the funniest shit ever.

"Keep on with the jokes, nigga, and I don't know exactly what I plan to do just yet. I know I'm not going to lose Ray over this bullshit. So, the first thing I gotta do is break things off with Chandra since she is the only one of them hoes

that Ray knows about. She is cool and all to kick it with, but you and I both know she has always been convenient. Pussy on demand and low maintenance. I just have to tell her we're done," I said, causing K-O to burst out laughing.

"You really have no idea how complicated your situation has truly become, do you?" K-O asked, shaking his head at me.

"What do you mean, complicated? I just have to cut Chandra off and roll up on Ray and apologize. Simple as that," I stated with confidence.

"Zy, you cannot be this slow on the uptake. Chandra is not going to be understanding or accommodating about you cutting her off. You may not be breaking bread with her, but she has bragging rights just by being in your circle. Shit, no other guy in our age group even asks her out because they know she's taken," K-O said, looking at me like I was crazy.

"That's not my doing, though. Chandra just likes to run her mouth about us being together, even though she knows we're not a couple. I can do whatever the fuck I want to, and so can she. We're not exclusive, and she knows this," I explained to K-O, getting even more frustrated about the situation.

"I understand what you're saying, but when you step on the scene whenever there's an event, she's usually the one you shut down the night with. Even when you started to date Ray, you never cut her off, so in the eyes of the people around you, she's your girl. Not only that, you have been fooling around with her for over a year, and she knows things about you and your brother's businesses that can hurt him." K-O told me stopping me dead in my tracks.

"Fuckkkk!" I shouted. Grabbing ahold of my braids and feeling the dirt in my hair. *"Shit."* I rubbed my head brushing off more dirt.

K-O released a long-tired sigh, *"Zaylar needs to change things around, get new stash houses and traps set up before you stop fuckin' with that girl. I told you having that hoe in the trap, and all that pillow talking would come back to bite you in the ass,"* K-O explained, making me realize just how bad a situation I have put Zaylar and the crew in.

"Fuck! Fuck! Fucckkkk! I have to call Zaylar and let him know what's going on. Come on, man. Let me get showered and changed so we can head to the spot and get things rolling. Thanks, man, for reminding me of my fuck up. This will never happen again. We won't be entertaining no more bitches at the trap. This shit is ridiculous," I said to K-O as I rushed back into the house.

I called Zaylar, and he answered on the third ring.

"Zaylar, man, meet me at the spot on Cole Street in about an hour. I need to run some urgent business by you," I said into the phone, relieved that Zay wasn't just sending my call to voicemail like he usually does when he's making moves between cities. He'd just bought five new houses and was moving between them to monitor traffic flow, so he rarely had time to do a pop-up.

"Sure, lil' bro. What's good wit'cha? You know I just made it back." I heard him take a deep breath and wheeze. I knew he had to be hitting some of that good Exotic.

"You sound upset. Who I gotta fuck up?" Zay said, his words somewhat calming my fear that he'd put a hurting on me when he discovered my need to see him.

"I really need to speak to you about this in person. I'll run everything down when I see you in a little while," I told him, not ready to explain the situation I'd unwittingly put us all in, especially not over the phone. Too many ears could be listening and catch us unaware. Shit, he might even change his mind about giving me more responsibility after this, but I have to make sure our tracks are covered. This shit with Chandra can't fuck up our business.

"Say no more, bruh. Meet you there in an hour." Zaylar ended the call, leaving me thinking just how I could fix my fuck up.

On my way to the shower, I heard my mother call me from the kitchen. I turned and made my way down the long hall to find her standing at the stove, fixing one of my dad's favorites: oxtails, collards, candied yams, and cornbread. She occasionally cooked one of his favorites whenever she said he was heavy on her mind. I guess she's having one of those days.

"What's up, Ma?" I asked, knowing she was probably upset with me about me and Raylexia clowning in her front yard. I still can't believe how that all played out. That was completely out of character for me.

Ma turned around to face me and burst out laughing. I was covered in dirt from head to toe; so, I knew I looked a mess, but her laughter just hit wrong. It took her a couple of tries to get herself back under control.

Once she gathered her composure, she spoke, *"Zylar, I love you, but I have to warn you. Raylexia is not like the other girls you've been with. In the short time you two have been together and she's come over to visit, we've talked. She won't let you have her while you're playing with your little friends on the side. That girl is a different breed. She would make you kill her before she submits to you or lets you disrespect her.*" Ma paused to see if I was listening.

I gritted my teeth. I didn't say a word. I just nodded to acknowledge I heard what she said.

She continued, "*she's not impressed by what you have, and she doesn't care about your status in these streets. She cares for you, but she loves herself more. She has a lot of responsibility for someone her age and has lived a hard life. If you don't plan to do right by her, let her go before one of you ends up dead,*" my mother told me and went back to cooking, giving me food for thought.

I am never letting Ray go. That girl has my heart. I just have to fix this shit. Us breaking up is not an option.

I kept replaying what my mother said in my head as I showered and changed to head over and talk to Zaylar. I couldn't get all the dirt out of my hair and my braids looked a mess. I did what I could to make them look presentable and headed to the mancave to get K-O. I would just have to get it washed and braided tomorrow. Talking to Zaylar is more important right now.

MY BROTHER, ZAYLAR "Stone" Crewens, is the plug for Louisiana. At 24, he stands 6'3" with a dark chocolate complexion, marble gray eyes, a thick muscular build, a broad chest, and our father's deep dimples. I respect him to the fullest because he stepped in and took over the family business after Pops' death without missing a beat and him and Nico always have my back. We all were grieving and going through our own anguish, but he pushed through and soldiered on. Most of the old heads that used to work with Pops gave him hell when he tried to make changes. Too set in their ways they refused to follow Zaylar and took offense at him taking over and running the business. They all felt like they should have been next in line since Zaylar was so young. Zaylar had to make an example out of them niggas, so he retired their asses permanently and kept it moving. No one saw that coming, when he introduced every one of them to that nigga "Stone."

Our older brother, Nico, is twenty-seven, but he wouldn't help with the business because he wanted to work in law enforcement, and we had different fathers. He would always say, *"I don't have the level of calm needed to live that life, but I can and will watch your back. If I were in the game, I'd have killed off half the state by now. Zaylar has to deal with too many grimy ass niggas. I wouldn't even try to deal with that bullshit. I'd just kill them all."*

True to his word, Nico went to law school, and now he's the current D.A. He works with the lawyer we have on retainer to keep our workers out of jail, and she just so happens to be his girlfriend. Now, just by looking at him, you couldn't tell Nico is black, because he takes after his father, a full-blooded Italian from Sicily. He's a little over 6'6", with forest green eyes, a dark olive complexion, and the lean, athletic build of a swimmer. So, any time we have cases that come up, no one knows the connection. We fly under the radar between Nico, our lawyer Josie, and the cops we have on the payroll.

At eighteen, I'm the baby of the family, and those niggas are always trying to keep me out of the loop. I only got a chance to work at the various spots because Zaylar needed someone he trusted to watch over things until he cleared out all the older crew members that wouldn't follow his lead. That was how I formed my own crew. I have eight young savages on my team, and we stay ready for whatever.

35 MINUTES LATER WE pulled up to the spot on Cole Street, and I could tell right away that Zaylar was pissed off just by his facial expression. His brow was furrowed, and he was pacing back and forth like a raging bull, barking orders into his phone. Zaylar was usually chill and never did anything flashy, but everybody knew he was that Nigga. He had this aura that screamed he was not to be fucked with, and people took heed. Me and K-O jumped out of my royal blue, pearl-finished 2011 Ford Mustang convertible and ran up to him to see what was going on.

He didn't give us time to speak; he just started talking.

"I need to switch out all the spots and move all the stash houses because we have a snake in this muthafucka. The spot on Woodrow Street got hit, but luckily for us, I changed things up there months ago. I no longer have any safes or product at that house because it was one of the few the old crew knew about. I wasn't taking any chances on the few niggas left catching me slipping. I just wish I

would have stopped Deuce and Jay from going there to smash from time to time. They got my boys, but luckily them niggas not dead. They were able to bust back and fend them niggas off until AnDro and Shane showed up."

After hearing that, I felt even worse about my news, but Pops didn't raise no coward, so I stepped up to tell Zay what I came there for. *"Yo Zay, I know this is the last thing you wanna hear, but I have to tell you why I needed to see you."*

"Nigga, I done already heard about your little problem. Moms called me to tell me your girl whipped your ass on the front lawn after she caught you on the phone with one of your jump-offs. Shit, just looking at your head I can tell she put in that work," he said and started laughing hysterically.

I didn't see the humor in the situation, but if it took his mind off his boys getting hit up, I guess I could take one for the team. Ignoring him laughing at my expense, I finally told him what I came to say. *"That's part of what I needed to talk to you about, Zay. I plan to cut Chandra off completely, and that hoe knows some of what goes on at the spot. I've smashed that hoe in the back room enough for her to see some shit and know some shit. So, I wanna make sure we cover all bases before I drop her for good."*

Zaylar looked at me hard before nodding his head and starting toward the door to the spot. Me and K-O followed behind him and entered the house to see damn near everything packed up and ready to be moved.

Zay turned to me, *"I told you we were changing all the spots and switching shit up, but it makes me proud as fuck that you came clean, even though you didn't have to. That's the mark of a man, and it lets me know you and your crew are ready to handle your own spot. Get started on the shit in the back. The van will be here in an hour. The new setup will belong to your crew exclusively. Choose your people wisely. You need a nine-person crew. The hours will be long, but the payoff is sweet. Just remember keep your grass cut low, so you can see the snakes trying to approach."*

That was the last thing Zay said as we all got to work cleaning the place out like we had never been there.

CHAPTER FIVE Zylar
Crewens

April 21, 2011

Over the past three weeks, I barely had time to eat or sleep as we got things up and running at the new spot. I handpicked my crew of young hitters who were hungry and deadly. All of them have been part of my unofficial crew since I first started working for my brother after Pops was killed, so I knew that each of them was loyal and ready to get this paper.

Kayden "K-Boy" Blake is the nigga who busts his gun first and asks questions never. He's eighteen, like me, with a baby girl that he takes care of.

Next is Cree "C-Lo" Logan, the nigga on my left. He's nineteen and loves to fight. He's deadly with his hands and has an aura that screams danger, so everybody in the street knows not to fuck with him.

Then there's Myron Dax, a twenty-year-old who used to work for Pops and has watched my back as I learned the game from Zaylar. He stayed in the shadows, showing us how to move in silence with violence. He has degrees in business and is smarter than anyone else I know. Both he and C-Lo are smart and have all kinds of business ideas.

We also have Jayce, Kamden "Kam," Lance, and Jamie Shaw, who are all cousins. They are eighteen, nineteen, and twenty years old. They have been hustling with us over the years but never got the chance to step up until now. They're loyal and like us, all about their paper.

Finally, there's my eighteen-year-old right-hand man, Karel "K-O" Ogan.

That sums up our team, and so far, the setup that C-Lo and Myron put in place works great. It's to the point where we have been making more money than we have time to spend.

It's just K-O and me in the trap today, with C-Lo making runs. Our trap has been producing good numbers, even on the slow days, Monday through Wednesday. I can't complain about much, but I really miss my girl. Raylexia has disappeared on me, and her friends and I are worried sick. K-O told me she would reach out when she had time to cool down, and I want to believe him. It's just hard when she hasn't even been in contact with her closest friends.

"Zy, what the hell has you so preoccupied in this bitch? If I was coming to rob you, you wouldn't have seen me coming. You'd be dead, not even knowing I was ever here," C-Lo asked as he pulled out the counter and got situated to start separating the cash in the duffle bags he collected from the runners.

"Nigga, you can't sneak up on anybody with that menacing ass aura coming off you in waves. I might not have seen you, but I felt yo ass. I don't know where Raylexia is, and that shit is starting to make me wonder if she planned this. I know she caught me cheating, but that's no reason for her to leave and not even contact her friends. I'm beginning to think something may have happened to them," I told C-Lo as K-O walked into the back.

"Nigga, Ray is off somewhere doing her. She ain't worried about you. You might as well chill with Chandra since messing around with those other hoes is what caused you to break up with Ray," K-O said.

"I see you got jokes nigga. Raylexia will forever be mine. I don't care what I did. I haven't been fuckin with Chandra or anyone else. I just need to find my girl and make things right," I told them, and they both fell out laughing.

"Well, good luck with that. Let me know how that works out for you," K-O quipped and changed the subject. *"Man, this place is poppin'. We are almost out of product,"* K-O said and handed me the money to separate and prepare for the drop.

"I know. We've been selling out, so Myron asked Stacy to up us to 5 kilos a week. We've been supplying the corner boys and the drivers with their weight, so we're light by Friday. Especially when the first of the month falls on a Friday. We get all the money from the dopefiends that get checks on the first and third, along with the ones that get paid on Fridays. It's not convenient to call and wait for a drop when the traffic is that high. That's how niggas get caught slipping. I'd rather have too much product than too little," C-Lo added.

"*Yeah, I'm with you on that one. Having to wait for more product is not the way to move. Did y'all see how they just posted up and waited outside until Jayce brought it in? That shit was crazy. They all damn near bum-rushed him when he left,*" K-O added.

"*Yeah, and that shit is dangerous and caused a big commotion outside. We definitely don't need to draw that kind of attention to this spot. If not for Shanna serving meals outside, the neighbors would have probably called the police,*" C-Lo mentioned and glanced at me. "*Zy, why you so quiet?*"

"*Nigga, didn't I just tell you that my girl is on my mind? If not for working here, I would have lost my mind with worry. This at least keeps me busy. Her mom stays gone for months at a time. I just hope everything is alright with them,*" I told them, and both K-O and C-Lo kept quiet while we all counted and bagged up the money for the drop. No one had anything else to say.

Zylar Crewens

July 2, 2011

The layout for this spot is totally different from all the other traps because we run three two-man shifts and have four different pick-up times that rotate daily. Since five of us attend college, we switch out the various jobs daily to work around our class schedules. No two people ever run the spot consistently, nor does the same person handle the money. Zaylar watched how we moved and said he liked the new changes we made, and that he might have me help him set up the spots in other cities. As much as I would have loved to take credit for our new system, I had to tell him it was all Myron and C-Lo's doing. Those guys had plans and a vision that had us running the new spot like a top-line burger joint. Even with the large amount of traffic going through the place, it all seemed normal because Myron had a shortie named Shanna who sold plate lunches and dinners that changed daily. The sweet thing is she was none the wiser about what we really did. She was 100% about her own paper, so other than selling us plates to eat, she didn't talk to anybody but Myron.

"Zy, why are you looking like death warmed over in this bitch?" Zaylar asked as he came into the backroom of the spot. He didn't normally pop up without giving me a heads-up, so I looked at him to see what kind of visit we were having.

Looking him over, nothing showed on his face, so I answered with what I was feeling. *"Nigga, I haven't seen my girl in over four months, and when I call her number, it says it's disconnected. I went by her apartment, and they have moved. Her girlfriends can't even tell me where their new spot is because her mom moved them out without leaving any phone numbers or their new address. What's even worse is I can't get rid of Chandra's thirsty ass for nothing. I told that hoe we were done, and she turned into a straight-up stalker. I had about five of them in rotation, so dropping her was never an issue. She was just convenient because she would drop everything and come whenever and wherever when I called. She just wants to hang out and brag to her bird-ass friends that she still spends time with me. That never mattered to me before, but now things have changed, and I can't have that shit getting back to Ray."*

"It's bad enough that the last time I saw her, we had our little fight, and she thinks she's single now. Just the thought of another nigga touching that girl has me having murderous thoughts. I can't and won't allow her to be with anyone but me, and I put that on everything I love. The craziest part of all this shit is that I was only still messing around with those hoes because Ray refuses to go to the club and socialize with me. She said I'm surrounded by a bunch of fake-ass people, and she doesn't want to be around that shit. Now that she's gone, I barely want to go anywhere, and I can't stand to be around any of those hoes," I expressed as I kept getting the money for the drop ready.

C-Lo would be here in 30 minutes, and we had to do a double drop. The crazy thing about the new setup is with the food we offer outside; the fiends think it's a one-stop shop. They buy food and product, making us double our normal numbers.

"That's because you are finally beginning to figure out quality over quantity. With Ray, you had a good, solid female who loved you for you and didn't care about your status in these streets or the amount of money you have in your pocket. Those other hoes only want to be with you for what you can give them or the perks that come from being in your circle. With Ray gone, you can finally see the difference, and now you know what you've lost. Now that you know better, you'll do better... if it's not too late." Zaylar just made my blood boil.

"Nigga, what the fuck do you mean, if it's not too late? Ray is mine, will always be mine, and I refuse to let her be with anybody but me. I just have to find her," I told Zay, making sure he understood my meaning. *"Ray and I are 'til the casket drops, and I mean that shit. She can't be with no one but me. She can play with it and die around this muthafucka."*

"Yeah, whatever you say. Good luck with that." Zaylar spoke looking at what I was doing. *"What the hell are you doing? Why do you have two drops? Did y'all miss a pickup?"*

I laughed at this nigga's abrupt change of subject, knowing I was about to blow his mind with my words. I didn't even get the chance cause he was checking me again, sounding even more annoyed about my laughing. *"Lil bro, what the fuck is so funny? I know y'all niggas aren't slacking off on the new system y'all put in place already?"* Zay sounded like he was getting more heated by the minute.

I decided to put him out of his misery. *"Bruh, chill. It ain't even like that. We have a double drop because of the traffic flow in this place. We don't hold no cash over, so if we make enough for two drops, we send two drops."*

Zaylar looked at me like I was crazy because of what I just said. He had to come check both drops because he didn't believe we were moving weight like this. After he examined both, he sat down at the table and stared at me.

"What's wrong, Zay? Why are you looking at me like that?" He had me worried the way he just sat there looking crazy.

"First, how many times a day do you have to make double drops, and how long have you been making double drops?" Zaylar asked with a demonic look on his face. His eyes turned black, and I could tell that my answer would change something in my brother forever.

I had to think about how long we were doing the new system and when the food started. *"We started doing double drops two and a half months ago. On average, we have double drops three to four times a day. I assumed Biz made you aware of this our first week with the new setup because I called to let him know we were not going to hold the money here since you always increase our pay based on our profit,"* I explained, causing him to spring from his chair just as C-Lo walked in, yelling for me to get Myron here now.

I wasted no time pulling out my cell phone to hit Myron up. He answered on the third ring, sounding tired as hell. That nigga did a double shift last night and this morning since K-Boy couldn't work cause his daughter had to get shots today. Myron volunteered to work his shift since he was already here and just stayed over until I relieved him three hours ago.

"Hello," he said, sounding like he swallowed glass.

"Aye nigga, we need you to come back and bring the books with the drop charts. Zaylar wanna look at that shit right now." That woke him up fast as hell.

"I'm on my way," was all he said, and the line went dead.

C-Lo had just been standing there waiting for us to turn over the drop.

"What the hell is going on, Zay? You act like this is your first time hearing about the extra drops, and that makes no sense. We have been getting extra product for over two whole months. I know for a fact you, Eric, or Biz have to okay that in order for us to receive the right amount of increase. So, what's the deal? Don't leave me and my crew hanging."

Before Zay had a chance to say anything, K-O came in to do a safe drop and noticed the drop still sitting on the table. *"What's good? And why the hell is the drop still sitting here? Myron's gonna have a fuckin' fit about us messing up his timetable for the drops,"* K-O said until he laid eyes on Zay pacing the room like a caged animal. He turned to look at me like I could shed some light on the situation, but I was just like him, wondering what the fuck is going on.

MYRON FINALLY WALKED in twenty minutes later with the drop schedule and the drop amounts for each day we had been in business. Zaylar was impressed and made Myron explain the system to him and how it works. Myron started talking, and we all listened.

"Aight, first off, we do the drops at different times every day, so no one but us knows our drop schedule. Since it changes so regularly, no one, not even us, knows whose turn it will be. It's based on who comes in at the drop time, and we don't know that until we walk in the door. Keeps us all honest. Each drop holds between $5-10K, depending on the sales for the day. If you look here, you'll see the first two days of sales were high, and that's what made us switch to double drops after having a $50K drop at the end of our third night using the new system."

"The corner boys and drivers make their drops to us after they have more than $500 in cash. We didn't feel comfortable holding all the cash in one spot for long periods, so we came up with the double drops. Up to today, not including today's money, we have dropped off $1.2 million," Myron stated, showing Zaylar the amounts from all our drops with dates, times, and each person doing the drops and who received the money. Myron even had each person receiving the money initial the drop sheet with totals on it, making sure our tracking system was airtight.

After Zay had a chance to go over all our information with Myron, I could tell something was off. Zay looked more hurt than anything.

"What's really good, Zay? From what I can see, you had no idea about the increase, nor have you been informed of any of the changes we made damn near three months ago. That's a serious breach in your inner core, my nigga. From the looks of it, they have no plans to clue you in on these changes. My question is, are you ready to clean house?" C-Lo asked, voicing the thoughts running through all our minds.

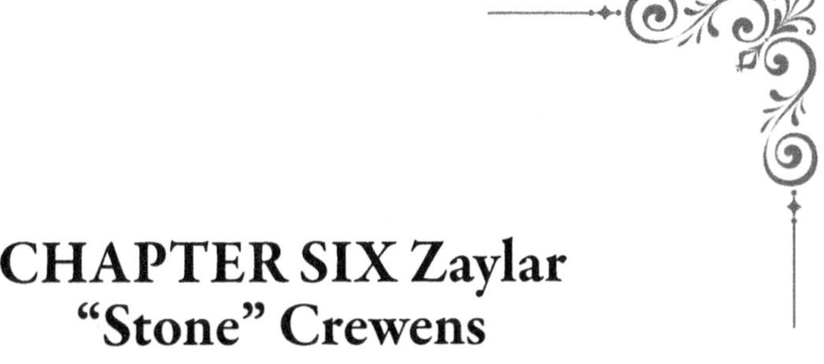

CHAPTER SIX Zaylar
"Stone" Crewens

Let me introduce myself. I am that muthafucka, Zaylar "Stone" Crewens, and I run shit in one of the deadliest southern states. If it's about moving that product, I'm your man. The shit that has me so stuck right now is that the snakes in my camp are my so-called right and left-hand men. Them niggas, Stacy "Biz" Clay, Eric Taylor, and Antone "Red" Flakes, have been with me since I started hustling at fifteen, learning the craft from my dad. We came up in this shit together, and I treated all of them niggas like my family. We ran this shit together until Red caught a drug charge a couple of months after I took over for my Pops. Come to think of it, Red maintained all through his trial that he was set up. He said he never transported drugs in his personal vehicle, and I believe him. It was something Pops put in place long ago. After this shit happened, I believe they had something to do with him getting locked up. But I cannot for the life of me understand why they thought they could steal from me and get away with it. Now it's time for me to reintroduce them to that nigga "Stone."

That lil' nigga C-Lo spoke up on what I'm sure everyone in the spot was thinking. My right and left hand have my whole inner core team looking foul as fuck because they on some other shit. I have to make an example out of them bitch-made niggas or retire from the game. I am nowhere near done making this bread, so them niggas finna pay dearly for the disrespect and all-around griminess they displayed. I just have to figure out who I can and can't trust around this bitch. This just makes me wonder if the hit on the spot on Woodrow Street was actually to rob the spot or to take out my loyal crew. Going with what my gut is telling me, them niggas were trying to kill off my soldiers. I have no choice now but to bring in my hitters. Kahmala, Killian,

Khiershan, and Kilayla O'Shae have been moving between the other cities in Louisiana, training new hitters and setting up slaughterhouses for just this type of occasion. Now I gotta have them come help me clean house.

Looking over at Zylar and his crew, I think I just found my new right-hand man. *"Say, Zylar, I need you to get your whole crew here now. I have a proposition for you and your team, and I need this done like yesterday,"* I instructed, and all them niggas got on the phone calling the rest of their team.

While we waited for them to show up, I decided to speak to Myron and C-Lo about the first part of my plans. *"Say, Myron. You and C-Lo let me holla at y'all about some changes we need to make."* I had barely started speaking when Myron and C-Lo approached me with expectant looks on their faces.

"Zylar told me that you guys are responsible for the new setup. First off, I want to tell you guys that the system you have here is the best I've ever seen. I want you two to go from city to city and set up the other houses that I have the same way. This system makes it super easy to keep control of the money. Plus, as you said, it keeps the workers honest."

"With the shit I have going on right now, I need nothing but loyal muthafuckers around me. The other thing I need is for you guys to change up the system on the top level to reflect the profits from stash house to stash house, and the input and output in the warehouse. Can y'all system be utilized on that level?" I asked, referring to them changing our whole setup.

⁓

Myron Dax

I couldn't believe our luck as C-Lo and I listened to Zaylar run down what he wanted us to do. This is our chance to finally show Zaylar what we can do and how much better we can make this operation run. I've been in the game since I was twelve, working on the side for Zaylar and Zylar's dad, Big Z. I used to score genius level on tests in school, but none of that paid the bills. Mom has been working two jobs all my life, but we could barely keep the bills paid and food on the table. So, I started doing small runs for Big Z at twelve years old, earning $200 to $500 a run, twice a month. That's how I got my start in the game.

I've been lowkey since then, only doing enough to help Mom with the bills and keep us with food. I got full ride scholarships to pay for college at the age of fourteen and graduated with a master's degree in business administration at eighteen. Now, I'm working on business plans for when I build up enough money to buy a couple of businesses and start flipping houses and small businesses. If I can get Zaylar to invest and fund the project, I can make us all very rich.

"To answer your question, yes. We can make you an even better system for the warehouse and other houses, but first, we must get a new warehouse and additional houses set up. Leave what you have in place, so they think everything is still good. Do they know the connect, or are you the only one with that information? Depending on how you answer, we can determine how easy it will be to weed out the snakes in your camp." I hoped they didn't know the connect.

"No, they don't know the connect and have no idea when or how we receive product. I met the connect when I first started learning the business from my dad, and I learned how we receive product and pay the connect. No one other than me and Zylar knows who the connect is," Zaylar answered, looking offended.

I smiled, showing all thirty-two of my teeth because Zay just made my day. *"Okay, that's music to my ears. First, we get a new warehouse set up. Preferably a truck rental business and storage facility with at least three levels. If we can purchase the Move-It Company for sale over off Hollywood and 12th, that would be perfect for our needs. They are already established and have a good reputation for quality service. We would just have to build on and improve by adding more services.*

Second, we need to start doing pickups from all the houses and stop the product flow for two to three months. None of the houses in Louisiana can re-up until we have everything in place under the new system. This will give you time to find out who you can trust, and who we need to take out. Next, we need all new spots in all the key subdivisions in the Shreveport area, so they won't know anything when we start back up. C-Lo, what do you think?" I asked because he was being a little too quiet.

Cree "C-Lo" Logan

Sitting back, listening to that nigga Myron talk, I knew that we thought so much alike it was creepy. I was thinking the same thing. If them niggas don't know the connect and we cut off their supply of money and product, they are done. We just have to change everything up fast enough to catch them unaware.

Since I was fourteen, I've been on my own. My mom went to jail, and none of her folks would take me in. My dad had a hand problem and beat my mom so bad one night that I got tired of that shit and bashed his head in with a bat. Mom took the charge, thinking since she was all beat up, they would let her off. Too bad for us, that wasn't the case. They charged her with involuntary manslaughter and sentenced her to five years. I've been staying in her apartment since she went to jail, but my aunt has been renewing the lease for me every year, so I don't have to live with them. Hustling came easy, so I've been straight. This is just my first time being able to make some real money. Just listening to Myron's plan, I know exactly what else we need.

"Since Myron already recommended the storage and trucking setup, we had our eyes on, you also need to purchase a strip club. We recommend Mimi's over on Bayed Road. They have a steady clientele, and the place is clean and well-lit. We'd have to do a small remodel to update the restrooms, add VIP sections, install video surveillance, and expand the bar area, so we can reopen in about three months. That way, we have a safe location for the soldiers to kick back and let loose while spending money with you. You also need a car dealership. We recommend Shortie's because he has top-quality merchandise and makes a profit each year off his foreign whips. He is only selling the business so he can retire to Florida with his new, very young wife."

"The car lot will serve dual purposes. First, we can add on a chop shop to break down cars that we need to dispose of, and we can buy and sell our

merchandise to our soldiers. That way, the money comes back to you in trade. Acquiring these businesses will also help clean up the drug money and make it look legit on paper. While you own several car washes, barbershops, and laundromats, none of those will bring in enough daily revenue to adequately clean up the money fast enough to have cash on hand to use with ease."

"By adding these businesses, we clean it as we make it. Next, leave your boys where they are, just slowly remove all your money from their control, and never allow anyone but you or your brother to have full control in the event you're out of pocket. You gave them niggas too much power, and it went to their heads. They forgot that you don't bite the hand that feeds you."

Zaylar "Stone" Crewens

Just listening to C-Lo and Myron explain their plans for my operation, I was floored. Them niggas had to have been working on this for some time. I'm just glad I have them on my team now.

"Okay, when do we start, and how long before we can have everything in place?" I was ready to give them the go-ahead.

Myron was the first to speak. *"If you have enough legitimate cash on hand to make the purchases for all the businesses, we can get the properties bought and remodeled within about three months. The setup for the warehouse will be the most extensive because we will have a legit rental, storage, and moving business, along with divisions for our drug manufacture and distribution center combined. The business itself takes up three and a half blocks, including a parking lot across the street from the warehouse. Adding the area for manufacturing and distribution will take the most time because all the walls will have to be insulated and soundproofed. We have a contractor on standby; his prices are reasonable, and he does top-quality work."*

C-Lo hung up his phone and took over. *"I just called Nina. She is getting the paperwork started on offers for each property with the amounts we agreed on. Zaylar, she has been talking to each of the owners on our behalf for the last six months. She believes she can buy them all for 1. 2 million. Do you have that in the bank as legit cash on hand?"*

"Yes. My brothers and I have over 2.5 million apiece from Dad's life insurance policies alone due to his accidental death. I can have that amount cleared from the bank first thing tomorrow. Let's do this," I told them to get the ball rolling.

As we finished up, I noticed the rest of Zylar's crew had arrived and were patiently waiting at the back, giving us privacy. None of them knew what they were here for, but they dropped everything and came as quickly as possible. I liked the level of dedication they all showed to making this money. I guess I should explain why I have them all here.

"Come here, Zylar." I pulled him aside to ask about his crew.

"Can I trust your crew to handle this job? They will be responsible for helping me clean house and reshape our traps throughout the state. Do you believe they are ready?" I asked as soon as he was within reach.

Zylar looked over his crew and replied without hesitation. *"My crew has been ready, Zay. They have been for some time now; you just never gave them a chance. Not only are they hungry, but every one of them is loyal to you and me. They all had the utmost respect for Dad and grieved when we lost him. They are some of the coldest young niggas we have in this state. More than that, they are down for whatever and loyal to a fault."*

"Alright then," I replied as I turned to address his crew.

"What's up, my niggas?" I gave each one dap.

"I called you all here because I am promoting your whole team. I like what you all have been able to accomplish at this spot. I wanna see us do this at each spot throughout all of Northern Louisiana and then take it to the other cities in the Eastern, Western, and Southern parts of the state. To make that happen, I am promoting you all. You will be responsible for several traps in the different cities throughout the state that we control. I know most of you are young, and before seeing what you all have been able to accomplish at this spot, I would have never entertained the idea of letting you all control your own crews. With that being said, Myron and C-Lo will be working with each of you to get you ready to control the crews and maintain your new traps. We first have to get the new setup up and running, so this spot will only be open another two days. Don't worry about pay because, as of right now, you all will be getting paid even after we close the spot down in two days."

"Some of you will also be going to the other spots I have set up to pick up all drops and bring them to the location Myron and C-Lo set up with our new stash house. It is now going to be your job to clear all money from every trap we have in Louisiana. We will no longer be making drops to the old warehouse. The drops from all traps will all be coming here until the new safehouse is put in place. Also, we have some snakes in our camp, but we are going to leave them be until we have everything in place and them completely disconnected from the business. That way I don't have to worry about them turning rat after they realize the

money train has stopped. I know this goes against street code, and I am itching to make them bitch-made niggas pay for the disrespect, but protecting what my father built is more important than killing them hoe-ass niggas right now. Any questions?"

Zylar's crew jumped right in, asking questions about the new setup and what they could do to make it run better. All of which I deferred to C-Lo and Myron. I know good and well what my strengths are, and organization is not one of them. For them to be so young, their main goals seem to be centered around making the setup work better for all of us. Not one of them asked anything about how much of a pay increase they would be getting for the additional work they would have to put in. That by itself made me decide to give them all a bonus and promote them all to lieutenant, which comes with a pay increase. Listening to Zylar's team made me go back and reevaluate all the niggas I have on my team. Off the top of my head, I can only say about ten of them are somewhat close to the members of my little brother's team.

CHAPTER SEVEN
Raylexia Gavion

August 30, 2011

I have been totally and completely cut off from all the people that I have come to rely on to help me through these fucked-up situations my mother always seems to put us in. She never has to deal with any of the fallout, so she just changes shit for us and goes on about her business. These past four and a half months have been some of the hardest for us, and things just keep getting progressively worse. Three days after I found out Zylar was cheating on me, Mom had us packed up and moved to this three-bedroom, two-bath duplex in the Queensborough subdivision. She was approved for Section 8 that paid over 95% of her total rent cost. The problem with this move is that Mom seems to have forgotten that she would still have to pay utilities and rent when staying in a house. We now have gas, lights, and water to add to her portion of the rent that equals $39.25, and that's just the rent. Which doesn't include the essential household bills needed to sustain normal living conditions. Thank God Raquon brought Rodereck a Nintendo game system with plenty of games because Mom didn't get cable or a phone setup, leaving us without a way to contact anybody.

The first month started off fine, or so we thought. Mom got us all transferred over to the area schools. Reign now goes to Queensborough Elementary, Rodereck goes to Midway Middle, and I attend Fair Park High. The first issue we have is that I need to be at school by 7:15 a.m, and Rodereck must be there by 7:30 a.m., which leaves no one to put Reign on her bus that usually comes between 7:15 a.m and 7:35 a.m. I have been putting Reign on the bus and then going to school, which causes me to completely miss my first class. The school has sent home four letters for Mom to come to parent conferences, but she has not been home since she got us all moved in, and I have no way to contact her without a phone. The school now has me on suspension until Mom comes to the conference. Mrs. Joy, the principal's secretary, lives down the street and has warned me that by law, she will have to report Mom if she's not home soon.

The second issue we have is that we are running out of food. Grandma Etta and Raquon taught me how to cook most basic foods, so I have cooked all but three packs of meat, but we have no more cold cuts and bread. Normally one of the uncles would have sent us some money by now, but mom didn't even do a change of address form for our old residence, so nothing is being forwarded to our new address. I have a sneaking suspicion that Mom moved us to keep Raquon from finding us when he gets out on some ole vindictive type bullshit. I truly don't understand why she would put us in a situation where we have no one to help us, and we don't know anyone around us to ask for help. I can't even use my side hustle of doing make-up and arching eyebrows because we don't know any of these people out here and I'm unknown. It's like she wants to make us suffer.

The third issue is we found out I was three months pregnant during the move when I started throwing up because of the bumpy ride. Mom took me to the doctor to get my prenatal care started but didn't say anything else. It was as if she didn't care one way or another. I know that I am nowhere near ready to be anyone's parent because I can barely keep me and my siblings together. Now I'm seven and a half months pregnant with no bus fare to get to the doctor to keep up with my prenatal visits. I used all the money that I got from Zylar on the rent, food, and utilities over the first three months, but there's nothing left. The gas and water have been turned off for nonpayment. We don't have any food left in the house, and Mrs. Joy has decided to tell the school tomorrow that we've been home alone for over three months.

There is nothing I can do about all the other things that's going on, but I can at least try to get us some food.

"Rodereck, I am going to walk up to the Price-Lo and get us something to eat for tonight and tomorrow. If I'm not back in two hours, it means I got caught. We can't go another day without something to eat or drink in this house. I know you and Reign have been getting breakfast and lunch at school, but you still need

water and at least a sandwich for overnight," I explained to my brother as I grabbed my backpack and duffle bag to put food in at the store.

"I don't like this, Ray. You are too far along to be trying to do this." He fussed.

"Believe me when I tell you, I don't wanna do this either, but I have no choice. We can't risk you going back up there Rod. It will be okay." I tried to comfort him.

He looked upset. I know he would have normally been the one to go and run out of the store with something for us to eat, because he knows I couldn't outrun the guard in my current condition. But he can't go because they know his face and would have him sent to juvie on sight.

I made the 10 min walk in 15 min in a full sweat, with my ankles swollen and hurting. I made sure to head straight to the hand baskets to sit my duffle inside and kept my backpack on my back. Moving through the store, I got ham, cheese, bologna, smoked sausage, bread, chips, juice, and water. I made sure to keep an eye out for the guard while making my way up front. Grabbing the bag out the basket, I left it at the end row of chips and headed for the front exit. Just as I turned to make my way past the last checkout, the security guard stepped out in my path.

The security guard, looking down at me, asked, *"what do you have in the bags, young lady?"*

I looked him straight in the eyes, took a deep breath and spoke, *"food to feed my brother and sister."*

He seemed taken back by my response and looked at me again to see if I was serious. When I just held his gaze, not blinking and looking him straight in the eye, he grabbed my arm and escorted me to the front office. Once inside, he called the police and began to question me again.

"So, why are you stealing food out of the store? I didn't actually see you take anything, but I have seen your younger brother run out of here several times with bags full of food. If not for seeing you guys together when you came to make groceries, I would not have even stopped you." The guard asked me while holding my gaze like he really cared.

Not having anything to lose, I answered him with the truth. *"My mother moved us over here from the Jackson Heights Projects in the Lakeside Subdivision about 4 and a half months ago, and she hasn't been home in over*

3 months. We don't have any more food at home, and they cut off the gas and water 2 days ago. My brother has been running out of the stores up here because we have nothing to eat, and we don't know any of the people around here to ask for any kind of help." I sighed.

"I haven't been to school in two and a half weeks because they need her to come for a parent conference, because I have been missing the first period since starting school to put my baby sister on the school bus. That about sums it all up. I am stealing from the store because we are hungry and have nothing at home to eat or drink."

When I finished talking, the guard excused himself and went out front to speak with the store manager.

Gerald Gains

Gerald Gains had heard some pretty crazy stories coming from the different shoplifters over the years. Never had he heard one that made him want to purchase the products for the thief and let them go, until now. Shaking his head, he lifted his arm to get the manager's attention to discuss the issue before the police arrived.

"Mr. Wells, I really don't think that jail or juvenile detention is the right place for this young lady. After hearing what she has been through over the past 4 and a half months, I believe we should see if the police can possibly get her and her siblings some help," Gerald said, hoping his boss would consider helping the young lady out.

"What do you mean, Gerald? I thought you caught a shoplifter stealing in the store?" Mr. Wells asked, trying to understand what Gerald was talking about.

"Yes, Mr. Wells, she was indeed shoplifting, but after you hear the circumstances, I think you will agree that this young lady and her siblings need some help out of the abusive situation they are living in," Gerald replied, happy that Mr. Wells was at least willing to listen to and maybe consider a different alternative.

"Okay, explain to me what's going on." Mr. Wells listened while Gerald told him what the young lady told him had been going on that led her to these dire circumstances. Just as Gerald finished recounting the facts for Mr. Wells, the police walked up.

After hearing the story, Mr. Wells also wanted to find out if the police could do something to help the children out of this situation. So, with that in mind, they both spoke with the police and explained the situation hoping the police could do something to help.

Officer Nelly showed up on a call for a shoplifter and got a possible case of abuse and neglect. Just listening to the store manager and guard explain the young lady's situation, he knew it was a case for child protective services. *"Let me call this in and get someone out here, so we can go to the house and check on the other children involved. I take it you no longer want to press charges but want to help them get out of their current situation?"* He asked the store manager to be sure they were all on the same page.

"Correct," Mr. Wells replied, hoping that everything would work out for the young woman and her siblings.

Raylexia Gavion

October 16, 2011

To my shock and surprise, me going to Price-Lo Foods to try and steal some food for us turned out to be a blessing in its own way. The police called Child Protective Services, and they took me back to the house to find everything I said to be true. We were then placed in foster care with Mrs. Chance. She allowed us all to stay together for the time it took for me to go to court and get me emancipated so I could get full custody of my siblings. I missed so many days from school and fell off track in the accelerated magnet program that I was in. Even though I am only 16 years old, I skipped two grades and am classified as a senior in high school. They allowed me to take the GED test and graduate early. Mom was charged with abuse and neglect of three minor children and lost her parental rights, along with having to serve two years' probation for child abuse and neglect.

On September 13, 2011, I was emancipated and awarded full custody of both Rodereck and Reign. We were able to get the mail held at the post office from our old address and information for my uncles. After they found out what happened with mom, they all sent me over $10,000 to help me with expenses. They spoke with child services and set up accounts so they all could send me money each month to pay bills and provide for my siblings while I finished school. Working with Child Protective Services and Section 8, they helped me get my own place in a newly built apartment complex in the Southern Hills Subdivision. They made sure to get a place with electricity and appliances included to minimize the amount of bills I would have to pay each month. So, I added a combo bill of internet, cable, home phone, and cell phone service. That way me and Rodereck can have a reliable way to keep in touch with each other.

With the help of Mrs. Chance, we managed to get everything in place just in time for me to give birth to my son Zander Zylar Crewens on October 16, 2011. Mrs. Chance helped me purchase all the new bedding and towels for the apartment and got everything moved over from my mother's house. The landlord allowed me to have it all since Mom never came back, and he was just going to have it thrown away. She set it up and had everything moved in while I was in the hospital. She even made sure to spend money on all the necessities we needed, including a washer, dryer, and microwave.

Raylexia Gavion

October 19, 2011

Today I was released from the hospital with my baby, and Mrs Chance came to help me get settled in. She agreed to let Rodereck and Reign stay with her while I was recovering to help get them transferred over to the schools in the new district. She has truly been a gift from God to me and my siblings, and she has the kindest heart. Mrs Chance is a 55-year-old divorcee who became a foster parent to help children in need and to have the income to pay her bills. She was a homemaker for twenty years when her husband decided to divorce her and marry a woman in her 20's.

"How are you feeling?" Mrs Chance asked me as we walked into the four-bedroom apartment on the south side over by the main office to the apartment complex.

"I am a little sore, but I'm not in any real pain. How long before I am well enough to get around, and sign up for school? Since I got my GED and they let me graduate early, I want to apply for the Business Management program at the University of Shreveport," I told Mrs Chance, ready to plan out my next moves. *"I need to apply for the Pell Grant and have one of my uncles submit the information for my military dependent subsidy grant as well. If I can help it, I don't want to apply for any loans to cover the cost of school, because I don't need any added expenses."*

"You should be able to move around like normal in a couple of days or so, but you won't be able to resume your normal activities for six weeks. That gives your body a chance to heal and return to normal." Mrs Chance looked at me with a worried expression.

I nodded and took off my shoes by the door. Then I walked over to take a seat on the couch as Mrs Chance sat the car seat holding Zander down next to me. *"That's a relief,"* I sighed.

"Raylexia, I know you want to become independent as soon as possible, but please don't rush it and cause yourself to have a setback. I know from the conversations we have had over the past few months that you never want to find yourself in the same situation again, but you need not worry. I am here for you, and you can use me as a reliable support." Mrs Chance laid a blanket and pillow down for me to sleep on and arranged all Zander's things for easy access in the living room near the sectional.

I laid down on the blanket and curled up ready to get some rest. *"Thank you Mrs Chance, I really appreciate all you're doing for us."* I told her and closed my eyes.

We decided I would sleep on the sectional for the next few days to be close to the bathroom, kitchen, front and back doors. This new apartment is really wonderful and in a nice upscale area over by where Zylar's mom lives. I have to be careful not to run into her while I'm out or she will surely inform her son of my whereabouts.

Thanks to Zylar teaching me how to drive and Mrs Chance taking me to get my license, my uncles purchased me a used 2009 Ford Expedition. Mrs Chance put it in her name for me since I am technically still a minor and to keep the insurance reasonable. I now have transportation for me and the kids. Hopefully I'll be able to maintain it. I know no matter what I'll never let us return to the way we lived with Mom.

Raylexia Gavion

January 11, 2012

It has been twelve weeks since I came home from the hospital with Zander, and I must say things have been going really well for me and my siblings. I have fully recovered from giving birth and started the winter/spring semester at the University of Shreveport for a master's degree in business administration with a strong concentration on Finance. Rodereck loves the new school he goes to and has made several new friends in the neighborhood. I think that because of his thuggish appearance and constant use of slang, he is the one all the middle schoolers over here look up to. Reign likes her new school as well, but it takes her time to make friends because she don't fuck with people she don't know. I also think a lot of her issues come from missing her dad. I was finally able to get his information from the Parish jail, and we all wrote him a letter letting him know where we were and what happened to us after he got locked up. He was upset that we went through all that, especially when he said his mom would have taken us in. I ignored that because Reign is four years old and has never met this mother he's talking about. He told me he has a little over two months left to serve for his violation, and he'll be released. I told him he could come visit Reign whenever he is free, and I added call time on the phone for him to talk to her once a week. I thanked him for all he did for us and let him know we really appreciated it.

Mrs. Chance has been watching Zander and my siblings for me to go to school and work. The foster care service pays her because I qualify for the service until after I have finished school if I maintain at least a 2.5 grade point average. They also send me a check every month for $500 to help with expenses since I exited the program with no solid support. Thanks to Mr. Wells at Price-Lo Foods, I have a job as a cashier that pays me $7.50 an hour for 25 hours a week that I started in December. We now have a little over $12,000 in our personal savings bank account. In addition, I have been able to add $1000 a month to the checking account the uncles set up for me to pay bills that has a little over $8000.

For the first time in my life, I feel that I might just survive. The only thing that has been troubling me lately is I really miss Winkie, Johnya, Deana, and Shamena, but I don't know if I can trust them not to tell Zylar how to find me. I know it's wrong for me not to tell him about Zander, but I feel he would try to use that connection to come back in my life. We can co-parent, but I refuse to play the dummy for him or anyone else. Besides, he may have just been a fluke because I haven't been able to find anyone other than him and Daylon's mean ass attractive. Maine, Mr. Wells' son, has been trying to ask me out since I started working at Price-Lo Foods back in December, but I'm not interested. He acts like I should be grateful that he asked me out. That's a total turn-off.

Throwing caution to the wind, I decided to call Winkie. She picked it up just before it switched over to voicemail, speaking carefully since I know she does not recognize my new number. *"Hello, who is this?"*

"Hey, girl. It's me." I waited to hear how she would respond.

"OMG! Raylexia, where the hell have you been, girl? We have all been worried sick about you and the kids. Zylar has been over here every other week to see if we have talked to you. Are you, Rodereck, and Reign alright? Why the hell did it take you close to ten months to reach out to us? Me and Johnya damn near messed up in the program over worrying about you. Let me call the girls, hold on," Winkie asked, barely even taking a breath.

"No, don't call the girls because I'm short on time, and yes. We are all fine now, but that wasn't the case a little while ago. I'm sorry you guys went through that, but I had a good reason for not getting in touch with you guys. I must ask that you please do not tell Zylar that you have spoken to me, and whatever you do, don't give him my number. We broke up before we moved, and I have no intention of ever speaking to him again," I told Winkie in all seriousness. If she couldn't do this for me, I would have to cut ties with her for good.

"I had no idea you guys had broken up. Does it have something to do with the girl Chandra that keeps popping up on him whenever he's out in public or there's a party going on? That hoe be all in his personal space, even though he

tries to push her away and tells her to get the fuck on. Me and Deana were at the mall last week, and that hoe and a handful of her friends were there. Zylar and K-O walked out of Footlocker and that hoe followed that man from store to store trying to talk to him. He just ignored her and continued on about his business. That shit was hella embarrassing. Shit, I was ashamed on her behalf." Winkie just further let me know I was making the right decision to stay away from him with his cheating ass.

"That day you watched the children for me, I caught him on the phone with her making plans for her to come over to the spot the next day. We had a fight about it, and I told him we were over. He made threats about there being no leaving him and killing me if I fool around with somebody else. Then Mom moved us, and he doesn't know where I am, and I plan to keep it that way." Winkie remained quiet on the phone.

"Anyway, enough about all that. I have so much more to tell you, but I want to tell you, Johnya, Deana, and Shamena at the same time. Can you guys meet me at the Pierre Bossier Mall next Saturday at about 12 p.m.? I have to get Rodereck the new Jordans that come out next week, and Saturday is my only chill day. Will you see if everyone is free for me? Cause I really want to explain everything only once. Make sure they know not to say anything about me to Zylar or anyone else." I tried my best to express the importance of them, not mentioning me to anybody.

"This is my personal cell phone number, so store it and call me back to let me know if everyone can make it on Saturday to the Mall at 12:00 p.m."

"I will, and it's so good to hear your voice. I really missed my bestie, and I have something important I need to tell you too. Talk to you later," Winkie said before ending the call.

I released a deep breath; glad I got a chance to reconnect with one of my friends. I just hope and pray I'm not making a big mistake.

CHAPTER EIGHT Zylar
Crewens

January 18, 2012

I can't believe it's been over nine months since I saw my girl. It's like she disappeared into thin air. None of her homegirls in her old neighborhood have heard from her or seen her since they moved, so they are all just as worried about her as I am. There must have been some truth to what Ma said about Ray being different from all the other girls I've been with, cause none of them would have let a week go by without calling. Here it is damn nearly ten months later, and I have yet to get a single phone call from her. I wonder if this is what she meant by showing me better than she could tell me about us being over. Did she know they were moving? If so, she had me fucked up if she thinks I'm going to just let her go. I meant what I said. We're both in this until the casket drops, and I refuse to let her be with anyone but me. Ironically, all of them hoes that I used to spend time with, can't even make my dick get hard since Ray has been gone. I used to smash that hoe Chandra at least four times a week, and now I can't even stomach the sight of the bitch. Ray left me, and I have no desire to have sex or entertain any of them hoes. If it wasn't for the added responsibility of being Zaylar's new right-hand man, I think I'd have gone crazy.

The new setup that Myron and C-Lo put in place proved to be more effective than expected. We now have multiple thriving businesses and a completely sustainable legitimate income. In addition to the moving & storage warehouse, strip club, and car dealership they had us purchase, they also had Zaylar open a real estate and construction company he named Zander's Realty and Key Stone Construction. Using those companies, along with independent contractors, Myron has been able to purchase and flip several failing businesses and help his girl open a soul food, Cajun, and seafood restaurant and sports bar combination in the West Gate Shopping Center called "Shanna's Sports Bar & Grill." That bitch stays packed. He was also able to purchase and flip homes for the crew all in upscale neighborhoods that he obtained through foreclosure and sold to the crew at a discounted rate, well below market value. C-Lo even brought both him and his mom homes not too far from each other over in the neighborhood where Ma's old place is and had Mrs. Janie's ready to move in after her release next month.

With all the positive changes them niggas were able to make business-wise, Zaylar had Myron and C-Lo practically running this shit. If they say we need to change something, it's done. No questions asked. He has just that much trust in them niggas. The only issue we have is them fuck niggas managed to slip away before we could catch them muthafuckas. Everyone in the organization is on the lookout for them snakes and anyone they are associated with. Zaylar took it a step farther and put a $500,000 bounty on each of them niggas heads, dead or alive.

"Zylar." Hearing Ma call my name snapped me out of my current train of thought, and I exited my new royal blue pearl finished 2012 Mercedes-Benz SL-Class. We had to go ahead and move her to the new gated community in the plush area down off Ellerbe, where we all purchased land after Pops passed since them fuck niggas knew where mom lived. We weren't taking any chances with her safety. The houses we purchased down here sold for more than $2,500,000 and came with five or more acres of land. They also have armed security and 24-hour surveillance. Mom has a five bedroom, six and a half baths that she claims she is waiting for us to fill with her grandbabies.

"What's good wit'cha, ma? I haven't seen you in a whole week, so I thought I'd come by and get me some of your good cooking." I kissed her on the forehead on my way to the kitchen. I could smell something good as soon as I crossed the threshold. Mom must have been thinking about me because I smell crawfish etouffee.

When I made it into the kitchen, I could see Ma really did have me in mind while cooking today. She had a Cajun buffet set out around the island with all my favorite foods. I wasted no time running to the half bath off the foyer to wash my hand so she could fix me a plate.

"Ma, I love you lots. What made you cook for me today?" I asked Ma as she passed me a plate filled to the rim.

"I needed to speak with you about something important, so I figured I'd feed you while we talk."

"Oh, so you were going to call me over today?" I asked.

"Yes, I did something a while ago, and now that I have the information, I'm glad I did."

"Ma, what did you do?" I asked Ma as I began to get a restless feeling in my gut.

"I talked to Nico. He helped me hire a private detective to find Raylexia, and what happened to her since she's been gone. His findings are a bit disturbing," Ma paused before looking at me with an expression I couldn't decipher.

"Zylar, what exactly happened out in that yard the last day Raylexia came by to visit? I know you guys had an argument, but what was said to make her completely cut all communication with you?" Ma asked, looking at me with that same odd expression she had a minute ago.

"Ma, do you know where she is? Is she doing alright? Why would you ask me something like that?" I really didn't want to answer.

"Boy, I didn't just fall off the boat yesterday! Answer my question. What did you do?" She asked more forcefully.

I sighed before looking up at her with a confused expression. *"I hit her after she said something that took me by surprise. I didn't even realize I had hit her until I started feeling the blows that she was throwing back at me. I also told her I would kill her if she left me,"* I sighed.

"I'm not proud of what I did and I'm sorry, Ma. You know I don't hit girls, and I'm embarrassed to even have to tell you that I did something so out of character for me, but Ray just makes me feel and do things I've never done before. Just thinking about her with someone else is driving me crazy."

"But you thought it was okay to cheat on her though. I keep telling you men that us women can do anything you can do better." Ma smirked.

"I admit I was wrong and my actions felt foreign to me. Ray's the only person to evoke that reaction." I grumbled.

"Yeah, yeah, whatever you say," Ma chuckled. *"That may explain the information contained in the file. I was wondering why she didn't call you when*

things got bad." Ma looked at me with a stern expression that I had never seen aimed at me before and shook her head.

"What did you find, Ma?" I asked, ready to know what was going on with Ray. The way she was acting. It can't be good.

"First, I want to know what are your intentions where Raylexia is concerned? I know you have been searching for her, but what do you plan on doing when you find her?"

"That's simple, Ma. I plan to take care of her. She's my girl and I love her. I have been so lost without her these past 10 months. I just wanna make everything right with us. Did you think I had you fix up that house for her on a whim? I love that girl, Ma, and I just wanna do right by her. I never expected her to up and leave like she did. Especially without saying a word or contacting me," I said to Ma, not trying to hide my feelings about Ray.

"Okay, son, I believe you. And if I didn't, I would never share the information about her with you, regardless of you being my son. That girl has been through some really bad things, but she is a fighter." Ma went to the side bar and came back with a legal size manila envelope.

"Raylexia's mom moved them to the Queensborough Subdivision three days after her last visit over to the house. They stayed there for four and a half months until the utilities were turned off, and they had no food. Raylexia was caught at the Price-Lo Food Store trying to steal something for her and her siblings to eat. When the store manager and security guard found out what she had going on and asked the police for help. They called in child protection and she and her sibling were placed in foster care," Ma paused and looked over at me before continuing.

"She was emancipated and awarded full custody of her brother and sister last September. They could never find her mom, so they charged her with abuse and neglect, and sentenced her 2 years of supervised probation. Raylexia lives in Southpoint Plaza Apartments #1106, off the Interloop, and attends the University of Shreveport for business administration. She owns her own SUV and works part time at Price-Lo Foods." Ma finished on a sigh.

I truly did not know what to say. To think that Raylexia went through all of that when she knew perfectly well that she could have called me at any time is unbelievable.

"Did she really believe that we are done? Can she really not understand that she is mine, and that we are in this until we take our last breath?" I said under my breath.

I looked over at Ma to find her watching me closely.

"What else, Ma? Cause I know there's more I can see it in your eyes?" I asked, not quite sure if I could stand more.

"There is more, but I'm not sure if I should be the one to tell you or not," she replied, making me look at her to see if I could gauge her meaning.

That's when it hit me. *"No."* The word came out of my mouth as a hoarse whisper.

"She was pregnant when she left. She had my baby."

Ma just looked at me and nodded her head in the affirmative.

The bottom just fell out beneath my feet. She hated me enough to keep me from my child. Did she really hate me that much?

Della Faye Crewens had seen a lot of things in her 55 years of living, but never had she seen such a look of bewilderment on her youngest son's face.

"Zylar, I ask you again. What did you do, or say to Raylexia to make her believe that she can't trust you with her care?" She asked again, and for the first time, I paid attention.

"Could she really believe she could run and hide from me? That I wouldn't eventually find her?" She is mine, and I refuse to go even a day more without her. I jumped up from the table, leaving my half-eaten meal, and headed for the front door.

"Zylar, wait!" I heard Ma calling as I made my way out to my car. She came running out the door after me.

"You can't just pop up on Raylexia. She goes to school and work on Wednesday, so she will not even be home right now. Will you stop and listen with your hard headed ass. There is no reason for you to go off half assed in this situation. You don't even know where she is right now!" She yelled, making me stop in my tracks.

"Where is she right now, Ma? I really need to see her. She has been hiding my baby from me, and I don't even know if they are okay. I need to find out what is going on with her, but more than any of that. I need to see her and my baby with my own eyes to relieve this restlessness that I have in my soul," I asked after she caught up to me as I opened my car door.

"*I found out from the detective that on Mondays, Wednesdays, and Fridays, Raylexia goes to school from 8 a.m. to 1 p.m. Then she goes to work at Price-Lo Foods from 2pm to 7pm. Right now, she would still be at work, but you can't go up there and cause a scene. Wait until she gets home from work and gets settled in. The sitter she has is the foster parent they placed her with when they removed her and her siblings from their mother. She keeps the children at Raylexia's apartment and goes home when she gets in from work,*" Ma told me as I settled in my car, preparing to do a pop-up on Raylexia.

"*I'll go to her apartment and wait for her to get off. Thanks, Ma. I really appreciate you finding her for me. We'll all be over tomorrow for you to meet your grandchild. It's crazy. I don't even know if it's a girl or boy-*"

"*Well,*" Ma started to say, and I cut in.

"*No. I don't want you to tell me. I'll find out when I see them. Thanks again, Ma. Go inside so I can get over to her apartment. It's almost 7 p.m.*" I waved bye to Ma as she made her way back inside.

Raylexia Gavion

January 18, 2012

This week turned out to be harder to complete than I expected. I keep thinking about meeting up with my girls and explaining what has happened to me since we've been apart. I know they are going to be upset since I didn't reach out to any of them for help, but I couldn't take the chance of Zylar finding me before I had the time to get myself together. I know I was not in love with Zylar, but I had come to care a lot about him since we had become a couple. I expected him to give me the same level of respect I gave him and not cheat on me. Since he did, I have no desire to see him, so I did what's best for me. The shit he did really hurt me, and finding out he cheated on me the entire time we were together was a major slap in the face. I don't know if I trust myself around him right now, and I don't want to end up in jail for fucking him up. If he can cheat on me, get caught, and then expect me to just accept it and keep it moving., he got shit twisted. I care about him still, but I love myself more. I will never be one of many. If I can't be his only woman, I'd rather be nothing at all.

"Ray, are you listening to me?" I heard Maine ask as I continued to clean my station so I could go home.

"I wasn't, but what do you need?" I replied to Maine in a dry voice. He has been trying to get my number since I started working here, and sadly I am not interested. He comes off as one of those spoiled rich kids that's used to getting what he wants, and me turning him down seems to have made him work harder to change my mind. Too bad for him I'm just not interested.

"I was asking if you're free this weekend. I'd like to take you to the movies and out to eat."

"Oh, sorry, Maine. I have plans for this weekend and lots of homework, but thanks for thinking of me," I replied, trying to let him down easy.

"Please don't start asking me personal questions?" I chanted in my head.

Maine tends to ask me out repeatedly like he can change my mind if he keeps asking, but all he ends up doing is making me not want to speak to him at all. Not to say he's not fine, because he's cut the fuck up. Standing at 6'3 with a babyface, hazel brown eyes, muscular build, sporting a low-cut Caesar with sickening waves. He just comes off thirsty as hell, and it's a complete turn off for me.

"Well, can I at least get your number to call you and see when you're free?" He asked the same question he's been asking me the past two months. Maine and I attend the same college, and for some reason, he acts like the word "No" does not compute with him.

"No, Maine. I have told you this before; I'm not ready to date. I just don't have time right now, and I don't like you like that. I have tried to be nice, but you act like you have a problem understanding English. My answer is no. I don't want to go to the movies or out to eat, and I'm not giving you my number. Now, will you please leave me alone? I have not told your dad about you harassing me, but I will. You're up here every day I work, and my coworkers see that I am not into you like that." I finally lost my cool and snapped on Maine, venting some of the penned-up frustration I have from thinking about Zylar's cheating ass.

"Is there a problem over here, Raylexia? Maine, what's good? Does your dad know you up here tonight?" Mr. Gains came over after hearing me raise my voice.

"No problem, Gerald. I'm on my way out. I just dropped in to speak with Ray. We cool," Maine spoke up, trying to save face.

Me, on the other hand, was not having any more of this shit from him. *"No, we are not Cool!"* I snapped. *"Mr. Gains, I have told Maine I'm not ready to date, and he keeps coming up here and to the school to ask me on dates. I'm tired. I've had a full day, and I still have to go home to complete my schoolwork, plus take care of my son. I've tried to be nice, but I feel it's time to let Mr. Wells know about what's been going on."*

I finished my rant breathing hard and looking upset. Mr. Gains stepped between me and Maine and put a hand on his shoulder to restrain him.

"Maine, I'm going to have to let Mr. Wells know that you have been harassing one of our employees, and that it's best if you refrain from visiting the store. Raylexia is not the only female employee who has complained about

this type of behavior from you. I can no longer ignore that you seem to have a problem. Let me call your father and see how he wants to handle this." Mr. Gains escorted Maine to the office.

I continued to clean my station and recover my area. At 7 p.m., I removed my till and took it to the main office so Jane could verify my receipts and close down my lane. When I entered the office, Jane took my till while giving me funny looks.

"What's wrong with you, Jane? Do I have something on my face?"

"No. There is nothing on your face. I'm just wondering what happened with you and Maine. He had everyone believing you guys were dating, and now they're in here calling Mr. Wells about possible harassment charges. You know that's a serious accusation to make, Raylexia. Especially when we have seen you guys talking throughout all your shifts," she stated while looking at me like she just knew I was lying, and Maine couldn't possibly be bothering me.

"Did this bitch just have the audacity to accuse and question me about lying on this punk muthafucker? Relax, Raylexia, and take a deep breath. Jesus, take the wheel because I really need to keep my job. I can't let the ghetto out on this hoe, so please guide me." I told myself as I put my hands on my hip and gave that hoe the "Bitch please" face.

"I find it amazing that you have the nerve to tell me that Maine had everyone believing that we were dating, and that I'm making accusations of harassment. How many times have I worked, and Maine came to see me, and I excused myself to talk to him? I'll tell you none, because I have no need to talk to him or any other guy that comes around. You are the Assistant Manager and you have heard me tell Maine on more than one occasion that I would not be giving him my number, so how the hell do we go from me telling him he can't have my number to us dating."

"Hold on Raylexia, that's not what I meant." Jane tried to explain, but I was too far gone.

"Well, I need you to explain what you meant to me, Jane, because it seems like you have a problem with me letting Mr. Gains know that I can barely work my shift without Maine coming up here like he owns the store, standing in my lane blocking the customers' path to the checkout. Did I miss the memo that said I have to deal with him while I'm at work? If so, I need to see it in writing," I yelled at Jane as Mr. Gains returned with Maine in tow.

"What's going on, Raylexia? Why are you yelling at Jane?" He asked when he took in my facial expression and level of aggression.

"Jane here seems to think I'm just making accusations of harassment against Maine for no reason. It seems he's told people that we are dating, according to Jane. Which is crazy because I know you, her, and everybody in this place have heard me tell him I'm not ready to date. I have too many other things to worry about to add a man to the mix, especially one I'm not even attracted to," I added to make sure they all know just where I stand with the situation.

"Jane, you had no right to question Raylexia about what happened with Maine, and you know better. You could lose your job for trying to influence Raylexia in any way, and you know that. It stands to reason how the last case went left. I think I need to call the district manager to be on the safe side," Mr. Gains stated as he exited the room to go back into his office.

Jane stood there looking stupid. *"Are you going to count my till so I can go home? In fact, let me call Mrs. Chance and let her know I'm running late."*

I left Jane standing her stupid-looking ass in the office, went to get my purse from the locker, and called Mrs. Chance. She answered on the first ring, sounding worried.

"Are you okay, Raylexia? If you are calling it must mean you'll be running late, since you never come in late without warning me in advance. Is something wrong?" Mrs. Chance hit me with question after question, not giving me a chance to answer any.

"Sorry to make you worry, Mrs. Chance, but I don't know exactly when I'll be leaving here since I have to wait for the manager, and district manager to show up. Maine kept asking me out, and for my phone number, so I finally reached my breaking point today. I let Mr. Gains know he's been borderline stalking me. When Mr. Gains went into the back office to call Mr. Wells, I finished up out front and took my till to Jane. She had the nerve to accuse me of lying about Maine harassing me and said he claimed we were dating."

"So, I started to tell her off, and Mr. Gains came in to check why I was yelling at Jane. I told him what she said, and he told her she had no business trying to interfere with my statement. He needed to call the district manager to make sure it was handled properly. Come to find out I'm not the first girl he has done this to," I explained as I saw Mr. Wells coming in the front entrance facing the parking lot.

Zylar Crewens

*"*W*here the fuck is this girl at? I've been waiting outside this apartment for more than an hour. It's after 8, and Ma said Ray got off at 7pm. Let me go up to her job and see if I still see her car there."* I drove up to the Price-Lo Food Store and spotted Ray's car right away, so she must still be at work.

I got out of the car and made my way inside the building. I saw Ray exiting the office in the back looking upset, so I made my way in her direction.

"What's wrong, Ray?" I asked as soon as I got close enough that I didn't have to raise my voice to be heard.

Ray looked like a deer caught in headlights. Then she just looked angry again. *"Not now, Zylar. I can only handle one thing at a time,"* she said, making her way to the front exit.

An older white female, two middle-aged black males, a black female in her late 20's, and an older teenage black male came out the same office Ray just exited. The white female called out to Ray. *"Ms Gavion."*

"Yes, Mrs. Coleman. What else can I do for you?" Ray asked in an icy tone that made me take notice.

"I apologize for what you have experienced, and I promise that we will make sure it never happens again. Had we been made aware sooner, it wouldn't have gone on this long. Enjoy your weekend and we will see you back at work on Monday." Mrs. Coleman told Raylexia as she prepared to leave the store.

I remained calm as I peeped the situation. The younger guy was grilling Ray like she was his bitch and did him dirty. Then he had the nerve to look over at me like he was upset with me being here with her. This nigga had me all the way fucked up. Ray is my woman, and I'll kill her and any other nigga that thinks he can take my spot. Not willing to deal with the disrespect any longer, I had to check that nigga before he got ahead of himself.

"Say, playa. Do you have an eye problem? 'Cause you grilling Ray like you have a problem with your fuckin' eyes. I can help you with that by snatching them bitches right out the sockets." I kept my tone calm, letting Ray know I was ready for whatever.

Ray's head snapped in my direction, *"Really, Zy? Not right now, please. I have had enough bullshit to last me a year today alone. I don't need you adding to the chaos,"* Ray pleaded like it was supposed to move me in some way.

Then Fuckboy finally found his voice. *"I thought you said you weren't ready to date, but this nigga pops up here all of a sudden after you've been turning me down for months. Have you been seeing him all along? Is this why I can't get your phone number or take you out?"* Fuckboy kept talking and I let him. He had all but confirmed for me that my baby wasn't dating anybody else.

"So, now you admit to harassing Ms. Gavion?" Mrs. Coleman questioned after letting Fuckboy say his piece.

"Wait, what? Harassment? Ray, has this nigga been bothering you?" I stepped into her personal space.

"Zylar, please not right now! Let them handle this please. This concerns my job, or I would have handled it differently myself. He has been constantly asking me out here on the job and at school, but you know I have to feel a certain way to date, and sadly no one else has caused me to have those feelings besides you and—." She mumbled. *"Can we please discuss this later? I just wanna go home, do my homework and take a bath,"* Ray whispered in my ear so only I could hear her, sounding upset and thoroughly pissed.

I let go and placed my hand at the small of her back. Instantly I felt her shiver at my touch.

"Okay, Ray. You got that. Are you done here? Can we go?" I decided we could talk when I got her home. Her reaction to me was enough to somewhat calm my anxiety.

"Mrs. Coleman, is there anything else you need from me? If not, I'm going to clock out and go home." Ray asked the lady who seemed to be in charge.

"No, Ms Gavion. I don't need anything else from you. Mr. Wells all but admitted to all the charges he previously denied in his little rant. I will be

contacting human resources first thing tomorrow to find out what they need us to file on your behalf in the system. Mr. Gains will be contacting the police to see what we need to do to proceed with the stalking charges. You have a good weekend, and we'll see you back on Monday." She told Ray as Ray headed to the back to clock out and collect her personal items to leave.

Fuckboy kept grilling me, so I had to speak up. I took a step forward almost into his personal space. *"Bruh, this ain't what you want over here, so I suggest you stop grilling me like you about that life. I don't know what you have going on, but Ray ain't the one for you to play with. I understand you find her attractive, but she belongs to me. I don't have to be around for her to make that known."* He bristled and I smirked, continuing.

"The fact that you couldn't get a date or phone number lets me know nothing has changed. So, it's best that you keep it moving where Ray is concerned or you and me gone have a muthafuckin' problem." Ray walked by and grabbed my arm when I finished speaking, leading me to the front exit. I kept my eyes on fuckboy as she pulled me away. I wanted that nigga to know, I'm Dead Ass Serious!

"Come on, Zylar. I'm ready to go. I need to get home; Mrs. Chance is worried. I never come home this late and she's about to throw a fit. She really doesn't like me driving once it gets dark out." Ray explained, talking about her sitter.

Just looking at her walk ahead of me, I can see all the changes to her body. My baby added a good amount of weight to her slim, thick frame, making her ass shake and jiggle when she walks. She has wider hips and thighs to match. Her breasts went up two cup sizes, but her stomach was still flat. Other than the weight gain, I couldn't tell she just had a baby. My girl definitely has that snap-back.

"Ray, do you want me to follow you home so we can talk, or do you want to go park at our new crib, and we talk there? I'm good either way. So, what's it gonna be?" I had to let her know I'm going with her no matter where she decided to go.

We walked slowly approaching her SUV. I could tell by the look on her face she was pissed, but she was not unresponsive to my touch. Even while upset and angry about my actions, she still wants me.

"Zy, I really have no desire to speak with you at all, but I guess I have no choice now. How did you find me anyway?" Ray asked, looking me directly in my eyes. If looks could kill, I'd be dead.

"My Ma hired a private detective to find you. I only found out where you were today. How could you disappear on me like that without reaching out once in the last 9 and a half months? I was worried sick about you, and so were your friends. Or did they know where you were all this time and just lied to me?" I asked, getting heated just thinking about the nights I couldn't sleep wondering if she was okay.

I watched as Ray looked back at the entrance to the store only to see Fuckboy coming out, followed by one of the older black males. They were in a heated discussion. Ray sighed heavily and looked at me with an annoyed expression on her face.

Crossing her arms over her chest. She snapped, *"how could you cheat on me and have the nerve to tell me I belong to you and to get over it, like that shit was okay? How did that work out for you over the past nine and a half months? I will not just sit back and accept you doing whatever the hell you want. I'll leave your ass first, and no, my friends have no idea where I am, and they didn't have the means to contact me either. I knew they would be the first place you'd check, so I made sure they would have nothing to tell. Sadly, things got really bad for us not having anyone in that place,"* she stated and then seemed to remember what I said.

"I guess you can follow me home. I have a lot I need to tell you about and a lot I need to make sure you understand about me going forward. I see you in a totally different light than when we started our relationship. So, I want to make sure we both know where we stand." Ray proceeded to get in her SUV and drove off.

CHAPTER NINE Raylexia Gavion

As we pulled out from the store, I couldn't believe I had been betrayed by my own damn body. I ain't felt a tingle or a single twitch in my pussy since I left Zylar's crib over nine and a half months ago. Now he pops his ass up today, and she's on fire. This shit is completely wild. I been around some of the finest niggas in the city, but my body only reacts sexually to him and Daylon's fine ass. Can it really be that he and Daylon are the only men I'll ever be attracted to? If so, some shit's gotta change. I refuse to let Zylar have his cake and eat it too, and I don't even understand what's going on with my reaction to Daylon. Zylar has to decide if he wants me or them other hoes, 'cause he can't have both. Simple as that.

We pulled up to my apartment fifteen minutes later, and I parked in my assigned spot. Mrs. Chance was already in one of my guest spots, so Zylar took the other one. He got out and walked over to open my door.

"Let's head up. Mrs. Chance just called to check on me again, and I told her I was just pulling up. She's been here since 7 a.m., so I know she's tired and ready to bounce. Good thing she's off tomorrow, so she can get some rest. Although knowing her, she'll be doing laundry and cooking a feast for the kids on Friday," I explained as we walked up the stairs to my second-floor balcony.

When I finished unlocking the door, Rodereck was standing there, looking all anxious. I forgot he'd be just as worried as Mrs. Chance with me coming home this late.

"Hey, Rod. Everything's good. I just had to finally handle that business with Maine. Sorry I made you worry." I tried to console him knowing he takes everything I go through personally. He visibly relaxed.

"Okay, Ray. You know I can't sleep unless I know you're straight. W-A-A-W-G," he said, and I flashed him a smile, showing all my teeth at our little mantra.

I kicked off my shoes and walked farther into the living room with Zylar right on my heels.

"You should have reported that dude a long time ago. I think he was just trying to save face with his boys since you turned him down publicly. His little feelings were hurt. You shoulda let me punch that nigga in the face and we tag that ass together." Rod finished, then noticed Zylar for the first time since we entered the apartment.

"What's up, Zy? You finally came to see Zan? The lil nigga getting big," Rod said all in one breath. *"Talk to you later, man. I gotta get to sleep. Ray ain't gonna let me stay home tomorrow from school, and that bus comes hella early."* He leaned his fist out.

"Nothing much Rod. You good?" Zy spoke and dapped Rod's fist as he nodded.

"Boy, you better watch your mouth. You see Mrs. Chance standing over there." I reached over and slapped him across the back of his head before he had a chance to back up from Zylar's hand.

"My bad, Mrs. C. You know I don't mean no disrespect." He smiled, looking down at Mrs. Chance as he turned headed to his room.

"It's okay, Rod. I know you were just caught up in the moment." Mrs. Chance giggled calling after Rod just as he exited the room.

"So, I assume you are Zylar? Nice to finally meet you. I'm Anna Chance, Raylexia's foster mom." Mrs Chance spoke and shook Zylar's hand.

"It's nice to meet you as well. Thanks for looking after my family when I couldn't. I appreciate it." Zylar greeted choked up.

"Don't mention it. I love them like they are my own," she paused. *"Glad to see you guys are talking. Zander just went down for the night, so you should be good for about four hours. I'm gonna get out of here. Ray, you know I have a full day planned for tomorrow of cooking and cleaning so we can have movie night Friday."* Mrs. Chance gathered her things and headed for the door.

"Oh, I almost forgot to tell you. You don't have to work Friday night 'cause I'm off until Monday, so they can handle things with Maine. I only have school

from 8 to 1, and I'll be home." I hurried to tell Mrs. Chance as she opened the door.

"Okay. That just means I'll only have Zander on Friday, so no need for me to cook. See you Friday morning. Call me if you need me." Mrs. Chance gave me a hug and headed out the door with a wave.

I locked the door and set the alarm before turning to face Zylar. I knew he had lots of questions, but I really wanted to take a shower and get ready for bed.

"Zylar, I know you have questions, and I'll answer them. Just let me take a shower and get ready for bed first." To my surprise, he gave me a head nod and took a seat on the sectional by the hall, pulling out his phone.

I stopped by Reign's room to find her fast asleep, hugging her pillow. In my room, I found Zander sleeping peacefully on his back in his crib. Satisfied that all was right with the kids, I grabbed my sleepwear and stepped into the bathroom connected to my room to start the shower. Once the steam filled the room, I took a long, hot shower, washing some of the day's stress away. When I stepped out, I found Zylar leaning on the bathroom sink, watching me.

"What the hell are you doing in here? I told you to let me shower first." I hurried to grab a towel and wrap it around my body. Just having Zylar standing there made my body come alive. My clit felt like it was about to burst, and my juices started flowing down my legs. The towel even felt rough against my skin, making my nipples extra sensitive.

"Ray, you can't believe that I could wait another minute to touch you after being away from you for damn near ten months. I know we need to talk, and we will get to that, but first, I need to be inside you in the worst way." Zylar began stripping his clothes off like we were about to fuck.

"Zylar, you seriously think I want you touching me after finding out you cheated on me throughout our entire so-called relationship. You made me look like a complete fool for trusting you and taking you at your word. A man is only as good as his word, and you lied and cheated, proving you ain't about shit. I haven't let a single person touch me in any way, be it sexual or otherwise. You were all I needed, but I guess we can't say the same for you." I spat the words at him, my anger boiling over.

"That's not true Ray—" he started, and I cut him off.

"That shit you did has no bearing on me as a woman. I know I kept you satisfied sexually, and I stimulated your mind mentally. You always had a need to go to the club and hang out with muthafuckers that grin in your face while plotting on you behind your back. I told you what I could handle, and you agreed. No one put a gun to your head and said we had to be together. In fact, I know for certain that you brought up the subject of us belonging to one another. What you really meant was I belong to you, and you can do whatever the fuck you want," I snapped as he finished taking off his clothes and walked across my room to throw them over my desk chair in the corner. He walked back to me dick just dangling everywhere.

"Ray, you may not believe me, but I haven't been with a single girl since you've been gone. Shit, my dick refused to even rise for the occasion. No one has been touching my body and I haven't been touching anyone either. I told you that the relationship thing was new for me and we could learn together. Like you said, I enjoy going out clubbing. It was not something you would do with me, so I would chill with Chandra, just kicking it and having fun. It was never about sex. I just liked chillin' with my boys and wanted my girl at my side. Why can't you bend a little and do some of the things I enjoy with me? You going out to the club and hanging out with me and my boys every now and then would be a small compromise. Shit, you can even bring your girls," he walked up to me and tried to caress my cheek. I slapped his hand away and he sighed.

"That way you don't have to even socialize with people you don't know because you'll have your own girls with you already. Can you do that for me? I promise you from here on out it's just me and you. I don't want anybody but you, Ray, and I put that on my pops. I can't and won't live without you, and I refuse to let you live with anybody other than me. So, what we gone do?" Zylar asked, standing there looking yummy in all his naked glory.

How the hell does he expect me to concentrate on what he's saying with those nine inches of steel wrapped in skin calling me?

I had all types of arguments ready for him about his cheating and what I would and wouldn't take from him, but he addressed them all. Then he had the nerve to put it on his Pops. Knowing I know how he idolized that man. Looking up from his dick on full display, I found Zylar watching me as I took in his whole body. He had to be hitting the gym hard because he's a lot more buff than usual. His six-pack has become an eight, and his chest, arms, legs, and back are more muscular. I could even swear his dick has gained an inch. He caught me looking at it and it jumped, making my mouth go dry, and snap my head up to meet his gaze. Flustered, I shook my head, releasing a low moan. I'm sexually frustrated as hell.

"What do you say, Ray? Can we try again and work on a compromise about the club and social gatherings with my friends?" Zylar asked, looking deep into my eyes.

I could see the love he has for me, but Zylar is spoiled and used to getting his way. Me not going to clubs and hanging out with his friends was one of the issues we argued most about, but as he said, I am willing to compromise somewhat.

"If I go, I can bring my friends, and I don't have to have fake-ass people in my space, right? 'Cause we both know that I will embarrass a bitch quick. If you are cool with that, I will try. I'm not making no promise that this will work, but I'm willing to try. That's the only compromise I'm willing to give. No cheating, Zy. If I find out you are fuckin' around with somebody else, whether it's sexual or not, then we're done. If I'm not the only woman you have, I refuse to settle for being your main. Am I understood? It's me and only me, or nothing at all?" I demanded, feeling a knot of anxiety tighten in my stomach.

I could feel the fear creeping in, the fear of being hurt again, of putting my trust in someone who had already shattered it once. My voice wavered slightly, betraying the strong front I was trying to maintain. I searched his eyes for any sign of deception, any hint that he wasn't being completely honest with me.

"Done." That's all I heard from Zylar before he picked me up and wrapped my legs around his head, attacking my clit. My back arched, and my body began to shake and jerk after ten minutes of Zylar licking and sucking on my pussy like it was his last meal.

I forgot where we were until Zylar cut on the shower. Water began to cascade over my legs as he walked in and positioned my back against the tiled wall. Zylar tried to add a finger, and my body squeezed and creamed more, making me feel lightheaded. Just when I was about to voice my fear of passing out, an orgasm hit me so hard I blacked out for a second or two. Zylar wasted no time and lowered me down his body straight onto his dick, making me let out a startled gasp at the intrusion. Zylar was indeed bigger than before.

I hadn't had sex in over ten months, so he could only work in about three inches before my shit closed up around him like a vise.

"Ray, baby, your pussy is soaking wet and so fuckin' tight, let me in. I don't know if I can control myself long enough to give you gentleness right now, so I put you on top so that you're in control. Ride your dick, baby. Make me cum," Zylar said in a strained, pleading tone.

The urgency in his voice matched the desperate need in my body. I clung to him, my nails digging into his shoulders as I tried to adjust to his size. The pleasure and pain mixed together, creating a whirlwind of sensations that had my head spinning. I began to move, slowly at first, then faster, the intensity of the moment driving me wild. The sound of our bodies coming together echoed off the tiled walls, each thrust bringing us closer to the edge.

Letting Zylar hold up my weight, I began to bounce up and down on his dick, taking more of him inch by slow, agonizing inch. It felt like I was being split in two. Zylar had indeed grown in length and width, making it challenging to work down to his base. Once I took all of him in and found my rhythm, Zylar grabbed my ass cheeks and spread them apart, slamming into me without mercy. He was going so deep I swear I could feel him in my chest. Not willing to let this nigga outdo me, I started to clench my walls while rotating from side to side, back and forth, round and round, slamming down hard on his dick, making Zylar shout out.

"Fuuucckkk! Ray, you got that snapper, baby. Your shit is biting my dick. I'm about to cumm!" Zylar exclaimed as a tremor rocked his whole body. We came together, and he settled us both on the shower floor, breathing hard as hell.

"I love you, Ray, and you never have to worry about me cheating again. These past ten months of living without you have shown a nigga that I definitely don't want to ever experience that shit again. I'm sorry about the cheating and even more so sorry that I put my hands on you. Something just snapped inside me at the mere thought of you being with someone else. I can't take it, so I apologize for doing that shit to you. I was wrong for that, and I'm man enough to admit it," Zylar apologized, rubbing my back.

Just listening to him voice his feelings made me feel somewhat like shit for keeping Zander away from him. *"I'm sorry too about not telling you about Zander, but you have to understand that you hurt me, and I didn't care too much about your feelings at the time. Hearing you talking on the phone to that girl and telling her about how you had new responsibilities draining your pockets hurt me more than you will ever know,"* I sighed trying to organize my thoughts.

"So, when Mom upped and moved us, and we found out I was pregnant, I honestly had no plans to ever tell you about him. Then things got really bad, and I promised myself that me and my siblings would never have to depend on anybody else ever again as long as I have breath in my body." I got up to take another shower. Once finished, I grabbed towels for us to dry off.

I finished drying off and walked into my bedroom to see Zander awake and kicking his feet in his crib. I kissed him on the cheek, making him give me a gummy smile, looking just like his daddy. Zylar came out of the restroom, headed for my desk chair, and put on his boxers. Once finished, he came around the side of the bed and looked at Zander awake and smiling up at him. I could tell Zylar was choked up because he had tears in his eyes at the sight of our son.

"Ray," he called out to me in a hoarse whisper, and I knew he had all types of emotions running through him right now. I went through the same thing the day I had him, and they placed him on my chest for the first time. Having him put everything into perspective for me. Nothing else is more important to me than taking care of him and making sure he has everything he needs.

"I know, Zy. I felt the same way the day he was born. It's all about him. Nothing else matters." I checked Zander's diaper to see if he was wet, before picking him up and handing him over to Zylar.

Zylar Crewens

I almost panicked when Ray placed my son in my arms. I've never held a baby before, and he's so small, I'm worried I might break him. This little guy looks just like me, right down to the peanut butter skin tone and gunmetal gray eyes. I can even see that he has my mouth and nose. Ray didn't do anything but carry this guy because he's all me. I can't wait to show my guy off to Ma and my brothers. I'm someone's dad.

"Ray, I need to call Ma and let her know I have a son and make arrangements to take you guys over tomorrow to meet the rest of the family. What time is good for us to go over? I know you have to get the kids after school, so any time after that is good, right?" I asked, making sure before telling Ma to invite the family over to meet my son.

I watched my son and I felt a tightness in my chest. I almost lost the chance to meet him. Ray left and never came back. *"What would I have done if Ma hadn't had Nico hire a private investigator to find them?"* I thought.

"Zylar, we can go over after we get Reign off the school bus and change her out of her uniform. Rodereck gets home around 2:45 p.m. and changes into his street clothes, so we just have to let him know to get dressed and be ready to go before he leaves for school in the morning. That way, he'll be ready before Reign's bus gets her home at 3:30 p.m. Are you sure you want to invite people to meet Zander? He's just a baby."

"Ray, what are you talking about? Zander is the first grandchild of our family and the first great-grandchild for our grandparents. We have to celebrate his life and introduce him to his uncles, cousins, and grandparents. In fact, let me call Ma and let her know to get things set up for tomorrow." I pulled out my phone and dialed Ma on speakerphone.

Ma answered on the fourth ring, making me think she had already gone to bed. *"Hello,"* Ma answered, sounding wide awake.

"Ma, what took you so long? I almost hung up thinking you had gone to bed. What are you doing over there?" I fired question after question at her.

"Boy, don't question me about what I'm doing. I'm the parent. I'm minding my business. What do you want? I am planning a meal for tomorrow. How are Ray and the kids doing? Did she agree to come over tomorrow?" Ma asked, fussing at me.

"Hi, Mrs. Della. I'm doing fine. How are you?" Ray responded.

"Hey, Raylexia baby, it's good to hear your voice. Are you and the kids doing okay?"

"Yes, we are doing fine. I finally have the means to support myself and take care of my siblings, so God has been good to me. I have no real complaints at the moment."

"That's good to hear, Raylexia. Now, what has you and that big-headed son of mine calling at this time of night?" Ma asked Ray like I wasn't on the phone.

"Ma, I'm calling so you can get the family together tomorrow so everyone can meet my son and my woman. The kids will be home from school by 3:30 p.m., so we'll be over after that. Is that enough time for you to let everyone know and get the food ready?" I asked, confirming our plans for tomorrow.

"Yes, Zylar, that's more than enough time. I plan to put the meat I'm marinating now on to barbecue first thing in the morning and fix the sides to go with it. I'll be at my old residence by 4 a.m. to start setting things up and let the caterers in. There's no way I could cook all this by myself and call everyone about the gathering. It would be too much. I'm only inviting the immediate family members on my side and your father's side, so that's over 40 people right here in town. Everybody else will just have to be content with getting a picture of him. I can't wait to meet my new grandbabies and spoil them rotten." Ma sounded excited.

"We only have one baby, Ma. Where you get multiples from?" I chuckled at Ma getting carried away.

"Boy, I know what I'm saying. Raylexia has a brother and sister she's accepted guardianship for, making them her children. That gives me two more grandbabies to love on. Bring my daughter-in-law and grandbabies to meet the family tomorrow. Let me get off this phone so I can finish preparing my food." Ma hung up before me or Raylexia could reply.

I turned to see Raylexia crying, and it scared the shit out of me. Ray didn't cry ever for no reason. So, I was stuck trying to figure out what the hell went wrong. We were just talking to Ma, and I thought things went well.

"Ray, what's wrong? You don't want to go to the gathering tomorrow? I told you Ma would want to invite the family to meet Zan and introduce you guys to everybody. Have you changed your mind?" I asked, not knowing what made her feel bad enough to cry. I thought she would be happy to meet my people.

"No, everything is perfect. No one has really treated us like family since our grandmother died when I was eight years old, and then we had to move in with our mother. That was the last time we had someone other than me take care of us. After she died, the full responsibility of caring for us fell to me. It wasn't so bad when Mom had Reign because her dad, Raquon, moved in and stayed to care for her and us by default. The problem is, I think if Reign wasn't there, he never would have made sure me and Rod were good. It was the little things, like when the new Jordans would drop, and he'd get him and Reign a pair, but nothing for us."

Damn, what can I say to that? Him doing that set a divide between the kids that Ray and Rod couldn't help but to notice.

"We understood from then on that his only responsibility was Reign. He just paid the bills and brought food for the house because he was there. Me and Rod accepted it for what it was and treated him as such. He was the first person to really make sure the bills were paid, and we had food, so the other stuff didn't really matter. The uncles would send us gift cards for Wal-Mart to get whatever me and Rod needed twice a year, so in that regard, we were good. We didn't have name brands, but it was clean and in good condition, so we were good. So, your mom calling us her family means so much more to me than any other form of acknowledgment," Ray explained, giving me a radiant smile.

Listening to Ray talk about feeling touched enough to cry let me know that I need to find out more about the things that happened in her past. Ray is very strong and rarely shows any form of real emotion unless it's humor or aggression. I know that she cares for me, but not because she has told me. I know by her actions and the way she treats me. When I'm in the room and we are surrounded by other people, I am her focus. Not only that, my girl is only attracted to me. What other man out here can say with 100% certainty that his woman has never looked at another man without a lick of interest and mean it? Ray's body only reacts to me sexually. That shit is more potent to me than any drug on the market, and I'll kill a mutherfucka for touching her, let alone having a sample of her.

Raylexia Gavion

After my mini-meltdown, I didn't know how to feel. Mrs. Della accepting me and my siblings into her family simply because I'm with Zylar and have her grandson means a lot to me. We've been alone in the world for the last eight and a half years. Not even our uncles have ever really made us feel like family. While they may send us money and ask about our well-being, I can tell they don't really care. They just don't want to have to come back and accept any form of real responsibility for us. That was made clear when they learned we became wards of the state and were in foster care, and all they did was send money and set up bank accounts to help me pay bills. Not that I don't appreciate everything they have ever done for us, because I do. I just know that there is no real love there, so I treat them as the distant relatives they are. My friends are the only ones that really feel like family to me. That's why I want them there with me tomorrow.

"Zylar, I want to invite my girls tomorrow because they are the closest thing I have to a real family on my side. They made sure we had food and helped me take care of Rod and then Reign after she was born. So, will it be okay to give them a call and invite them over to your mom's place?" I asked, not wanting to overstep by having people show up without clearing it with him first.

"Yeah, that's cool. I'm inviting my niggas too. K-O, C-Lo, Myron, K-Boy, Jayce, Kam, Lance, and Jamie are all like family to me, so I know what you mean. I need to let them niggas meet you and my little man. I forgot that the only one of them you've met is K-O. Let me call them and tell them what time to be there. I'll have K-Boy bring his little girl since it's a family affair." Zylar pulled out his phone and started calling his boys.

I took a deep breath and went to retrieve my phone from my charger to call Winkie. She answered on the third ring.

"Hello, is something wrong, Raylexia? Are the kids alright?" Winkie asked, sounding concerned.

"No, Winkie, everything is good. Better than good, in fact. I need you to call Deana and get her to call Johnya, and Johnya to call Shamena, so we are all on the call. I have some things to tell you guys, and I want to do it all at once," I told Winkie and heard her click the line to call the other girls.

It took about three minutes for everyone to get connected, and Johnya went off. *"Raylexia, why the hell would you leave and not keep in touch with us? We are your friends, and no matter what, we will always have your back. You have been gone for more than nine months, and I have been worried sick. When we started back up at school, I almost fell off track to graduate this year because I couldn't concentrate on my schoolwork worrying about you."* Johnya sounded close to tears.

"I'm sorry, Johnya. Part of the reason I'm calling is to explain what happened to us and to ask you guys to come to a family gathering tomorrow after school. I told Winkie to tell you guys to meet me at the mall on Saturday so I could explain in person. Zylar found me today, and I didn't have to worry about putting you guys in the middle of the conflict between us now."

"That's no excuse for the foul shit you did, Ray. We have feelings, and you just leaving and not staying in touch hurt us all deeply. We didn't care about being put between you two, that's what friends are for," Johnya answered, full-on crying now.

"Johnya's right, Ray. You shitted all over our feelings by keeping us in the dark right along with Zylar, and now you say we can see you just because Zylar has found you. That don't sit right with me. We are sisters and are supposed to have each other's back. We would have helped you kill his ass and hide the body," Shamena added, not bothering to hide her anger.

"Look, y'all. I broke up with Zylar three days before Mom moved us out of the projects, and it wasn't a good split. I caught him cheating, we had a fight, and I left. He said some shit to me that I didn't agree with, so when Mom moved us, I felt it was the perfect way to get away from him for good. I decided not to tell any of you so he couldn't use our connection to find me. Not that I believed for a moment that you guys would tell him where I went. I just didn't want you guys at odds with him on my behalf," I tried to explain.

"You should have given us a choice though, Ray. We've been worried sick not knowing if you and the kids were okay. You can't justify that by saying you were trying to keep us out of the conflict between you and Zylar. You just created a conflict between us," Deana said, making me realize for the first time that they might not forgive me for this.

"I was not trying to cause conflict, period. Especially not between the five of us. I just did what I thought was best for me. Mom disappeared for four and a half months after she got us moved in, like she usually does, and things went from bad to worse during that time. The little money I saved up to pay bills ran out after three months because things are more expensive in a house than in an apartment, which caused the gas and water to get turned off. Then the school suspended me because Mom didn't attend a parent-teacher conference to address me being late for school every day putting Reign on the bus. When we ran out of food, I got caught trying to steal from Price-Lo Foods, and they placed us in foster care," I took a breath and continued.

"Shit, in my opinion, that was the best thing that happened because after going to court and explaining my situation to the judge, he emancipated me and gave me full custody of Reign and Rod. When I went to live with Mrs. Chance, they tried to sort out me going back to school. However, the guidance counselor arranged for me to get my GED because I no longer qualified for the escalator program with my absences. Right after we got everything squared away and our new apartment, I had my son Zander. I started attending the University of Shreveport in January for the winter/spring semester, and I just got back together with Zylar today." I finished and prepared for them all to go off. It didn't take a second.

"Ray, what the hell! Your mom is grimy as hell. Why did she move you guys if she was just going to leave you all alone to fend for yourselves?" Johnya yelled.

"Bitch, you shoulda called me. You know Mom woulda took you guys in. We have more than enough space, and you know she loves you like a daughter," Winkie screamed.

"Why, Ray? You always have to do things the hard way. We are friends, and we would have never left you out there alone. You know you could have called," Deana cried.

"Ray, you're wrong for this, and you know it. How can you sit up here and tell us that you suffered all this, and we knew nothing, so we couldn't help? How

do you think that makes us feel? We have always been more like sisters than friends, so telling us we have a nephew that we have never seen is foul. That shit stinks through the phone. How old is nephew, and can we see you guys now? Are we off punishment?" Shamena said, snarkily making me feel like shit.

"You were never on punishment, Shamena, and yes, you guys can see him. He is three months old. That's why I'm calling you all tonight instead of keeping our shopping date for Saturday. Zylar's mom is throwing a family gathering tomorrow for everyone to meet us, and I want you guys to be there with me. You are all my sisters and my only real family, so I want you to be by my side. Can you guys make it after 3:30? Do I need to pick you guys up?" I asked, anxious to get their reply.

"Of course, we'll be there. We all have a test in second-hour Calculus class, and we can check out after that. What time do you want to come get us? We'll all be at Johnya's house. Can she bring Tylan?" Winkie asked, putting my mind at ease.

"Yes. My nephew needs to come, and I can pick you all up at 12 and bring you back to my apartment to wait for Rod and Reign to get out of school. That will give me time to reconnect with you guys and let you get to know your nephew before we leave. How does that sound? Is 12 p.m. good for you guys?"

"Twelve is fine, Ray. Let us get off this phone, so we can find something nice to wear. It's cold outside, so dress warm, guys. We all want to look sexy but classy, so sweaters and jeans should work. What do you say, Deana?" Johnya asked, knowing Deana is the fashion police. She plans to study fashion design in college, and thanks to her, we have all been able to keep up with the current fashion trends. Deana can make damn near any design by famous designers like Chanel and Gucci, so our gear may not be name brand, but it's on point. None of us are label whores, so what we have works for us.

"Sweaters, jeans, and ankle boots ought to work nicely. We all have at least two pairs of ankle boots we bought at the beginning of last year. Do you still have yours, Ray?" Deana asked after telling us all what to wear.

"I still have all my things from Mom's place after I was emancipated, so I pretty much have everything we had from our old place. Mom left everything and didn't come back, so the landlord let me get all the furniture. When we moved in here, I only had to buy a washer, dryer, and microwave. I still have the

bar and everything," I answered, letting them know we're good. I can't wait for them to see that we are doing fine so they can stop worrying about me.

"Okay then. Ray, we will see you tomorrow, and I'll chew on your ass then. I know you ain't been taking care of your hair, so I'll bring my bag and dryer so I can take that shit out of that ponytail. Love you, girl," Shamena stated before we ended the call. I could tell she was still really upset by her tone of voice, but I'll make it up to her somehow.

I turned to go back to my room, and Zylar was standing there holding Zander, who was asleep on his shoulder. *"You finished talking to your girls?"* he asked, looking at me with a strained expression on his face.

"Yeah, it went a lot better than I expected, but that's only because we were on the phone and it's getting late. They all have to get up at 6 to get ready for school tomorrow, so they couldn't really get in my ass like I know they wanted to. They all agreed to go with me tomorrow and need me to pick them up at 12. I said I'd get my homework done after Rod and Reign leave for school, then clean up the house. How'd it go with your boys?"

"It's all good on my end. My niggas will be there at 4. That gives us time to get there and get settled just in case Ma needs us to do something for her before the family starts arriving. But check this, Ray. I really wanted to take you by our new place and show you where we would be living. Hopefully, you guys will be staying at the new place with me soon. I know we just got back together today, but I don't want to spend another night apart from you and Zan ever. So, either I'll be staying with you or you'll be staying with me."

"I'm okay with you keeping your place, because I know it's important for you to have your own shit, but can we move back and forth between the two? That way you don't have to uproot the kids again, and we can start rebuilding a solid relationship. We can stay here Monday through Friday and Friday through Sunday; we can all stay at our new place. What do you say? Is that okay?" he asked with his whole heart on display.

"I hear what you're asking, Zylar, but it's not that simple. We have to rebuild the trust that was broken between us and figure out if we can live together full time under the same roof. We've never done that before, so you have no idea if we can even get along for a long period of time." I tried to explain some of the issues we could face by jumping in headfirst without giving us time to

learn each other's habits. I don't want to have to kill this nigga behind not letting the toilet seat down.

"Ray, we won't know if we don't try. Are you at least willing to try and see how it goes? We can always make adjustments as different issues arise. I know for a fact I'm willing to compromise on anything if it means we'll be together," he said, letting me know that the time we spent apart affected him.

"We can see how it goes, but I don't know how us staying over at your place on the weekend is going to work when Mrs. Chance has to clock in and out on the system that's connected to my home phone. The State pays for my childcare, so I have in-home care with someone I trust to watch the kids for me to be able to work and go to school. We can go to your place on Friday after I get off work and come home Sunday morning so I can leave for work by 1:15 p.m. That way we don't disrupt the kids' routine too much. Is that okay with you?" I tried to somewhat accommodate him.

"That's fine. I just want us to get used to both places and hopefully eventually settle on our new place that belongs to both of us. I also need to let you know about some changes that happened while we were apart. I am now Zaylar's right-hand man, so my business phone rings all times of the night. I may have to leave in the middle of the night to handle a problem. That nigga still be from city to city randomly, so they mostly call on me to handle issues that arise."

"We also have to move a little differently. I'm going to assign you a security team to protect you and the kids. That will be in place when you go back to school on Friday. Don't worry, you won't even know they're there." He just further proved my point about us having issues going forward.

"What the hell, Zylar. You should have told me about your promotion first. Will we be safe living here with you being as deeply involved in your brother's business as you are now? This is a whole other level, and I know how dangerous the lifestyle can be," I asked, now worried about our safety living in this open area as exposed as we are.

"Ray, that's why I wanted you to see our new place. We have a six-bedroom, seven-bath home in the same gated community as Ma's. Me, Zaylar, and Nico had homes built over there along with Ma's a little while after Pops was killed when the plots of land became available for sale. We all have five acres apiece, so there's no chance for us to invade each other's privacy. The best thing about the place is that it has an armed security gatehouse with 24-hour surveillance. I

don't have to worry about your safety there; that's why I asked you to come see it with me tomorrow. I just don't want to push you away by being overbearing, but it would be safer if you moved into our new place."

He made me think about how long it will take to pack our shit and get moved in.

"Zylar, I don't have to go see the place; we'll move in this weekend. My son, brother, and sister's safety are more important to me than any differences we may have cohabitating. I will get my girls to help me start packing tomorrow and get the information for the schools in that area to have the kids transferred by Monday. I also have to inform Mrs. Chance and break my lease, unless my girls would like to move in and take up the rent next year. My uncles paid the whole year up in advance, so they don't have to renew the lease until December." I could not believe that he didn't tell me about his change in circumstances earlier.

"Do you have security with you now, or are you out here naked?" I asked Zylar, getting heated at the fact that he didn't tell me this shit sooner.

"Ray, calm down. My security detail is always with me. If you could see them, they wouldn't be doing their job. I didn't tell you sooner because my main concern was getting you to take me back and meeting my son. I had no idea that you would actually take me back, but I was determined. Now that you have agreed to move, I can have what you want moved on Friday while you're at school. You just show me what you want moved tomorrow after we get back, and we'll handle the rest on Friday," Zylar replied, sounding entirely too calm in my opinion.

Zylar Crewens

"*Ray, let's get some sleep. We have a busy day tomorrow, and you have a long list of things to get lined up for me to take care of on Friday. Let's get some rest and start fresh tomorrow. Besides, I need you to show me how to change Zan's diaper. He just let out a foul-smelling load that I'm more than ready to get rid of. What the hell are you feeding him to smell like this?*" I complained about Zan's diaper cutting up.

"*I see you have jokes, nigga. Don't do my baby. He is still adorable, even stinky,*" She chuckled. "*Let's go make his bottle first, and then we'll change his diaper, because if we change him and don't have his food ready, he will act a fool until we feed him,*" Ray added, switching off heading to the kitchen.

I watched her hips sway thinking about getting back between them thighs. Zan gurgled and I looked down at him chewing on his hands grinning at me. I smiled down at him and laughed to myself. This lil nigga already cock blockin.

Ray took a bottle out of the fridge, placed it in a round object on the counter, and hit a switch on the side. In less than a minute, I heard steam coming from the device. "*What the hell is that?*" I asked, my curiosity getting the better of me.

"*It's a bottle warmer. It saves time and comes in handy when you only have two hands and a screaming baby ready to be fed.*" She explained. It made me feel like shit.

"*I'm sorry for hurting you so deeply that your start in motherhood with him was so hard. If I had never cheated, you would've had me, my family, and your girls for support. I can't change the past, but I promise you, I'll spend the rest of my life making sure you never regret taking me back.*" And I meant every word. I'm determined to make her happy from here on out, no matter what hardships come our way.

Ray just nodded. I could tell she was being cautious. I couldn't blame her for that. Talk is cheap, I will just have to show and tell.

"Okay, his bottle is ready. Pull it out of the warmer and shake it up to mix the milk. Then shake a few drops on the back of your hand to make sure it's not too warm for him to drink." I did what she said and frowned at the smell.

"Ray, this shit stinks. I don't know how my little man tolerates that smell to drink this. It smells something serious," I see now I gotta train myself for feeding time if I gotta smell this for any length of time because this shit stinks.

"Nigga, come on. Let's go change his diaper. If you're bitching about the milk smell, how the hell are you gonna deal with his shit? That smell coming through that diaper ain't got nothing on the full smell while changing it." Ray laughed her ass off while heading to a room off the side of hers.

When she opened the door, I was surprised to see a bedroom set up for my son, decorated in Blue's Clues. She went over to a strange-looking table and patted her hand on top for me to lay him down. *"Now, you have to be quick when changing Zan 'cause he likes to piss on you when you pull his diaper off. I can't tell you how many times he's got me already, so I get all his stuff ready before I start trying to clean his butt."* She reached over and grabbed a pamper.

"Here's his diaper. Pull about six wipes out and lay them next to his butt for easy access. Here's his powder and cream. I'll change him, and you just watch this first round." Ray coached me through changing Zan for the first time. When she finished, I picked Zan up off the table as he started to fuss. Now I can see why Ray insisted on having that bottle ready.

We went back into Ray's room, where she had me prop up at the head of the bed to feed Zan his bottle. He was sucking that stuff fast, and before I knew it, he was done. Ray showed me how to burp him, and he fell back to sleep. After laying Zan down, we got in bed, and I wrapped my body around her in the spoon position. For the first time in over nine months, before my head could hit the pillow good, I was sound asleep.

CHAPTER TEN Zylar
Crewens

January 19, 2012

We all woke up around five a.m. and did our personal hygiene. Ray changed Zan and fed him a bottle before laying him back down to sleep. Then she went into the kitchen and prepared a light breakfast of biscuits and sausage for Rod and Reign. Once done she woke up Rod, who ate and then got dressed for school. She moved quickly, completing each task efficiently. I could tell this was something she'd long grown accustomed to.

"Rod, before you head out, I want you to know we're going to a family gathering at Zylar's mom's house after you guys get home from school. She wants to introduce us all to the family and finally meet you and Reign. So, when you get home, dress up a little when you change out of your uniform," Ray told Rod before he grabbed his backpack to leave.

I just stood there and silently observed waiting to see if I could do anything to help.

"Okay, Ray. I'll be ready. See you later, Zy. Will you be riding with us?" Rod asked before he made it to the front door and put in the code.

"Shit, Rod. You, Reign, and Zan might be riding with me since Ray is going to pick up her girls. That Expedition can carry some passengers, but not that many," I replied.

Rod paused before unlocking the deadbolt. *"What! Ray, you're picking up the Rude Girls?"* Rod asked, surprised. *"We haven't seen them in forever."*

"Yes, I'm going to get them at 12. That will give us time to hang out and chill before getting ready to go. Oh, I almost forgot. We're moving in with Zy this weekend, so be ready to pack when we get back this evening," Ray

explained before Rod crossed the threshold. He turned back around to face Ray frowning. I couldn't tell if it was from aggression or fear.

"What! We just moved in, and you said this was our place, that no one was going to make us leave!" Rod yelled at Ray, making me look at him like he was crazy. I didn't get involved, just gritted my teeth, continuing to watch silently.

Ray sighed and walked over and put a hand on Rod's shoulder. *"No one is making us leave, Rod. Zy's place is just safer for us to live in than here. I'll explain more about it when you get home from school. Believe me when I say, nobody is making us do anything we don't want to ever again."* Her explanation calmed him down immediately. He steadied her expression for a minute then nodded.

"Okay, we'll talk about it when I get home," he said, turned, then left.

I released the breath I had been holding. If Rod disagreed, Ray would not be moving anywhere, ever. I could tell Ray was feeling some kind of way about Rod's reaction, so I moved closer trying to gauge her mood. *"Ray, what's wrong?"* I asked, watching her closely.

"Rod is scared, and I can't blame him for feeling that way. We've all been through a lot in the last year, and things just settled down to something somewhat normal. Me telling him we're moving again just brings back memories of Mom moving us and leaving us alone for months at a time. The difference now is that I can support us," she sighed. *"He just needs reassurance that we're going to be good no matter what,"* Ray explained, making my heart hurt for them.

I'm not gonna lie. The shit was sad. I can't even begin to understand what they've been through for Rod to have such a grave look on his young face at the mention of moving. I can only support Ray and them as much as they allow.

"Ray, you know you can depend on me from here on out, and I will not betray your trust again. When you were talking to your girls and I came back into the room, I overheard some of what you said, and I felt like shit. Knowing that you allowed yourself and your siblings to become wards of the state rather than call on me for help made me feel like less than a man. I'm supposed to be the one you call on when you're in need, and you chose homelessness over me. I will restore your trust and become someone Rod can trust too. I promise you. Just trust in a nigga," I told Ray, vowing to prove every word.

Ray gave me a long look before she nodded and headed to the back to get Reign up and off to school. I went down to my car to get my overnight bag, and Buck, my head of security, was parked by my car, putting me on alert.

He exited his car and met me at my trunk. *"Boss, that youngster from the young lady's job followed you guys here last night and stayed out here until about 4 AM. I had someone tail him home to get his address and vehicle information so we could have it this morning. He lives over in the gated community off East Gate in Bossier City. Nice upscale place with affluent families. I have our PI looking for more and should have something for you before noon today. I made Stacks stay with him just in case he is a problem we need to handle. We should have his routine down by Monday,"* Buck informed me of the fuckboy's movements.

"Buck, I need you to set up a security detail for my girl and both of her siblings. That's my world in that apartment, and I plan to protect them. Also, make sure someone whips that nigga's ass every time he is out away from home. I want that nigga scared to move. Get me five guys from the moving division to help move my girl Friday morning. She needs to be settled by Monday. Make it happen," I told Buck as I looked up to see Ray and Reign coming down the stairs with Zan in a bag strapped to her chest. She had my little man looking like a mini-Eskimo with all the layers she had him wrapped up in.

"I'll walk her down, just tell me where," I told Ray as they reached the bottom of the stairs.

"It's just right there at the opening of the apartments, Zylar. I do this every morning, so I got it," Ray told me and kept walking by with Reign holding her hand and Zan sound asleep laid out across her chest. I decided not to say anything right now, but we would be discussing this shit about her not letting me help her with the simplest things.

"Hi, Zy," Reign spoke while smiling at me and waving.

"Hey, Reign. See you later, munchkin." I waved back as they made their way to the apartment entrance where five other children stood with their parents. Ray stood down at the bus stop with Reign for about ten minutes before the bus pulled up. Reign gave her a hug and ran up onto the bus. She waved bye to Ray and stuck her head out the window to wave bye to me. I waved back, smiling at Reign. She wasn't overly friendly, so it surprised me that she spoke to me this morning.

Ray made her way back to the apartment and laid Zan down. Once she was sure he was sleeping, she started to clean the apartment, prompting me to ask, *"Ray, is there anything I can help you with?"*

"No, Zy, I'm good. I have a routine, and it's best if I just continue until I'm done. Thanks for asking, though," she said and continued what she was doing like I wasn't there.

"Say, Ray, I know you're used to taking care of everything on your own, but you have me, and you can share some of the load. There was no need for you to take Zan out in the cold while he was asleep when I could have watched him or taken Reign to the bus stop. You're not alone anymore, so let me help," I told Ray, hoping she would start to believe in me soon.

"I'll try, Zylar. I'm not used to depending on nobody but me and Rod, so it's not personal. It's just what I'm used to," was all she said before going back to cleaning.

I left her to it and went back to her room to shower and get dressed. When I got out of the shower, my business phone was ringing, so I answered while drying my hair.

"Speak," was all I said.

"What we moving, my nigga? We just got your shit set up and you're already moving stuff out," C-Lo asked.

"Naw, nigga. I'm moving my girl in. Did you not hear me say come to Ma's old crib for the gathering yesterday? She agreed to move in since her place is not as safe as mine," I told him, knowing he was checking on the truck and movers Buck set up for Friday.

"Congrats on your son, Zy. I know Big Z is looking down proud as fuck to have a namesake," C-Lo told me, making me feel good as hell.

"Thanks, bruh, I appreciate it. You got everything set up for Friday? I don't want nobody but you guys to know where I lay my head. Make sure the movers are part of the regular work staff that don't know shit," I told C-Lo, not taking any chances with my family.

"You know I got this. Now that I know it's family, I'm adding extra protection. I just put that shit in as an elite client, that way it's untraceable and the address and info will fall out of the system after check-in," C-Lo explained as he clicked away at the keyboard at the storage warehouse.

"Thanks, bruh. See you later on," I told him as I ended the call.

"Bet." was all I heard, then silence, letting me know that nigga hung up.

Ray walked in the room and went straight to her desk to start on her homework.

"Ray, while you do your homework, is there anything you need me to do?" I asked before I started checking on the spots.

"No, Zy, I'm good. If you need to leave, we're good. It should only take me an hour or so to finish, and then I can start packing. I know we don't have to move my bedroom furniture, but what about Reign and Rod's?" Ray asked while concentrating on the tablet and book in front of her.

"Ray, I had my house decorated with you in mind. Rod and Reign both have fully decorated rooms at the house. The only thing you need to move is your clothes and Zan's furniture. My Ma made sure everything else is done," I told her as she looked up from her homework in surprise.

"Really, Zy? You didn't even know where I was," Ray said, her tone skeptical, like that was supposed to change me preparing for our future together.

"Ray, when I told you it's you and me until the casket drops, I meant that shit. I had our home designed with everything you would need for Rod and Reign, and your cars are in the garage waiting on you to drive them. Just because I didn't know where you were at that time didn't mean I couldn't provide what you needed," I replied.

Ray rolled her eyes but smiled, *"Alright, alright. I'll give you that. But you better not slack off now."*

I laughed, *"Slack off? Nah, I'm in this for the long haul. You can count on that."*

I tried to reassure her while checking my incoming text messages from Myron, Jayce, Lance, Jamie, and Kam. They all wanted to know if it was okay to bring their girls to meet my girl.

"Ray, my boys wanna know if it's okay to bring their girls to meet you today. This is my crew, my close friends. Not them niggas that worked for Zay. Like you said, 'Them was some hating-ass niggas.' We only got about 20 niggas left from Zaylar's old team, and none of them will be at the gathering," I told her, hoping she wouldn't get upset about those fake-ass niggas.

She sighed, still looking unsure. *"I agreed to try, Zy. I'll meet them today and go from there,"* she told me, and I could do nothing but agree. Ray had been telling me that Biz and Eric were snakes since I met her. If I had listened and told Zay, maybe we wouldn't be having to watch our backs now. *"I texted all them niggas back, letting them know you said okay,"* I told Ray as I gave everybody the okay except for Jayce. That hoe Derricka ain't welcome nowhere near me. I texted to let that nigga know to stay home if he has to bring that hoe.

"Alright. Once I'm done with my homework, we need to go to Home Depot and get some boxes to pack our clothes. That way, I should have all Zan and Reign's things ready before it's time to go pick up my girls," Ray told me, prompting me to pull out my phone and call C-Lo back. Just as he answered, Ray's phone began to ring.

"What's wrong, Zy? I already changed things over in the system and made sure only regular movers are scheduled for the move tomorrow. You know I'm gonna make sure your family is straight," C-Lo told me before I could get a word in.

"Nigga, I know you got everything covered. I just wanted to ask if you had time to drop me off about 20 medium to large boxes so Ray can start packing? She'll be through with her homework in an hour and wants some boxes from Home Depot. If I'm gonna spend money on boxes, they're gonna come from our business," I asked C-Lo as Ray put down her phone and turned to face me.

"Zylar, can you run and pick up my girls now? They are done with second period and are ready to be picked up. They will all be at Johnya's apartment with their bags, so you just have to pull up to my old building and they will come out. Oh, and Johnya is bringing Tylan, so you'll have to use their car seat," Ray asked me while I was waiting for C-Lo to reply.

"This works even better, Ray. We may be able to get your stuff moved today. Hold on, let me check with C-Lo," I told Ray as I switched back to my call with C-Lo.

"I'm back, C-Lo. My girl wants her girls picked up from her old apartments. Can you swing by there and pick them up when you come to drop off the boxes? If we can get everything packed early enough, we can move their stuff today, right?" I asked C-Lo as he laughed on the phone, talking shit.

"Nigga, I never said I was dropping the boxes off, and now you want me to play chauffeur?" C-Lo came back, still laughing.

"Yeah, nigga. Handle that. I'm texting you the address now; just pull up in the center and call me. I'll have Ray tell them when you get there so they can all come down. Which one of your whips are you pushing today so I can let them know what you are driving?" I asked C-Lo while texting him the address to the apartments.

"That nigga told me he was in his Suburban and hung up. Ain't even say bye. That's alright, though. I'll remember that next time he needs a favor," I muttered, shaking my head.

Ray chuckled, *"Sounds like C-Lo said yes?"*

"Yeah, that nigga agreed while bitching the whole time. I should charge him for all the stress he puts me through," I said with a grin.

I let Ray know to tell her girls to be looking for a 2012 Matte Black Suburban with 24-inch chrome rims. I'm glad I caught that nigga before he left the warehouse heading this way so he could just scoop Ray's girls on his way here. Saves me a trip. Hopefully, we can get Ray moved today.

Raylexia Gavion

Right after I finished my homework and Zylar and I started to pack up Zan's room, the doorbell rang. I left Zylar taking apart Zan's crib and looked through the peephole to see my girls all standing at the door.

I swung the door open and started hugging my girls. *"Bitch, let us in. It's cold as hell out here,"* Johnya said, coming through first, holding Tylan, followed by the rest of my girls trying to get out of the cold.

"Ray, we can hug after we warm up. That wind is whipping outside," Shamena said, looking back at Zylar's boy unloading the boxes. *"Who is that fine muthafucker you sent to pick us up? The nigga got my pulse racing and kitty thumping when all I did was sit next to him while he drove us here."*

"Calm your hot ass down. Let us check on our girl before you start trying to make a sex connection, hoe," Deana told Shamena, giving her the stank face.

"Why the hell would I do that? My mom always said the early bird gets the worm, or in this case, the dick. I want that nigga in the worst way. Maybe he can tame this beast in me," Shamena said without a lick of shame.

"We won't know until we try, lil mama. I'm game if you are," C-Lo replied, standing in the door holding an armful of boxes.

His muscles flexin through the black long sleeved cotton shirt he wore. I can't lie he did make a fine attractive man in them acid washed black Levi jeans. Shamena was practically vibrating with raw sexual tension.

"Shit, you ain't said nothing but a word, my nigga. I'm ready whenever you are. I'm Shamena, by the way, and you are?" Shamena asked, looking at C-Lo like he was her favorite snack.

"Cree Logan is my name, but my friends call me C-Lo. Let me take these boxes to Zy but check it. Put your number in my phone and save it under 'My Beast.' Then call your phone from my phone and save mine," Cree demanded,

setting the boxes down and reaching into his pocket to give Shamena his phone.

After she stored her number and called her phone, she eased the phone back into his front pocket and pulled her hand out slowly while looking C-Lo directly in the eyes, licking her lips. The shit was so carnal we all could see their attraction.

Cree's green eyes changed to a darker shade and he licked his lips. *"We gonna explore me taming that beast you speak of,"* C-Lo grunted, picking the boxes back up and heading to the hall where Zy was standing there grinning at him.

I laughed, shaking my head. *"Looks like someone found a new friend,"* I taunted, smiling over at Zy.

"Yeah, looks like it," he replied.

Then Winkie spewed, *"well, bitch, so that's how we doing it now? You just gonna forget the rest of us here and say whatever the fuck you see,"* Winkie snapped at Shamena, her eyes blazing with anger.

"Really, Winkie? Does it really matter if I tell him what I want in front of you all or not? I'm just gonna turn around and tell you guys everything we say and do anyway. I don't see the problem. Cree is fine as fuck, and I want to climb that mountain and explore all the hills and valleys he has along the way. That man is every bit of 6'3 with milk chocolate skin, bulging muscles everywhere, and hazel green eyes. Do you know what our kids would look like? Don't get mad at me because your new boo didn't answer the phone for you earlier. You are being petty. Wasn't I happy for you when you hooked up with K-O? Shit, I was the one who told you to finally call him back. You had that man's number for months before you acted on it. Don't hate on me 'cause I see something I want and am not afraid to go after it," Shamena fired back, her voice dripping with defiance.

Winkie's face flushed with shame and anger. *"Really, Shamena? You gonna throw that in my face? Just because I'm cautious and you're reckless doesn't mean you get to rub it in."*

"Wait a minute, Winkie. You're dating K-O? Since when? I want all the tea," I said, trying to lighten the tension but feeling the anxiety of the situation.

"That hoe has been talking to him on the phone for about two weeks now, and I think he's really feeling Winkie, but you know that hoe still carrying that shit around from Marcus's punk ass and she is self-sabotaging." Shamena sighed, then her expression softened as she looked at Winkie.

"I still don't believe Marcus called himself getting mad she wasn't ready and tried to talk to Sonya, but you know she fucks with us the long way and told us about it. After we beat his ass with them bats, he ain't been back on our side of town since. I keep telling Winkie she gotta let that shit go with Marcus. Just because K-O didn't answer or call her right back don't mean he's up to no good. He may just be tied up with something and not have his phone," Shamena stated, her tone softening slightly but still intense.

We all knew Shamena could cut viciously when crossed so I knew she was taken it easy on Winkie. Besides, we don't attack each other like this. Winkie has to be hurting.

"She's right, Winkie. He might just be busy. You know he's heavy in these streets and not working a regular job. He might just be on the grind," Deana said, looking around my new place, trying to diffuse the situation.

Winkie took a deep breath, her anger giving way to a look of determination. *"You're right. I need to trust more and not let the past dictate my future. But Shamena, you gotta chill with the bluntness. We're all in this together."*

Shamena shook her head, *"I can only be who I am,"* she shrugged.

"Winkie, K-O is cooler than a fan and mellow as hell. If he wasn't feeling you or had an interest in somebody else, I think he'd tell you. Shit, I know for a fact them work phones ring all night. I could hardly sleep with Zylar's ringing every 30 minutes. So, work could be the reason, or he's at school. You know last year was K-O's senior year just like Zylar, right?" I told her, trying to get her to see the other side.

"I don't mean to act so insecure, guys, but he's fine as hell and I have no real experience with men. The one time I was interested in a guy he turned out to be a hoe, so I'm scared," Winkie voiced, sounding sad and anxious.

"Winkie, don't let your past ruin your future," I said, my voice full of determination. *"I know with recent events I might not be one to talk, but I gave my all to Zylar, and him deciding to cheat on me has no bearing on me as a woman. I know I satisfied him sexually, and I kept him stimulated mentally.*

Our issues came because I refused to hang out with his fake-ass friends," I paused to collect my thoughts.

"You guys all know I have a sixth sense when it comes to snakes, and I can spot them a mile away. His brother's boys are grimy as hell, and I just didn't see myself grinning with them like shit was all good. Zy found, or should I say kept fuckin' with, a hoe that would. So, I removed myself from the situation. I refuse to accept anything other than being his one and only. The thing is though, I don't think Zylar feels it was worth losing me," I told my friends, feeling a mix of anxiety and fear but also a strong resolve.

"No, it wasn't worth losing a day with you, Ray, and I'll never give you cause to leave me again. I promise you that," Zylar said, his voice filled with remorse and anxiety as he and C-Lo came out the back with Zan laying on his shoulder.

"Listen, Winkie," Shamena chimed in, her voice softer now. *"We've all been through shit, but that doesn't mean we have to let it define us. You deserve happiness, and you deserve to be with someone who appreciates you. K-O seems like a good guy, and you shouldn't let past mistakes keep you from finding out if he's the one."*

Deana nodded in agreement. *"She's right, Winkie, and like I said before. He might just be busy. You know he's heavy in these streets and not working a regular job. He might just be on the grind. But you've got to give him a chance and not let fear control you."*

Winkie took a deep breath, her fear and anxiety evident, but there was a flicker of hope in her eyes. *"You're right. I need to trust more and not let the past dictate my future. It's just hard sometimes."*

I hugged her, feeling the bond of our friendship strengthen. *"We're here for you, Winkie. You're not alone in this. We've got your back, no matter what."*

We all shared a group hug and I could feel warmth spread through me as I watched my girls settling in. *"I'm just glad to have everyone here. It feels right, you know?"*

Zy nodded, his eyes softening as he looked at me. *"Yeah, Ray, it does. We're building something real here. I can feel it."* He looked over the girls head at me with Zan resting in his arms. C-Lo stood there staring at Shamena.

I separated from the girls and Zy pulled me into a one armed hug. The other arm securely around Zan. In his arms I was feeling the care and excitement for our future together. *"We got this, Ray. All of us. Together."* Zy spoke, and I could somewhat feel that my girls were a part of that statement.

We separated and my girls saw Zan in Zylar's arms. *"OMG, Ray. He's gorgeous. Look at that hair. He's darling. Let me hold my nephew,"* Johnya said, reaching for Zan as the rest of my girls gushed over him. Our current conversation was forgotten for the moment.

"Wow, Ray, he looks just like Zy. Look at that inky silver and black hair, and it's soft as hell. My nephew is killin' it," Deana said, running her fingers through Zan's hair.

"She's right, Ray. You got a mini version of Zy. He has his eyes, nose, mouth, ears, everything. You must have hated that boy something serious for him to come out a complete replica of his daddy," Shamena joked, making us all burst out laughing.

"Ray, since it's only a little after 10 a.m., if we can get everything packed up before noon, we can move you guys in before the gathering at Ma's crib. Is that alright with you?" Zylar asked, bringing me back to the fact that we were packing.

"That's fine, Zylar. Let me call Rod and make sure it's okay to pack up his room. I respect his privacy and only go in there when he's home," I told Zylar, heading for my room to get the school number to call.

It took them about 15 minutes to get Rod on the phone. *"What up, Ray? Is everything good?"* Rod asked, sounding worried.

"Everything's fine, Rod. I am just calling to ask if it's okay if we pack your stuff in your room. Zylar said we can have everything moved this morning if you're okay with me getting your clothes together. Zylar got you a new bedroom set and stuff, so he said we just have to move your clothes. Is that okay?" I asked, making sure he was fine with this. I know we still have to talk about some things, and I refuse to rush him if he's not ready.

"It's fine, Sis. I thought about it after I got on the bus, and I realized that we are in a different situation than before. If you say we need to move, then it's fine. Just don't break my game systems," Rod told me, sounding full of confidence.

"Thanks, baby bro. See you after school. Bye," I told him and hung up to find Zylar standing in the doorway, listening.

"Was he okay with us getting his things together and moving this morning?" Zylar asked, looking a little worried as he eased up to where I was sitting.

"Yeah, he's good with us getting his stuff ready for the move, and I think he truly believes me now when I say I got us from here on out. As long as I have the breath in my body and can work, I got us." I sighed and stood up.

"Let me go get the girls to start packing the rest of the house. Do you have dishes, towels, sheets, and stuff, Zylar? Or will I have to shop for that? I'm asking so I can know what exactly I need to pack from here," I asked Zylar while heading out to my girls.

"Ray, the kitchen and bathrooms are fully stocked with everything we need to live in our house. Ma said, 'All you would have to do is add your own personal touch.' Whatever that is," Zylar told me as I made it back out to my girls still fussing over Zan.

"Guys, we are in the process of packing our stuff so we can move in with Zylar. I need you guys to help me get Reign, Rod, Zan, and my clothes packed and ready to go. We don't have to pack any of the dishes, towels, bedding, or food. Oh, and before I forget. Do you guys want to move in here as roommates and share the apartment until December when the lease is up? My uncles paid my rent up for a full year, so y'all will only have utilities to pay until then. We all complained about wanting our own spot when we lived with our moms; this is a chance for you guys to see what it feels like to have your own place before you start college in the summer. So, what do you guys think?" I asked them, smiling.

"Ray, are you sure you want to move in with Zy this soon? You spent 10 months running from him, and now you are moving into his place. Don't you think you should wait and see if he's really stopped fuckin' with them other hoes first?" Johnya voiced, completely ignoring everything I said about the apartment.

The room went silent for a moment. I could feel the tension building. I knew they would have some bold opinions about my decision. So now I just have to listen objectively.

"Johnya, I get where you're coming from, but I believe in giving people a second chance," I said, feeling a mix of caution and determination. *"Zylar has shown me he's committed to making things right, and I want to move forward with him."*

"I hear what you're saying Ray, but I agree with Johnya. You spent 10 months away from us hiding from Zy. Now you plan to move in with him out the blue. You guys just got back together yesterday, what if he's just trying to

make you give up your place, so you'll be dependent on him?" Deana asked not giving a fuck about Zylar standing in the room.

That let me know that Zylar not only has to prove himself changed to me, but my friends as well. I looked over at him looking anxious. There was nothing I could say to that, because her point is valid.

"I'm not sure if that is his motive or not Deanna, but Like I said, from what he has shown me so far. He's committed to making this work. So, I decided to give him another chance." I told her as Shamena stepped forward.

"Bitch I agree with them. How you hide from this Nigga for 10 whole months and then jump up and move with him the next day after seeing him again for the first time?" She folded her arms across her chest, and leaned back on her right leg, mugging me. *"That dick must be something serious to have you making dummy moves. I can understand you guys working things out slowly and rebuilding the trust, but this don't sound like you at all to be impulsive like this Ray. So, make it make sense."* Shamena spoke, making everybody in the room look her way.

I dropped my head. Shamena always speaks her mind no matter the cost. I can't even be mad at her, because I know she's coming from a place of love. She got me fucked up though.

"Really Bitch? I have never been. Nor will I ever be influenced by some dick. This move is motivated by our need for safety while we work on rebuilding the trust that was lost. Zylar is a lot deeper in the game than he was before, and this apartment is too exposed and hard to properly protect. I don't give a damn what issues Zylar and I may have. I want my brother, sister, and son safe." I paused to let that sync in.

"I had some of the same thoughts and concerns myself, but the deciding factor for me was even without us being together and working on our relationship, Zylar would still be coming around because of Zan. So instead of us living part-time in both places and being exposed here. We are just going to live at Zylar's crib that is in a gated community with armed security and surveillance 24-hours a day. You guys know me. I don't make impulsive decisions. I thought about all the pros and cons of getting back with Zylar before I made the decision to even talk to him last night. Shit Zylar didn't even tell me about his little promotion until after I took him back." I laughed while looking

over at Zylar who was watching me like a hawk. C-Lo stood next to him watching Shamena's every move.

"Ray, we're just worried about you. We don't want to see you get hurt again," Shamena added, her voice filled with concern.

"And what if he hasn't changed?" Johnya pressed, anger flashing in her eyes. *"What if he goes back to his old ways and you're left picking up the pieces?"*

"Look, I understand your fears, but this is my decision. I care for Zylar, and I want to build a life with him. But I also want you guys to have a chance to experience independence," I replied, feeling the excitement and unity of our friendship. *"No matter what may happen between us. I want to give it another go. If he fucks up again, I know I at least gave it one last try. I'll be good however it turns out."*

Deana stepped forward, breaking the tension. *"I think it's a great opportunity for all of us. We can support each other and make this work. Plus, we'll always be here for you, Ray."*

Johnya crossed her arms, not entirely convinced. *"I hope you're right, Ray. Because if he messes up again, it won't just be you dealing with the fallout. We'll all be there, and I'm not sure I can handle going through that pain again."*

"I get it, Johnya. I really do. But I have to follow my heart on this. I need to give Zylar this chance," I said, trying to keep my voice steady. My girls opinions mean a lot to me and I want them in my corner. If they are beefing with my man over me, it'll never work.

"Alright, let's do this," Johnya finally said, a small smile breaking through. *"But if Zylar steps out of line, we'll be here to back you up."*

I smiled knowing what she meant. Zylar's ass might come up missing if he fucked up again. *"Deal,"* I said, feeling a wave of love and gratitude for my friends. *"Now, let's get packing!"*

The tension lingered in the air, but the determination to support each other won out. We had a lot to do, but we were in it together, come what may.

Johnya, Deana, Winkie, and Shamena all looked at me and in unison said, *"Okay Bitch. We got you. Where do you want us to start?"*

I burst out laughing and showed them what all to pack and we finished in less than 45 min. C-Lo arranged a truck with 2 movers that came and loaded everything up in no time. Now we're all on the way to see my new place. The girls agreed they'd all like to move into the apartment and share the bills until December and make further plans after that.

Raylexia Gavion

It took us about 30 min to make it to the gated community off Ellerbe where Zylar said we'd be living. When we pulled up to the guard house Zylar had me get out and give the guard my driver's license to make a copy so they could give me a personal code to the gate. We then pulled into the subdivision and drove around the northside for about 5 min until we reached a second gate where Zylar had me enter my code to open the gate. Zylar took the lead as we drove for about a half a mile until we reached a two-story house on the hill concealed behind skeleton trees that line the drive. Zylar pulled around to the far end of the circular drive and parked. I followed behind and parked along the other side to allow the truck to pull past us to park in front of the door. We all exited the cars and Zylar walked over and pulled me to the door while handing me the keys.

"Open the door to our new home Ray. This is our first time coming home. so, we get to officially see it together," Zylar told me grinning wide as hell showing all his stacked teeth.

I opened the door to the house and Zylar swung me up into his arms and crossed the threshold. Once he sat me down and I got my first look around I was speechless. This house is the shit. The entryway had vaulted ceilings that branch off to the left and right both leading down hallways. The floors were a mixture of hardwood, marble, ceramic tile and carpet.

"Bitch you can gock at the place later. Let's get the unpacking done. Have you forgotten I still have to do your hair?" Shamena said, making everybody laugh at her including the movers who were bringing boxes in unloading them in the foyer.

"I see I can't with you right now Sha. Zylar, where are Reign and Rod's rooms so we can have them put the boxes in there? It will make it easier to unpack." I asked Zylar.

His reply stunned the hell out of us all. *"I don't know Ray. I've never been inside to see the finished result. I've only been to the garage to store your cars. I can't tell you where anything is. Ma did all this. I refused to come here until we could see it together."*

"Damn Ray. I take it all back. He has most definitely learned his lesson. Now let's go find these bedrooms." Deana said while heading up the hall followed by the rest of us.

I could tell Zylar liked what he saw because he kept checking each room and nodding his head in approval. My girls were all doing the same while we walked around the bottom level. We found a theater room, his and hers man caves, exercise room, laundry room, kitchen, formal and informal dining rooms, and three living room areas all setup differently.

"Well Ray this house is fire, but we need to head on upstairs cause ain't no bedrooms down here. Good luck with keeping this big bitch clean with your OCD having ass. I can see it now, your ass is gonna be cleaning from morning to night just to control the dust in this bitch." Shamena said, making all my girls burst out in hysterics knowing about my cleaning tendencies.

"You got jokes hoe. I am not that bad. Besides, I have all of you to help me keep the dust down, so I'm Gucci," I told Shamena as everybody except the two movers, Johnya, the babies and C-Lo went up the spiral staircase.

Once we made it to the top floor the view was breathtaking. The roof had a dome ceiling attached to floor to ceiling windows where we could see out over the property. The staircase opened into a sitting area decorated in large plush furniture that gave a view of the backside of the house. In the back there was an Olympic size swimming pool with what looked like a 3-bedroom pool house situated behind it. There was a paved sidewalk that led to a basketball/tennis court with a sauna and hot tub setup alongside.

"This muthafucker is bad Ray. I can see us out there in that pool soaking up the sun and doing laps to keep in shape, well everybody but your no swimming ass." Deana laughed.

"The summer gone be hype as hell out here with y'all Ray, with the pool parties and backyard barbecues throughout the summer. It'll be the perfect way for us all to destress from school on the weekend." Deana said as she headed down the left side of the top level.

"Come on y'all let's find these bedrooms so we can get started unpacking Ray's stuff. We can all explore the house over the weekend, since tomorrow after school we all agreed to get started moving into the apartment. We also all have to find jobs if we are going to be able to pay the bills at the apartment." Winkie stated while headed down the right side of the top level.

"Ray!" I heard Winkie yell out as she opened the door to the first room past the staircase. I rushed over to see what she was yelling about and damn near fainted when I went inside. The room had to be set up for Rod with a king-sized bed, big sturdy dresser and chest, built-in wall unit with 65-inch TV, DVD, PlayStation, Xbox, Nintendo GameCube, and state of the art Pioneer sound system. There was also a sitting area in front of the wall unit with couch, loveseat, and coffee table stacked with all kinds of handheld games. Rod was going to be in heaven.

I made my way to the next room across the hall and about four feet down from Rod's to find a room setup for a princess. Reign's room has a queen-sized white canopy bed in pink and gray with a wide variety of stuffed animals and pillows on top. It has a white dresser and chest with matching wardrobe cabinet situated opposite a large play area containing a kid sized doll house with miniature furniture inside. Over in the corner there is a table setup like the last tea party from "Alice In Wonderland," and all throughout the room there were toys in various areas. Directly across from her bed is an entertainment center with a 40-inch TV and a DVD collection of various children's movies. Just looking at the room and all the effort that went into putting it together for Reign touched my heart.

I checked out the third room which had a basic set-up for any would be guest with a lounge area attached. Mrs Della really did her thang in here.

I walked out of that room over to the other side and found Zylar in the last room at the far end of the hall. The sight that greeted me left me speechless. The room or should I say rooms took up the entire left side of the hall. On the far wall sat a California King Bed with black, gray, and white coverings sitting in-between two nightstands with arched lamps. At the foot of the bed is an oversized chaise lounge. Off to the left side of the bed is a recessed sitting area with wraparound leather sofa and loveseat combined facing a built-in wall unit with a 75-inch TV, DVD, Pioneer Stereo, PlayStation, Xbox, and video collection. The room has two closets/

dressing rooms with built-in shoe racks. The attached bathroom contained both his and her sinks, separate shower, bath and jacuzzi with the toilet in its own room. I was at a complete and total loss for words. Mrs. Della really out did herself. This place is so much more than anything I could have ever imagined living in.

I turned to see Zylar watching me to gauge my reaction to the room and I had to smile. *"Zylar, this place is beautiful. Thank you so much for creating a space for me and my siblings and making it a home. I never dreamed I would live in something like this, it exceeds all my expectations."*

"From now on Ray you will have nothing but the best, and hopefully we can give Reign and Rod the childhood that they have been missing. I don't know much about your past because you have only shared so much with me, but maybe now that you have the support you need things will start to feel a little more stable to where you'll open up freely and accept my help. We can take it one day at a time and I promise to earn back your trust," Zylar told me and I could see his heart in his eyes.

"I care about you Zylar and you hurt me really badly. This is the last chance, so it's our final dance. Remember me being with you is a choice, don't give me a reason to choose a different one," I told him while kissing him with my whole soul. If he fucked up again there is no coming back for us.

"Um, excuse me guys, but this little man just woke up and he's wanting his mom." Johnya walked in with a fussing Zander in his car seat.

"Give him to me girl, he's just ready to eat. Where's his diaper bag and Tylan?" I asked since I didn't see Tylan.

"He's downstairs on the couch asleep with C-Lo and the movers. I see you guys found the rooms so we can get started. It's after 11:30am and we still have to put everything away and get ready for the party before it's time to go pick-up Rod and Reign from the apartments. I don't think you thought this through, because you maybe should have kept them home today. It would have been easier than going back and forth." Johnya stressed while looking around the room. *"Girl, this place is beautiful."* She added.

"Thanks, and no, this all is last minute. We were planning to have everything moved Friday while I was at school but since you guys came over and we only had to move our clothes and Zan's furniture we thought it would be quick. We just got a little sidetracked." I giggled. *"Let me go get Zan's bottle and*

change him before I feed him. That way he'll go right back to sleep. Zylar Rod and Reign's rooms are on the other end, and you know this is our room. You and C-Lo can have the movers put everything in the rooms and let my girls have at it. They pretty much know what Rod and Reign like. They can change whatever they don't like when they get here after we come from the gathering or tomorrow after school," I told Zylar as I headed to the door to get Zan squared away.

"Ray before you go. Where do you want Zan's extra crib that you had in your room to go in here?" Zylar asked while looking around for a suitable placement.

"Just put it together and set it up anywhere for now. I'll decide after I look through the room more thoroughly," I told him heading to the stairs.

Zylar Crewens

Ma outdid herself with this place. Just looking around at the finished product I am more than pleased, and the look on Ray's face when she saw it put my mind at ease. Now that I have her back in my life, I won't be doing anything stupid to ever lose her again. Johnya gave me a weird look as we both followed Ray down the stairs prompting me to give her an inquiring look of my own.

"Is there a problem Johnya?" I asked not to familiar with this particular friend and talking to any of them without Ray present doesn't sit right with me.

"No. There is no problem. I just see now that you truly love Ray and really have no intention on cheating again. You have no idea how glad we were when she met you. Shit we all thought she would be gay because she had zero interest in guys. Ray has had a really horrible childhood and we were really worried about her after her Mom moved them away. She may never tell you the full extent of what has happened to her, but just remember that it shaped her into a fighter. Ray won't just except bullshit from you and stay. She'll run even if it means she'll have to do without and live off the grid, so don't make us have to live without our friend again. That's all I'm saying. We love her, in many ways for me her and the others are the sisters I never had. Don't make me have to live without my sister again. Her disappearing hurt more than anything I've experienced before." Johnya said and walked past me down the stairs.

It then dawned on me that Ray left everybody behind just to make sure that I couldn't find her. What lengths would she go to if it happened again? I know one thing for certain. I have no desire to ever find out. Was my last thought as I followed Johnya down the stairs to get the boxes moved up to the bedrooms.

Ray had the boxes labeled Zan, Ray, Rod and Reign so I had the movers put them in the rooms where Winkie and Shamena instructed them to. Winkie and Deana took care of Rod's room and Shamena and Johnya got Reign's room situated. They made such quick work of unpacking the boxes and putting the rooms in order that by the time Ray came upstairs and laid both Tylan and Zan in the middle of our bed surrounded by pillows, they were done.

"Ray, can you check out the other two rooms over here and let me know which one you want to use for Zander's room? The only thing left is to put his stuff in place in his room." I caught Ray before she could start sorting out her stuff.

"Sorry Zylar, I forgot all about Zan's furniture. You could have just chosen either one would have been okay. If we needed to change it later that would have been fine." She answered like she would have been fine either way. I wasn't buying that shit. I'm putting things where she wants them the first time, ain't no do overs.

Ray checked both rooms and chose the one right across and a little ways down from ours. The room was huge and swallowed his furniture, but I'm sure Ray will find more things to fill it up with as he grows. We had to move the bedroom suit out and placed all the furniture in the last bedroom stacked along the wall. That would have to do until Ray decides what she wants to do with it.

Once she had us place Zan's things where she wanted them, she got to work sorting out her things. It took her about 30 min in all after the girls came in and helped her. Watching them interact I now understand what Johnya was saying about their bond. They would literally say whatever to each other and no one took offense. It was like they knew no matter what was said the others didn't care. There was no pretense, no cattiness, or words said to hurt or demean. In truth just chillin with them I now understand why my girl refused to hang out with me. The hoes in the clubs are forever trying each other instead of having fun.

"Ray, are you and the girls getting dressed here or back at the apartment when we go to get Rod and Reign?" I asked to know how much time we had before we would have to leave.

"We're going to take our clothes and get ready back at the apartment. Shamena is going to do my hair first since it takes the longest and then the others. We'll then take turns showering and dressing since we have 2 bathrooms. I found Rod and Reign something to wear already so they will just have to shower and change once they come in from school and we'll be ready to go. I'ma let Johnya drive my truck and me and the kids will ride with you. They can just follow us since your Ma's place is not too far from the apartments." Ray told me as she laid an outfit on the bed to wear.

"Aight then let me get these Niggas so we can get these boxes and blankets back on the truck and get ready to leave," I told her while grabbing the boxes up in our room.

"Zylar, can we keep the truck until tomorrow after the girls get moved in at the apartment? We are gonna need more boxes cause they all are moving at the same time. Wait, I just figured out what to do with the bedroom set we took out of Zan's room. We can give it to the girls to put in Zan's old room at the apartment. Is that okay with you Zylar if I give them the bedroom suit?" Ray asked me like it wasn't her shit too.

"Ray you can do whatever you want to with anything and everything in this muthafucka. Everything in here belongs to you. You don't have to ask me anything. It's whatever you want," I told her, planning to show her the deed to this house with her name on it to prove my point.

"We don't have to keep the truck overnight. C-Lo can just reserve the truck and the movers for tomorrow after they get out of school. Just have them let you know when they are ready, and we'll have them there," I told her as I headed downstairs with the boxes.

I went downstairs to find C-Lo and the movers sitting in my man cave drinking sodas and watching the movie "Heat" on the 75-inch built-in to the wall. From the looks of it they had just robbed a bank and were laying muthafuckas down left and right.

"Man, how y'all Niggas gone watch my shit before me? This movie is the shit. C-Lo I'm telling Myron and K-O you busted that bitch open without us. We were planning to watch that the next time we chilled with all the fellas," I told C-Lo who was still engrossed in the movie and paying me no mind.

"Zylar fuck you interrupted the best part Nigga. We most def got to watch this with My Niggas. Them Niggas go hard in this bitch. Well, we don't need

K-Boy to see this shit cause he'll be trying to reenact the shit himself. We'd be reading about that Nigga on the news." C-Lo bust out laughing hard as hell.

"They're almost done, so we can gather all the boxes and blankets we used to wrap the furniture and put it all back on the truck. Ray wants to give the bedroom suit we put against the wall in the guest bedroom to her girls, so load it up and we'll take that bitch back with us and set it up in Zan's old room at the apartment. We need to head back to the apartment to wait for the kids to get out of school. Ray and the girls are going to get dressed over there. I'll get dressed once we get to Ma's house since that's where all my clothes are. Before I forget, Ray wants to get the truck and you guys to move her girls after they all get out of school tomorrow. Set that shit up C-Lo so we can handle it before we leave today," I told C-Lo as we all headed back upstairs to load the furniture and get all the used boxes.

CHAPTER ELEVEN
Raylexia Gavion

I thought we would be riding back with Zylar after we finished getting the house situated and prepared to leave. Zylar said, *"Since we have the car seat it was best if we used a SUV."* So, I'm thinking he wants us to take my Expedition, when he opened the garage and showed me a white 2012 Mercedes Benz G-Class SUV, a silver 2012 BMW X5, and a black 2012 Cadillac Escalade that he said all belonged to me. After I damn near fainted from the shock, we attached Zan's car seat inside the Cadillac Escalade and went back to the apartment.

The guys made quick work of putting up the bedroom suit and sent the movers on their way. C-Lo had a short conversation with Shamena then Zylar and he left as well. Shamena then got started on our hair. She washed my hair and braided me up into a high ponytail that hung to the middle of my back taming my edges to perfection. For Winkie she did a feathered style off to the left that brought attention to her gray eyes. Johnya and Deana both got bobs of different lengths. Shamena wore her hair down with a part on the left side hanging a little past her shoulders. We were all runway ready in our jeans, sweaters, and ankle boots.

"We are ready just in time. Rod should be here any minute. Winkie that black and gray really suits you. K-O ain't gone know what hit him tonight." I teased Winkie as she walked by grinning hard as hell.

"Shamena, where did you get those red jeans from? Those bitches look painted on. I want a pair if they fit like that." Deana said while watching Shamena move over to the couch and take a seat.

She wasn't lying, those jeans fit Shamena like a second skin. Every step she took her ass and thighs jiggled. With her thick frame on display everyone could clearly see all her dimensions. C-Lo is in trouble.

"Girl me and Johnya got them at 'Rainbows' when they had the buy one get one 50% off sale last month. Y'all know my Momma ain't spending no money on me like that. Mrs. Johnny Mae got me a pair along with Johnya's." Shamena said as she pulled fuzz out her sweater.

"Guys Price-Lo is hiring seasonal help right now for the evening shift that's usually from 2pm to 11pm at $7.50 an hour to start. If they hire you on a permanent basis it goes up to $8.00 an hour after your 90 days. The work is not hard, just a lot of standing and customers with bad attitudes. I'm using this job as a stepping stone, hopefully one day soon we'll all be working at Shamena's hair salon and beauty bar," I told them because all my girls are talented with skills that we have acquired from school and around the hood, we just need a chance to show it.

"I'm all for getting a job and working while going to school, anything beats being broke all the time and asking muthafuckers to do the most basic shit they should supply because they are our parents. I'm sorry guys, but y'all know my Momma ain't shit and I'm so tired of living like this." Shamena said and got up and went to the restroom.

We all knew that she needed a moment to collect herself, because thinking about the shit her mother does to her always causes her to become a little emotional.

"I really feel if you guys can get on at Price-Lo and we all save everything we can aside from bills, we'll be able to open the salon and beauty bar within the next year. All you guys already have your licenses and I'm taking the classes for business administration to learn how to run and manage a business so I feel we can do this," I told them all, more convinced than ever that together we can make it happen.

"Ray I don't mean to interrupt, but I happened to overhear what you were saying. If you guys are all licensed and really want to open a salon and beauty bar let me know what you need. We bought a real estate company and Myron flips failing businesses and properties. Just let me know what area you want to open a business in, and we'll start looking for properties on Monday. I'll tell Myron when we get to the gathering. If you guys have the talent and the

know-how. I'd rather you work for yourself than anybody else," Zylar told us, shocking the hell out of us all.

"We don't have the money Zylar. How can we buy a property and open a business? Just from the little I have learned so far in school I know we need start-up capital or money as we call it," I told Zylar not wanting to get the girl's hopes up.

"Ray, you have plenty of money. If I have it, you have it. Just let me get Myron on it. You guys just decide where you want the shop and how big. We'll take it from there," Zylar told us before going back into the room with Zan.

I looked at the girls including Shamena who came out of the restroom while Zylar was talking. *"What do you all think? Can we do this?"* I asked them not wanting to get too excited before we have definite plans.

"I say we go for it. We have nothing to lose. We don't have anything, maybe now we can make something happen for us all." Deana said as we all nodded in agreement.

Rod came home 10 min later and went straight to shower and change. When Reign got home, we rushed her through her bath and Shamena did her hair. Less than 20 min later we were all loading up to head to Mrs. Della's house when C-Lo pulled up and got out to get Shamena. She smiled and walked to the passenger side of the truck where he held the door open for her to get in. I could see the smile all over her face.

When we got to Mrs. Della's she was standing at the front door waiting on us. *"Come on in here and bring me my babies,"* she said as she hugged me tight and kissed me on the forehead while whispering, *"we'll talk later"* in my ear.

"Hi, Reign, it's nice to finally meet you. I've heard a lot about you from your sister. My name is Grandma Della or just plain old grandma, okay?" Mrs. Della spoke to Reign, shocking her because she'd never had a grandmother before. She kneeled down on the floor and gave her a hug.

She then turned to Rod who looked spooked. *"Hello Rod. You can call me Grandma Della too. Is that okay with you?"* she asked while holding his gaze.

"Yes Mam. We haven't had a grandma in over 8 years now. That would be really nice to have another real one." Rod answered while looking at me smiling.

I knew that Rod had missed Grandma Etta a lot, but I never thought he'd be this accepting of someone else in the role. Mrs. Della reached up and gave him a big hug making him grin even harder. I then introduced her to all my friends as my sisters and she gave them a warm and genuine welcome. The biggest of which was the hug and kisses she gave to Tylan. Zylar then brought Zander over in his seat and handed him off to his Mom so he could go shower and get dressed. Mrs. Della started crying and kissing all over his face and Zander was kicking and smiling like he knew he was getting love from his grandma.

After Mrs. Della calmed down a bit and laid Zander back down in his car seat, we began to walk around with Mrs. Della and check on the food the caterers were setting out. *"Is there anything you need us to help with before your guest gets here Mrs. Della?"* I was ready to do something to take my mind off meeting Zylars extended family.

"What are you talking about Ray? You and your family are the guests of honor here today. We are doing this so that everyone can meet my daughter-in-law and my grandbabies. Your sisters are just an added bonus. I want you all to know that you have family, and we take care of family." Mrs. Della told us all, including my friends. I could feel my heart swell.

"Thank you so much for saying that Mrs. Della. It means a lot to me and my siblings. We haven't really had anybody to take care of us or that cared about us in an adult role since our grandmother died when I was 8 years old. Just seeing the effort you put into getting Zylar's house ready for us means more to me than words can express. Thank you so much for welcoming us all this way," I said while giving Mrs. Della a very tight hug while smiling.

C-Lo made his way over and hugged Mrs. Della. *"How are you doing Mrs. C. I want you to officially meet My Beast. Her name is Shamena and she has charged me with taming her."* C-Lo told Mrs. Della while the rest of us burst out laughing.

"Mrs. Della, it's nice to meet you formally. I am Shamena Greene and Cree and I just made things official today. I still have to whip him into shape, so pay him no mind. I see I have some training to do. The next time we come over I'll have him house trained." Shamena grinned while winking at C-Lo.

"I'm sure you can handle it honey. The fact that you call him Cree and he allows it speaks volumes. You all make yourselves at home and get refreshments

if you need it. I'm going to lay Zander and Tylan down in my room. Come on with me Johnya, I know he's heavy and there's too much noise in here for him to get any rest. Reign, you and Rod can come to play the video game if you want. I don't want you guys to get bored just waiting around." Mrs. Della said as she grabbed Zan's car seat and headed down the hall followed by Johnya carrying Tylan.

Zylar Crewens

After I finished my shower and changed clothes, I made my way back over to Ma's side of the house. Ray and her friends were chillin talking to C-Lo and sipping on soft drinks. Before I could make it over to them the doorbell rang, so I detoured to answer it. I opened the door to reveal my boys and their girls. *"It's about time you Niggas showed up. What's up Lance and Awaii, Jamie and Sonya, Kam and Felisha. Jayce what the fuck you mean muggin' for Nigga? Don't come up in here with no bullshit, on God. I will fuck a bitch up today. My family is in attendance and y'all Niggas better be on your best behavior. What's good Myron? Hey Shanna."* I spoke to everybody but Jayce's bitch Derricka because that hoe cool with Chandra and I told that Nigga not to bring that bitch to my Ma's crib. I walked up to Jayce.

"Jayce let me holla at you Nigga." I snatched that Nigga by his neck and pulled him to the side. *"Didn't I tell you not to bring yo bitch to my Ma's crib? What part of if she had to come with you stay home did you not understand? You know good and well that I don't fuck with Chandra no more and yo bitch still hangs heavy with her. If that BITCH gets out of line that's on your body. I don't play about Ray, and I will kill a bitch before I let her leave me over some shit, I had nothing to do with. Control your bitch or leave,"* I told that Nigga before I pushed his ass away from me.

"Nigga don't be grabbing and pushin on me like I'm your bitch. I did leave that hoe at her house. She followed us here and snuck through the gate as we were coming in. I didn't even see that hoe until we were walking up to the door. I told you I stopped fuckin' with that hoe when I found out she was the one providing Chandra with our location every time we went out. That bitch is the new and improved stalker version of Chandra. I can't shake that hoe no matter how hard I try." Jayce told me while still mean mugging towards that hoe.

"Well, that hoe has to get up out of here. The only reason I let her in is because I thought she came with you and you are responsible for her actions. Get that hoe out of here now. You shoulda' turned around and escorted her out before y'all made it to the door," I told that Nigga not believing he let this hoe walk in Ma's house.

I walked off towards Ray and her girls while watching Jayce move and snatch up Derricka. He pulled her out the front door as she tried to tussle and draw attention to them. Everybody looked at them briefly and went back to mingling.

"Ray, let me introduce you and your girls to my boys and their ladies. Everybody this is my lady Raylexia and her homegirls Johnya, Shamena, Deana, and Winkie." I barely got out before Ray and her girls rushed Sonya and started hugging and talking like old friends.

"Ray?" I asked and she broke away from the group and grinned up at me.

"Sorry about that Zylar, but this is our homegirl from Lakeside Sonya. We all go back to middle school and haven't seen each other in a while," she told me, still grinning.

"Aight then Ray this is Myron and Shanna, Lance and Awaii, Jamie, and Kam and Felisha. Jayce had to handle something right quick and he'll be back. Everybody again this is my girl Raylexia." I introduced her again and this time everybody began to mingle. The ladies went over with Ray and the girls and My Fellas walked over to Ma's bar with me. So far everything was running smoothly.

"Man, why y'all let that hoe come in through the gate behind y'all. Jayce claimed he left that hoe at her house and she followed him here. If that hoe cause trouble for me tonight with my girl I'ma fuck Jayce up. He had no business showing that hoe where my Ma's house at. What the fuck is y'alls security detail doing if hoes can follow y'all to my Ma's place?" I vented upset that something could possibly go wrong tonight of all nights. Ray is happy and I wanna keep it that way.

"Calm your ass down Nigga. This is no longer your Ma's house and you won't be sleeping here anymore after tonight so that hoe don't know nothing. I do admit that his security should have stopped her from entering the gate and Black needs to address that. If they're just letting random muthafuckas follow us they serve no purpose." Myron said while texting on his phone.

He texts back and forth with Black and then put his phone in his pocket.

"Black said on several occasions Jayce has left home and she followed him to different spots that seemed legitimate. How do they know when it's something not planned when it happens more than four times a week?" Myron replied back to Black that her or no other female or anybody else is not allowed to follow us unless we hit up security to let them know it's happening in advance.

The doorbell rang again, and this time Ma went to get it, letting K-O in followed by Zaylar, Nico and Josie. They all hugged Ma and walked over to us to say hello, K-O then headed for Winkie like his ass was on fire. I laughed at the shit cause she's worried he is not feeling her like that.

"Zylar let me meet this woman that had you losing your mind." Zay said, making everybody laugh. I got up from the bar stool and gestured.

"Follow me Nigga, I'll introduce you to her and her girls. She comes as a package deal." I smirked at Zay as he laid eyes on Johnya. That Nigga's facial expression showed he had just marked his territory.

"Ray this is my brother's Zaylar and Nico, and Nico's lady Josie. Guys this my lady Raylexia." I made introductions while smiling hard.

"It's nice to finally meet you guys. I have heard some wild tales about you, Zaylar. I hope your reputation don't precede you." She smirked at his stunned expression.

"Hi Nico. I have heard nothing but wonderful things about you. Exactly how tall are you? I have to really look up to meet your gaze and you have some beautiful eyes." Ray told Nico while reaching past him to shake Josie's hand. *"Hi Josie. Nice to meet you. Hope to see more of you in the future. Now that we got that all out the way. Come on, go over here with us girls. We're just having girl talk,"* Ray said while pulling Josie along with her back over to the girls.

"Well damn. She just bypassed us and kept it moving. I like her Zy. No pretense. What you see is what you get, and she's blunt. I bet you never have to guess what she's thinking because she tells you straight off. You have a real one Zy. Don't fuck up again because I won't help you find her next time." Nico told me while walking back over to the Fellas. I just shook my head. I had no intention of ever making him use that threat.

"Zaylar what the hell is wrong with you? Why are you just standing there staring at Johnya like you are crazy My Nigga?" I asked that Nigga cause

he hasn't moved since Ray and Josie walked off and his gaze is trained on Johnya.

"She's My One Zylar. My heart started racing and my palms are sweating. Shit my dick feels like it's trying to jump out my jeans to get to her. Pop's told me that when I found her my body would let me know and I never understood what he meant until now. This shit is crazy Bruh. You have to introduce us and find a reason for her to run to the store with me. I have to be alone with her when I stake my claim." This Nigga told me like she can just leave with her son sleeping in the back.

"Zaylar, you know I understand what you're going through, but Johnya has a three-year-old son that's asleep in Ma's room. I'm sure she's not just going to leave with you without her son. Maybe you can take her over to my side of the house and talk to her there. It's private and no one is on that side of the house. Ma has it blocked off because of the caterers and high traffic flowing through here tonight," I told that Nigga as we headed in the girl's direction.

I walked up to Ray and pulled her over to where Zaylar was standing staring at Johnya. *"Ray Zay would like you to introduce him to Johnya. He is feeling her and wants to shoot his shot."* I laughed as Ray took in Zaylar's tense expression.

"Okay she's been watching him since he came through the door, so I guess she's feeling him too. He might be her one." Ray giggled as she went over and whispered something in Johnya's ear. Her head shot up and they both headed this way. Zaylar looked like he was going to devour Johnya with his eyes. His breathing got more labored the closer they got to us.

"You okay nigga?" I asked.

"Were you okay while Ray was gone?" He snapped back.

"Point taken," I answered and shut the fuck up.

When they made it to us, Zaylar was practically vibrating.

"Zaylar this is my bestie Johnya and Johnya this is Zylar's brother Zaylar." Ray made introductions and the two of them walked off towards my side of the house talking. That Nigga ain't wasting no time in staking his claim.

Me and Ray both chuckled and she walked back over to her girls and I headed back over to the Fellas. As I approached My Niggas, I remembered I needed to talk to Myron about the girls opening a salon and beauty bar.

"Yo Myron, let me run some business by you right quick," I said to him and we moved off to the side to talk in private.

"Ray and her girls all want to open a salon and beauty bar. They all have their license and just need a property in a good location and all the other stuff to start up a business. Ray is in school now for business administration and plans to act as manager. How can I make this happen for them? We can purchase the bitch for them, get everything setup and sell it to them for $1. I know C-Lo, K-O, Zaylar, and Me will all buy whatever they need since it's for our girls." I asked that Nigga eager to get started so Ray can quit that bullshit ass job. My Queen is a Boss and should only be working for herself.

"I just need to talk to them and find out how many services they plan to offer to know how much space they'll need. We just purchased the rest of the available properties in the strip mall where Shanna's restaurant is located, so we have many options for them to choose from. We just have to make sure the overall space will be suitable for the services they plan to offer. Our best bet is for me to talk to them and go from there. We are definitely doing this, so I just have to work out a working business model to have for the contractors get started on remodeling the building to accommodate the different procedures they provide. Can I ask them what services they plan to offer so I can know if we have to use more than one property to accommodate the business? That way I can get started tomorrow." Myron asked his mind already on getting the business started.

"Let me get Ray and the girls and ask Ma is it alright if we use the den for the meeting," I told Myron as we walked over to her and the girls talking a mile a minute.

"Ma can we use the den to talk about something important right quick?" I asked her first before letting Ray and her girls know we need to talk to them.

"Sure Zylar. We are all good over here." Ma said while she and Josie talked animatedly.

"Ray, can you and the girls come holla at Myron about what we discussed earlier. He needs your input to know how big a space you need, and to set up the business model," I told them and they all got up and followed me to the den.

Before Ray and I crossed the threshold, she stopped in her tracks. I damn near ran into her back.

"Wait Zylar. Johnya is still talking to Zaylar. We can't do this without her." Ray told me while looking at her girls expectantly making me whip out my business phone and call Zaylar.

That Nigga answered on the fourth ring right before it went to voicemail breathing hard as hell. "What?" He answered while speaking softly in the background to Johnya.

"Zay we need Johnya in the den to discuss the business they are trying to open. Myron said if they give him some particulars, he can get the ball rolling tomorrow. Bring Johnya to the den because the other girls won't discuss anything without her input. This is important to them." I stressed making sure he understood it's about her future and not no bullshit.

"We're on our way," he said and hung up.

"Their coming," I told Ray and the girls while checking on text from Buck. It would seem fuckboy went back over to Ray's place and four of the goons followed him until he stopped for food and whipped his ass good. I smirked just thinking about how long it's gonna take for that fool to give up on fuckin' with Ray.

We all waited for Zaylar and Johnya for 20 min before they made it to the den. Johnya was now sporting a high ponytail instead of the neat bob she left with, but no one commented on that.

Myron, ready to put that business degree to work, asked the girls questions about the services they plan to offer and how many stations each service would need. For Ray not to have finished school she was very knowledgeable about each girl's skill set and how many additional stations they would need to operate at capacity. *"We plan to offer a wide range of hair services that include haircuts, coloring, blowouts, braids, weaves, wraps, wigs, styling, sew-ins, and treatments. Shamena can do all that and has also made her own edge gel. We also want to provide a space for up to five additional stylists. Deana does nails, all services and we want three extra slots for more nail techs. Winkie does body waxing and will require a room setup for her use and two extra stations. Johnya does massages and facials so her area will require the most room because they need a changing room and massage room. We want two additional rooms for this service also so we can hire more techs, so we don't all have to work every day. We all can do makeup and eyebrows. We just don't personally wear it. They are also licensed in each field through the Career Center at Caddo that says we can practice in the state of Louisiana."* Ray finished leaving us all stunned. She looked over at all her girls. *"Did I leave anything out?"*

"Don't forget there needs to be at least 3 shower stalls connected to the dressing room in my section, Ray, because most clients like to freshen up before leaving after a massage. The facials are simple, but I will need a separate area from the massage area to do those. The specialized chair contains extensions and will need space to spread out. Other than that, everything you said sounds good." Johnya added, getting Myron's attention. Zaylar was sitting so close to her they looked stuck together.

"My area will need shower stalls and a dressing room too. That wax is a bitch to get off and most people like to shower because it's easier to remove it with water than pulling it off the skin when dry." Winkie spoke up, adding additions to her area. K-O sat next to her and laughed when she finished speaking. She turned to look at him and he reached over to grasp her hand.

Not trying to intrude on a private moment, I looked back at Ray. She too was smiling playfully at her friend.

"My area won't need a shower, but I do require at least three deep sinks and a raw drainage area to dump the used water and solutions after each client. Make that, 2 raw drainage areas and 4 sinks. If we get busy and we need to accommodate 3 other techs besides me the traffic at each station will be high." Deana told Myron after he brought out a notepad and started taking notes for each girl's section.

"Myron, since Ray wants to have 5 extra stylists in the shop, I will need at least 7 stylist sinks, with 1 set up between each stylist section and a free one at the end of the sections. That way I can hire a girl to wash hair and braid to cut time on sew-ins. Make sure you put my station in the middle so I can monitor everybody in the shop. We don't need no slackers working for us. Anybody not serious about making money will have to go. This will be our business carrying our name, so we only want people that are career driven and professional working with us." Shamena said, making C-Lo beam with satisfaction.

Ray and all the other girls looked over at Shamena frowning. They all opened their mouths to speak but Ray beat them to it.

"Girl what are you talking about? This shop will be carrying your name and your name only. You were the driving force behind us all getting involved in this type of business so we could support you. We just found out how profitable it can be by checking out the shops that offer the services and tagged along. This was your dream and passion, so "Shamena's or Sha's Salon and Beauty Bar" is what it will be." Ray spoke up and all the other girls nodded in agreement. They had a connection deeper than most familiar bonds.

I looked over at Cree as Ray finished speaking and he gave a little smirk at all of their responses. I could tell he was pleased to be here with Shamena, but I can't help but to wonder. *"What the hell does he plan on doing with Adrianna?"*

"Okay ladies we have some properties that we just acquired in Eastgate Shopping Center that might meet your needs. Just talking to you all I know what you want and feel four of the properties together will be enough space to provide for each service, but if we use a fifth property you can offer beauty supplies as well. What do you all think?" Myron asked them, causing them to look at him like he was crazy.

"Hell yeah." Shamena yelled.

"Let's do it," hooted Deana.

"Yes!" exclaimed Winkie.

"Fuck Yeah." squealed Johnya.

"Fuckin' Right," Ray whooped while doing a fist pump.

"Alright Ladies since Zylar has given me the go ahead to get started I just need you guys to set up a time tomorrow to come see the space and look at possible designs from the contractor. We should be able to get started by next week once you agree to the design." Myron told them as he made notes on his pad and whipped out his phone and placed a call all while standing up to head back out to the living area.

"We're moving tomorrow after school so after we're done with that, we can meet you then." Shamena told Myron as we all exited the den to a lot more people than when we left.

C-Lo had been sitting next to her quietly watching as they talked about the business. He has only known her for a couple of hours and I can already see the pride for her shining in his eyes.

"K-Boy when did you get here Nigga? I almost thought you weren't coming." I asked that Nigga as I walked up on him holding his baby girl.

"Shit I almost didn't My Nigga. Brea has been running a fever and Mom's said she might be getting an ear infection. I try to keep her home when she is cranky like this. I only came out to meet the Misses and run back in. I got that long ass drive down south tomorrow, so I plan to turn in early." Kayden "K-Boy" Blake said while suddenly staring at somebody across the room.

"Nigga what are you looking at so hard?" I followed that Niggas line of sight and thought he was staring at Ray until she moved to the side to reveal Deana laughing at something Ma was saying.

"Come on Nigga let me introduce you to my lady and her girls." I couldn't believe all my boys were hooking up with Ray's girls. This shit is downright crazy. I thought to myself as me and K-Boy headed over to Ray and her girls.

Deana saw us first and was watching K-Boy so at least the attraction is mutual. *"Ray, I want you and the ladies to meet my Nigga. This is K-Boy and his daughter Brea. K-Boy this is my lady Raylexia and her friends Deana, Winkie, and Shamena. Her other friend Johnya is somewhere around here,"* I told K-Boy as I looked around for Johnya.

"Nice to meet you K-Boy. What's your real name because K-Boy don't work for me?" Deana said to K-Boy while sizing him up like he's doing her.

"My name is Kayden and it's nice to meet you too." That Nigga said smiling wide.

"How old is she, and why are you toting her around?" Deana asked, referring to his daughter laying on his shoulder.

"I don't normally carry her four-year-old big butt around like this, but she has a slight fever and I think she may be coming down with an ear infection making her a little cranky." He explained as I stood there fascinated by their interaction.

"Did you give her something for the fever before you left home? If not, that might explain why she's a little cranky. Let me see if I have my thermometer?" Deana said while going in her purse to pull out a digital thermometer.

Feeling like I was a little too close to their conversation I walked off to see who else showed up for the gathering. Both sets of my grandparents have made it here, so I began to introduce Ray to the rest of the family. I doubt very seriously if she'll remember all the people she's been meeting tonight.

After introducing her to the remaining family members we brought Zander, Reign, Tylan, and Rod out to meet the grandparents and my Pop's folks were glad that Zander had Pop's name.

Deana had Johnya give Brea some Tylenol and she took her to the back to the playroom with Reign. The two girls hugged and started talking about their Dancie Dolls. All traces of irritability were gone from Brea as she played with the Barbie Dolls and Reign. Feeling sure she would be okay with Reign in the playroom, K-Boy and Deana rejoined the party.

Raylexia Gavion

The people in Zylar's family that I have met so far seem to be really nice and honest. They don't seem to have a hidden agenda or bad intentions. I can get with that. I was also pleasantly surprised that I got along with all of Zylar's boys' women. They all seem to be nice women that I wouldn't mind kicking it with if we find ourselves in each other's company often. My biggest shock is that all my girls have hooked up with Zylar's boys and his brother. Johnya went missing for an hour and came back in this bitch shining. I am so happy that she has someone to make her smile again, because that snake ass Nigga Tyrone made my friend miserable.

"Ray, let's sing and dance our routine and pull the guy's into it. We haven't done that since last year's talent show. Ask Mrs. Della if she has Ciara's "Body Party"? That is our shit. Me and Johnya will sing the main part and you, Shamena, and Winkie do the backup cause if you sing lead. No one will hear the rest of us. This shit is going to be fun. I haven't let my hair down in a while, I was really missing you bestie." Deana said and leaned over to give me a hug. I could tell she was getting emotional so I let her go. She rushed off to get the other girls.

Heart heavy I went and found Mrs. Della talking to her parents and pulled her away to ask. *"Mrs. Della, do you by any chance have the latest "Ciara" cd? We would like to do a small show."* I asked her and she said yes and took off for the entertainment center.

"Which song do you want me to play?" she asked while putting the cd in.

"Body Party" is the title. Let me get the girls," I told her as I met the girls in the center of the floor. I gave Mrs. Della a head nod to start the music and we took our places.

We had a little dance that we did to the song and for us to have not performed or practiced in over a year we still had it. Deana and Johnya did a slow grind and broke it down low. While Shamena, me and Winkie danced behind them doing a mixture of the slow grind down on them coming up. All while singing the lyrics in perfect sync just like the music video.

My body is your party, baby
Nobody's invited but you, baby
I can do it slow now, tell me what you want
Baby, put your phone down, you should turn it off
'Cause tonight is going down, tell your boys is going down
We in the zone now, don't stop
You can keep your hands on me, touch me right there, rock my body
I can't keep my hands off you, your body is my party
I'm doing this little dance for you
You got me so excited
Now it's just me on you
Your body's my party, let's get it started

Deana and Johnya sang in perfect accord while walking over to grab Zaylar and K-Boy to grind on them while singing the lyrics. They moved around their bodies doing wide legged squats and humping against their thighs and dropping low.

Boy, you should know that your love is always on my mind
I'm not gonna fight it, I want it all the time
Boy you should know that your love is always on my mind
I can't it deny it, I want you, I want you

Shamena grabbed C-Lo and bent over at the waist while rolling her hips up and down on his lap. The red jeans she had on made her legs look like strawberry jelly. Winkie pulled K-O up and did a squat on the floor in front of him while bouncing each hip up and down one at a time doing a pop like she was having a seizure. I grabbed Zylar and did an upside down split while wrapping my legs around his waist. I braced my hands on the floor and climbed his body like a snake moving all around him three times before landing with my legs wrapped around his hips grinding on his lap. All the while we were singing our part to perfection.

I can't lie, I won't lie, it's amazing
My faces, the places, you're taking me
Baby, take your time now, there's no need to rush

We can go another round, if that's what you want
'Cause tonight is going down, yeah you know it's going down
We in the zone now, don't stop
You can keep your hands on me, touch me right there, rock my body
I can't keep my hands off you, your body is my party
I'm doing this little dance for you
You got me so excited
Now it's just me on you
Your body's my party, let's get it started

Deana and Johnya let go of Zaylar and K-Boy and started doing a slow grind together while looking back at the guys and singing. When one wiggled her way down to the floor, the other would work her way back up doing a belly roll and hip shake.

Boy, you should know that your love is always on my mind
I'm not gonna fight it, I want it all the time
Boy you should know that your love is always on my mind
I can't it deny it, I want you, I want you

Me, Winkie, and Shamena broke away from the guys and started doing our signature slide and roll across the floor while rocking our hips from side to side going from squatting to crawling on our knees while humping the air singing loud getting fully into it.

The things I wanna do to you
My body's calling you
I'm having so much fun with you
Now it's just me on you
Your body's my party, let's get it started, oh

We all came together and walked up to the guys with a killer strut. We all grabbed their waist and rocked into them while rolling our hips making sure to bump and grind hard. All while singing our hearts out.

Then we all started doing a free for all using our nastiest moves on the guys. They all snatched us off the floor talking about how we are going too far. Making us laugh. Mrs. Della came over and thanked us for dancing and singing, saying her parents and in-laws loved it. We all were a little embarrassed because we forgot all about Zylar's grandparents being there. We were so caught up in the dance.

"Ray, I see you and your girls still are the life of the party. I haven't seen you guys perform since the talent show last year. You guys still got it." Sonya said while her and the other girls came over giving us all hugs while grinning.

"Girl, we haven't performed since that show. Deana just wanted to do something for Mrs. Della since she treated us all like her family. You all need to give us your phone numbers so we can hook up this weekend. We are all going to the Bossier Mall Saturday so I can get Rod the new Jordans and we gone do a little retail therapy. "You guys are all welcome to come," I told Sonya and the girls as we all pulled out our phones and exchanged contact info.

We were all just settling back down to chill when the doorbell rang and Mrs. Della excused herself to go get it. Me and the girls continued to mingle and talk to the other ladies when Mrs. Della brought a bitch over that looked familiar and Tyrone's ole snake ass.

"Ray this is my niece Stephanie and her boyfriend Tyrone." Mrs. Della introduced while smiling wide.

My mood instantly turned hostile. Just looking at that snake ass nigga anywhere near Johnya made my blood boil. I could barely contain myself enough to speak to Mrs Della with respect.

"Mrs. Della I'm sorry but if Tyrone is here, we all are gonna have to leave. He is not allowed within 25 feet of Johnya and we go where she goes. He has a restraining order against him that's good until Tylan turns 18. We don't want to disrespect your home by whipping him up in here so if you consider him family we have to go," I told Mrs. Della as in unison Me, Johnya, Deana, Shamena, and Winkie started to move to the back to grab our bags and go.

"Let me let Zylar know we're leaving guys. Johnya you drive the truck and we'll head back to the apartment" I told them as I took off in Zylar's direction.

"Wait, Ray. You guys don't have to leave." Mrs. Della yelled trying to get my attention prompting Zylar to look up and head my way.

"What's wrong Ma? What happened Ray? Why do you look so upset?" Zylar and the guys came over to see what the commotion was about.

"That snake ass Nigga Tyrone is here with your cousin Stephanie and Johnya can't be within 25 feet of that hoe ass Nigga due to her having a restraining order on his bitch ass. So, we are leaving," I told Zylar as I turned to head to the back to get Reign, Rod, and Zander I would have to apologize to Mrs. Della for my language, but that nigga makes my ass itch.

"You ain't going no muthafuckin' where. This is your party. Leave them kids alone and go back in there and get your girls. I'll handle this shit," Zylar told me as he snatched me to a standstill to listen to what he's saying.

"Zylar we don't want to cause confusion within your family, so we'll leave, but you better be careful letting that Nigga come around your people's houses and shit. He's a snake and is known to rob people and be grinning in their face the next day like shit good. I told Johnya that Nigga was a snake and she didn't believe me until he bit her ass. If he's up in this muthafucka you best believe it's gone, get hit within the next month or so. That nigga is grimy as hell," I told Zylar as I continued to try and head to the back because I wasn't trying to hear none of that shit Zylar was saying to me at the moment.

"Ray calm your ass down and go let your girls know they are good. I'm about to go put that Nigga out and have security escort his ass off the premises. Stephanie is our cousin on our Pop's side of the family and she always ends up with some ole bum ass nigga. Let me handle this. Go calm down your girls. You ain't going no muthafuckin' where. What it looks like you leaving a gathering setup for you. Stephanie and the Nigga finna get up out of here," Zylar told me as he left headed back out to the front of the house.

When I headed into the sitting room, I saw C-Lo had Shamena in the corner talking in low tones with her arms crossed over her chest giving him hell'a attitude. Winkie and K-O were off to the side talking with her gesturing with her hands swinging and pointing out the room. Deana and Kayden were standing by the door with her wrapped in his embrace like he was trying to calm her down. I didn't see Johnya anywhere and assumed she went to the playroom to check on Tylan. This shit is crazy. Who would 'a thought that Zylar was some kin to the hoe that Tyrone was cheating on Johnya with?

"Guys you all can calm down. Zylar went to put that Nigga out and have security escort his ass off the premises. I don't know how ole girl hooked up with that snake ass nigga, but I know I don't want that hoe around me if she is fuckin' with his foul ass," I told them and they all walked over to me to see what the fuck was going on.

"Y'all it is definitely a small world for us to see that nigga after all this time. If that snake ass nigga is still with her now, she has to have some kind of connection that he can use." Deana said while shaking her head.

Mrs. Della stepped into the room and came over to talk to us. *"Girls I am sorry about that? I had no idea what was going on and I would have never intentionally put Johnya in that type of situation. Zylar had him removed by security and they had to drive him since they came in Stephanie's car. She refused to leave with him and asked to speak to Zaylar and Zylar. Nico is out there talking to her now since I don't know where Zaylar is at, and Zylar is handling something with security down at the entrance to the property gate."* Mrs. Della told us all looking worried.

"I'm sorry about my language earlier Mrs. Della, but Tyrone is a foul individual, and we can't be around him at all without violence. Zaylar went back to the playroom with Johnya. I can get him if you need him," I told her because I have never seen Mrs. Della look so worried.

"Thank you, Ray. Tell him it's important or I would let him continue to bond with his new family. I don't know what Stephanie has going on, but I know it's bad." Mrs. Della told me as I walked to the back to find Zaylar and Johnya sitting on the floor in a heated embrace. They both looked so happy I hated to interrupt.

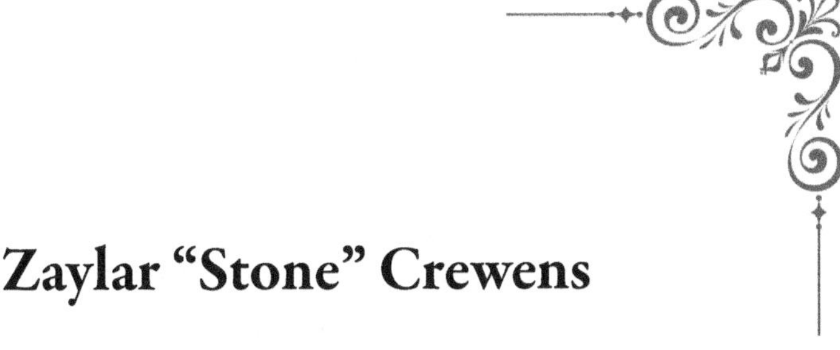

Zaylar "Stone" Crewens

Ray saying that Johnya had to leave because she has a restraining order on the nigga that showed up with my cousin didn't sit right with me at all. If she has a restraining order, it means that coward ass nigga put his hands on her, and I don't play that shit when it comes to my woman. I followed Ray and the girls to the back and found Johnya packing a diaper bag and backpack with kids' toys while talking animatedly to a handsome toddler that looks every bit of her. He has her honey complexion and big hazel brown eyes and wide nose sitting in a round face. He could be her twin.

"Johnya let me holla at you for a minute," I told her while stooping down to look into her son's eyes. *"Introduce me to my new son Johnya,"* I told her while watching her reaction to what I said. How she decided to play this will set the tone for our relationship.

"Tylan, this is Zaylar. Say hi," she told him while watching us closely.

"Hi little man. I see you are playing with your blocks. Can I join you? Is it okay if I play too?" I asked to gauge his mood.

"Red." He handed me a red block to connect to the red ones he had lined up attached on the floor. I sat down next to him and started to connect my red one to his collection and let him pass me the ones he wanted me to connect. Johnya watched our interaction, but I could tell her mind was somewhere else.

"You can sit down and join us or go and continue to mingle with the girls like you were doing. I can guarantee that nigga is gone from this house, and he won't lay a hand on you ever again," I told Johnya as Tylan handed me a blue and green block together. I guess we are mixing these two colors together. Sure enough, he passed me another blue then green block to attach.

"Well, I guess now would be as good a time as any to tell you about what happened to me while dealing with my ex," she told me while taking a deep breath and releasing it on a long sigh.

Johnya seemed to contemplate what I said before taking a deep breath and turning around to face me and Tylan sitting on the floor. She twisted her fingers together, then rested them on her thighs. Gripping her thighs and squeezing her eyes shut she finally sat back up composed. I watched her not saying a word. I needed her to talk to me when she was ready. I won't force her.

Finally, she released her breath and spoke, *"I met Tyrone when I was 13 and he was 18. I didn't find out how old he really was until long after he tricked me into dating him and I ended up pregnant. He would meet me after school to hang out and buy me snacks while we sat in the park talking about our future dreams and goals. It never really dawned on me that he talked about stuff for his right now while I talked about stuff for my future until he took my virginity and got me pregnant on purpose."* She paused while staring at Tylan with a far-off expression on her face before she turned to face me and continued.

"I had no idea that what we were doing was wrong until I fell out at school and had to be rushed to the hospital only to find out I was four months pregnant, and he wouldn't answer the phone for me when I called him. My parents kept asking me what his name was and where did we meet? Why hadn't they met him if we went to school together? Have him come by and bring his parents so they could meet. It never dawned on me that he was stalling so I'd be too far along to have an abortion until he answered one of my calls and admitted to that shit. Like I would really kill my baby, what the hell kind of person did he take me for? I might have been young, but I still wouldn't have let anyone make me kill my own flesh and blood." She stopped again while squeezing her hands together like she was trying to suppress some dark emotions.

Just listening to the shit that nigga did to her, I already know that Killian gone have to make that nigga disappear for good. It's taking everything in me to calmly sit here with Tylan and connect the blocks he's handing me. My mind is filled with rage and the only reason I'm able to control it is because I know Johnya and Tylan need me right now. So, I pulled myself together and continued to listen to my woman telling me about that pedophile of a baby daddy.

"*Two months after I talked to him on the phone he agreed to meet with my parents. My Dad was so angry he tried to beat him within an inch of his life when he found out how old he was and barred him from coming around me until after the baby was born. I should have done what my father wanted but I thought I was in love, so I would sneak and see him using my girls as a cover. It wasn't until after I had Tylan and he tried to get me to move in with him that I learned his true motives behind trapping me with a baby.*" She laughed to herself while shaking her head.

"*That fool got me pregnant and messed up my plans to join the military and go to college on the hope I could influence my dad to help him get a job with the city. You see he heard from people around the way that my dad hired the maintenance people who work on the city trucks and wanted me to ask him to hire him.*" I was stuck. She could have said a million things, but this sounds so stupid that I paused in accepting a block from Tylan to look her in the eyes to see if she was joking.

"*Yes. He ruined my future plans because of a hope he had that I could help his grown ass get a job. After finding that out things changed for me. The feelings I had for him disappeared like they never really were there in the first place and I started to put distance between us. I still dealt with him on the strength of him being Tylan's father, but nothing more no sex, nothing. That is until the day Zylar met Raylexia and he walked up into the game with your cousin. I cut off all ties with him after that and he got upset and snuck me after the first day of school my freshmen/junior year beating me up pretty bad. We in turn jumped him with baseball bats and broke both his legs, both arms, his nose, and 6 ribs. My dad got the restraining order on him after he jumped me, and witnesses gave statements to the District Attorney. That nigga was lucky the District Attorney didn't pursue them statutory rape charges the state attorney wanted to file,*" she said while letting off a small chuckle like she thought of something funny.

"*I haven't seen Tyrone since we put that nigga in the hospital, and he faked out on doing right by my son. That nigga ain't seen my son in over a year and a half. His Mom was supposed to pick him up and drop him off to the supervised visitation, but she said that Tyrone was not showing up for the visitation, so the state worker canceled it and had the judge give me sole custody of my son. I don't have to talk to that nigga at all, and the restraining order is good until Tylan turns 18. So as far as I'm concerned that nigga is dead to me and my son."* She spoke while looking me in the eyes full of conviction.

"Damn Lil Momma. I hate that you went through all that, but from now on I got you and my son for whatever you want and need. You're my lady now and I plan to treat you like the Queen you are," I told her while reaching over to pull her up in my lap. Our mouths met and she reached up grabbing my head to hold me in place while kissing me aggressively and placing small bites on my lips and sucking my tongue. We were so caught up in the kiss neither one of us heard Ray come in or clear her throat to get our attention. Until we broke away from the kiss breathing hard while grinning at each other.

"Hey, you guys I'm sorry to interrupt, but Zaylar your Mom needs you. It's something about what's going on with your cousin. I don't know what it is, but your Mom seems to be really upset. She said to tell you she wouldn't interrupt you while bonding with your new family but it's important." Ray told me as I stood to my feet holding Johnya. I put her down to pick up Tylan and walked out holding my new family in my arms.

RAY LED US BACK TO the sitting area where Ma was standing in the middle of the room talking to Ray's girls and a couple of the fellas in the crew. She seemed to be really upset so I gave Tylan to Johnya and headed over to find out what's got her so upset.

"What's wrong Ma? Why is your face all balled up like that?" I asked, getting straight to the point.

"Zaylar Stephanie is in some kind of trouble and needs your help. I don't know exactly what she has going on, but I know it has her scared enough not to want to leave the house. When Zylar told her, her boyfriend had to leave, she became hysterical and refused to leave with him or let him take her car. I'm not sure, but it looked like she had bruises on her arms and makeup covering the ones on her face. Nico is talking to her now, but you know he don't get involved in issues with Zan's family." Ma told me reminding me why we didn't really fuck with nobody on that side but our grandparents.

"Okay Ma. Let me go in here and see what she has going on. Johnya I'll be back," I told my girl as I passed by her talking to her girls.

"Alright Zaylar we'll stay for a little while longer, but we need to be getting back to the apartment soon. We are moving into the apartment tomorrow and we still have to go to school. I don't like to keep Tylan out that late and I need to talk to my parents about the move, so we're gonna go ahead and get our things ready to go while you handle your business," she told me as I exited the room followed by the rest of the fellas.

We found Nico and Josie talking to Stephanie over in the corner and most of the guests had left except for our crew and their girls and our grandparents. I went over and spoke to both sets of grandparents and assured them that we were going to get whatever Stephanie had going on settled. As I started to approach Nico Zylar walked in heated as hell. So, I changed direction to cut him off and find out what's wrong.

"What the fuck is wrong with you My Nigga? You look like you are about to blow this bitch up," I told Zylar because he had a crazed look in his eyes.

"Bruh shit is all fucked up and I'm going to have to kill that bitch to get her to leave me alone," he said looking me directly in the eye to let me know he meant that shit.

"What do you mean Zylar?" I asked for more clarification.

"That hoe Derrika followed Jayce stupid ass to Ma's house earlier and I had him put that hoe out and remove her from the property. Why did that hoe go and get Chandra and bring her back over here to the crib. They were causing confusion at the gate by trying to follow other people onto the property, so security called me down to handle it. When I get down there this bitch crying talking about, she loves me, and she is pregnant with my child. Then that hoe had the nerve to ask me, why did I treat her so badly? I told that hoe to get her delusional ass away from here. After that, she had a meltdown and some other residents threatened to call the police on her retarded ass, she left all the while spouting some disrespectful and incriminating shit about us being drug dealers." He vented, running his hands across his braids.

"You right Nigga you gone have to handle that hoe, and the sooner the better, but is there any way she can possibly be pregnant by you? Or do you think she just said that shit to get a rise out of you? Cause to be frank. If that hoe is pregnant by you, you can get ready to kiss your relationship with Ray goodbye. I can tell from meeting her and the little time I've been around her, she's not going to put up with the shit Chandra has going on. So, you need to decide if her

having that baby is worth you losing your family," I told Zylar and we stared each other down.

"But calm all that shit down and let us go over here and find out what Stephanie got going on. She got Ma all upset worrying about the shit she got going on with her Nigga. She is over there talking to Nico and Josie now so it must be really bad if he willing to step into anything for that side of the family after the way they treated him," I told Zylar as we walked up on Nico talking on his phone making arrangements for Stephanie to talk to a judge in the morning to get a restraining order.

"What's going on?" I asked that Nigga after he hung up.

"Man, this has got to be the craziest shit I have ever heard. Y'all cousin hooked up with this Nigga about two years ago and started helping him rob her family and friends. If she refused to do it, he would beat her ass and keep her locked up in the house while he takes her phone and car. She said he's gotten worse lately because she hasn't been going around any family members and his ass is broke. The saddest part about this shit is I believe she would have continued to help him rob her family if she wouldn't have found out he's been seeing somebody else behind her back. She has a very weak mind. Me and Josie peeped that out just from the first few sentences out her mouth. She's more worried about him moving on with someone new than she is about what he had her doing to her family and friends." Nico told us while shaking his head.

"Why are we helping her then? If she's that fucked up in the mind, why help her continue to do the same shit just with a different Nigga?" Zylar asked ready to leave Stephanie's weak ass to the wolves.

"Ma wanted me too." Nico stated and that said it all. Nico would do whatever Ma asked even if he really didn't want to.

"So, what's the plan since you seem to have handled everything?" I asked ready to be done with Stephanie and her bullshit.

"She doesn't have anywhere to go and she's not staying with Ma or any of us. If she can set up her own people without a lick of remorse there's no way, I'm trusting her with any of our crib's locations. We can put her up in a hotel until the judge puts the restraining order in place tomorrow, but in all honesty. I don't think she is done with him. She's more worried about the new young girl in his life than anything so I don't really trust her to be on the up and up about this whole thing. You might wanna put the Private Investigator you guys have on

retainer on him and her because this whole thing seems too neat to me. I think her goal was to spend the night with Ma, but that shit ain't happening. Ma has barely seen this girl in the past two years, she don't know nothing about her and neither do we." Nico stated making it clear that Stephanie ain't finna get close to Ma to use her kindness.

"I'll get Myron and C-Lo to get the PI to check things out. In the meantime, put her up at the Sheraton out on East 70th for two weeks. Make sure to add room service and get one of the guys to shadow her. Put that Nigga Jayce on her he between bitches at the moment. We can tell her he's her protection," Zylar said letting me know he's on that good bullshit. I laughed shaking my head at this nigga.

"Zylar you can't just drop one of our lieutenants down to bodyguard because you're mad at him. Who gone handle his crews while he's out playing bodyguard for you?" I laughed at Zylar's ass because he's dead ass wrong for trying to make that man babysit our cousin because he's mad about what his bitch did.

"He gone handle that shit himself, all he needs to do is check in with his crews on his business phone and have them drop off at the spot. Jayce is nothing nice with them hands, and this gives us a chance to see if Stephanie is on some setup shit for that Nigga, or she really wants to break free." Zylar answered, making sense. If she's done and just wants help out of the situation this gives her the chance.

"Okay Nigga but still Jayce has them out of town runs he has to make through the week. Who's gonna take care of all that? C-Lo and Myron mostly keep us running smoothly by handling all the stuff in S'Port and Bossier, plus they are trying to turn most of this shit legitimate. We don't have no one to spare," I told that Nigga cause I'm not doing his runs for him.

"Nigga his cousins, K-O, and K-Boy can split it up for one week. Let me call all them Nigga's in the den and ask them. Plus, this gives us a chance for him to disappear for a while, so Myron can find that Nigga a new crib that Derricka don't know about," Zylar said like he had it all figured out.

"That should work, but you gone have to make arrangements for them bitches to have an accident. When they start talking reckless in front of mixed company it's a problem," I told him while motioning for the guys to follow us to the den.

They all walked in and C-Lo was the first to ask. *"What the hell is going on with ole girl? Shamena is madder than a muthafucker. I had to restrain her from going after that Nigga."*

"Shit me too. Deana is small, but strong as hell. She was really upset about that Nigga being here." K-Boy spoke letting us all know he had claimed Deana.

"Who y'all tellin. Shayla was trying to go after that Nigga before Ray came back into the room and told them Zy went to put that Nigga out. He must have done some foul shit for them all to hate him to that degree." K-O announced letting me know that Johnya's girls haven't been discussing her business with their niggas.

"Nigga who the fuck is Shayla? I thought you were over there with Winkie." C-Lo asked, looking at K-O all crazy.

"Nigga Winkie's real name is Shayla Harris, Winkie is her nickname. What person you know out here walking around with a real name Winkie Nigga?" K-O told C-Lo looking mad as a muthafucka.

Zylar cut in on C-Lo and K-O because they seemed like they were about to set it off up in this bitch. *"I called all y'all in here because we need Jayce on guard duty for a week with our cousin Stephanie and we need everybody else to pick up taking care of his traps and crews. He only has two out of town runs to Lafayette and Alexandria. If we spread it out evenly it shouldn't take no more than a couple hours to make-up the time during your regular runs. This also takes Jayce away from home long enough for Myron to find him a new spot. Derricka and Chandra have become too much of a problem and need to have an accident soon. When bitches get to spouting off about us being drug dealers in mixed company it's time to handle that. Call Kahmala and let her know we have a job that needs taking care of ASAP. I know she and Killian are still on the hunt for Eric and Biz, but Killian gone have to do without her until she can get this shit with Derricka and Chandra handled. Ma has lived in this house since the community was formed 20 years ago and it takes bullshit from these thirsty hoes to draw attention to her home."* Zylar let them all know so it didn't seem like we were using Jayce for our family bullshit. We are helping him clean up his shit too.

"That sounds good to me cause I thought I was gone have to kill that girl behind all the shit she was doing. I don't see how Zylar been dealing with the

shit from Chandra this long. Derricka had me straight plotting to knock her ass off and bury the body in a shallow grave." Jayce said, looking serious as hell.

"That's why we told y'all don't be taking them jump offs to your crib. It's been two and a half years since when I started fuckin' with Chandra and she just found out about Ma's house today because of Jayce and Derricka. That was one of the first lessons Pops taught us about selling dope. Don't ever let a muthafucka know where you lay your head, not even family. Trust has to be earned and envy is a muthafucka, some of them Niggas that claim they your friends ain't nothing but snakes in waiting. Look at how Eric and Biz turned out, and that shit was totally unexpected," Zylar told them Niggas to remind them that we know from experiencing the shit personally.

"Aight then you guys can work out who gone do what and let C-Lo and Myron know who is filling in for what route and who is checking on which crews. That way there are no fuckups." Zylar stated and turned to C-Lo.

"You got the truck and movers on standby for the girls tomorrow? Ray said they gone be ready time they finish 4th period at 11am. They are all in the accelerated graduation program and only have four classes left to finish so they are only at school for about four hours each day. I don't want Ray stressing about getting them settled." Zy told that Nigga C-Lo.

"Nigga of course I got them covered. That's My Beast and her friends. I already got them set for whenever Sha calls me to say they ready." C-Lo answered like Zy offended him by asking.

"Zylar you got a good one and her friends are cool as hell. Shanna thought because they were so young, they wouldn't have much to talk about, but she said all of them are really intelligent and well spoken. None of them drink but they have a natural high out of this world. Shit she laughed and told me Ray and her girls are so blunt you never have to wonder what they are thinking because they are quick to tell you. She told me she's looking forward to spending more time with the group and that they all exchanged contact info so they can meet at the Mall this Saturday." Myron said, shocking the hell out of me. His girl Shanna didn't usually come to the gatherings because she said the females we dealt with were catty and immature as hell.

"Awaii told me the same thing and she never wants to come around when we're just hanging out or going to the club. She said that the girls y'all deal with

are too spiteful and nasty to want to be around." Lance said, referring to his girl.

"Hell, both Felisha and Sonya told me and Jamie flat out if it wasn't for them kicking it together with Awaii when we chill, they would not have come to hang out or go clubbing with us either. They said y'all were all fooling with some vindictive evil bitches. We had a lot of arguments about them spending time with us chillin." Kam said letting us know their girls really didn't want to deal with the hoes we use to fuck with.

"Shit guys I know Zylar feels happy just like me hearing y'alls ladies are looking forward to chillin' with our ladies again. That shit took a weight off our shoulders because we spend entirely too much time working to not spend quality time with our women when we want to play," I told them Niggas seeing them all nod their heads in agreement.

"Shit Ray refused to hang out with us because of Biz and Eric. She told me when she first met them Niggas that they were snakes, and she didn't fuck with fake ass people. If I would have paid more attention and told Zaylar about this shit back then, I wouldn't have had to spend damn near ten months apart from my girl," Zylar said and we all felt his pain. Ray left that Nigga and didn't look back.

"That just lets us all know that we have some strong women of quality who want be putting up with no bullshit. If we wanna keep them we all better get our shit right," I told them Niggas planning to cut off all the hoes I was dealing with as soon as we get this business handled. I refused to go through the shit Zylar just went through looking for my girl. I plan not to give her any reason to leave in the first place.

Myron called and made reservations for a two-bedroom suite at the Sheraton on our account, and Jayce left to go by his place to pack up enough clothes for a month. He said he won't be going back to that house period when he leaves. He'll just have Kam and Lance go get his shit and move it for him when Myron finds him a new spot. C-Lo worked out a working schedule with everybody to cover Jayce routes and crews for the next three weeks and called the PI and had him put someone on finding out what's going on with Stephanie and ole dude. Now we just have to wait for Jayce to get back so we can leave.

"I'm going to let Ma and the grandparents know we have something worked out to help Stephanie so they can all head home. Johnya told me her and the girls need to go back to the apartment to get some things settled before they go home, and that they all want to do some packing tonight. Is Ray letting them keep the Expedition tonight Zylar or do I need to get her something dropped off before the dealership closes at 9pm? Tomorrow I'll be getting her something of her own." I asked that Nigga while heading back to the main area where everybody is gathered. I had plans to put a bug in Killian's ear for him to take care of Stephanie's nigga because of the shit he did to Johnya and Tylan. No one else has to know.

"I don't know Zay but we can ask her when we get back in there." Zy replied as he moved over to talk to C-Lo.

CHAPTER TWELVE Cree "C-Lo" Logan

"C-Lo are you heading over to the apartments with the girls when we leave?" Zylar asked before we could make it to the door.

"Yes. I want to make sure Shamena's good and find out if she needs anything before I turn in for the night. Why what you need?" I asked that Nigga because today has been one crazy ass day.

"We're headed back over to the apartment too. Ray said she needs to give the girls a set of keys and show them how the alarm system works. Are you going to be with the guys coming to move them in tomorrow? I'm asking so I'll know if I need to be available to do it. I need to get all my stuff moved over when you have theirs moved to the apartment. We don't plan on using this spot anymore after I move all my belongings out. Ma said, "Myron can go ahead and put it on the market." It's too bad Biz and Eric know where it is cause it would have made the perfect stash house." Zylar asked letting me know this Nigga trying to make sure everything runs smoothly to please Ray. She scared the shit out that Nigga when she up and left his ass.

I laughed to myself as we both made our way to the main area, because he did that shit to himself. He should have dropped all them extra hoes he was fuckin' with when he decided to make Ray his girl. He just got used to having his cake and eating it too. Ray showed that Nigga she ain't having it. *"Yes Zy. I will be there. I want to make sure them Niggas get everything they want done and clean that shit up before they leave."*

"What's so funny My Nigga? You over there chuckling and shit. Let me in on the joke so I can laugh too." Zylar expressed while trying to mean mug a Nigga.

"I was just thinking to myself that you wouldn't be this worried about pleasing Ray had you not been trying to impress them nonrelevant muthafuckers that used to be a part of the crew. Now they are no longer around and you're wearing your heart on your sleeve. Please your lady only Nigga, and fuck what anybody else has to say about it, because I have a feeling that Ray don't give a fuck about what you got in your pockets or who you are out in these streets. If you fuck up again, she's done with your ass for good," I told that Nigga and turned to walk off. His next words stopped me dead in my tracks.

"It's funny you would say that bullshit to me, when you are walking around this bitch like Adrianna does not exist. So let's not pretend like I'm the only one with shit stuffed off in his closet," he told me and stood there mean mugging me in his feelings.

I paused for a second, then continued on my way. Him bringing up Adrianna hit me like a bolt of lightning out of the blue. She was the last thing on my mind, and I plan to keep it that way. Out of my sight, and out of my mind. I'll deal with that shit when I have to.

Once we made it back in the main room Zaylar was talking to his Ma, Nico, and Josie over in the corner. All the girls were sitting together conversing, and the fellas were together over by the bar. I made my way over to Shamena.

"Aye Sha let me holla at you for a minute," I told her and waited for her to get up and follow me off to the side.

"Cree what is going on? Can we leave now? I enjoyed kicking it with my girls but it's too much going on and I'm ready to end this day with you. Can we go by my Mom's place and pick up my things to bring back over to the apartment tonight, because I only have to get my clothes and hair supplies? I'm moving in tonight instead of tomorrow with the other girls. Ray told me she put a bedroom suit in the room that used to belong to Zan for me. She knows I don't have one at my Mom's place." Shamena told me while looking at me hopefully.

"Sure, we can leave. Let me tell the fellas we finna roll out," I told Sha and headed over to Zylar to tell him we were leaving.

Just as I was walking up to Zylar the doorbell rang, and he went to go answer it. He came back in with Jayce in tow. So, they both made their way back over to where we were all waiting. Zylar wasted no time letting Jayce know to come on so they could introduce him to Stephanie and let her know what's going on so we can all be on our way.

It took about 20 more minutes to get everything settled and we were on our way to Shamena's place to pick up her things.

"Are you sure you want to stay at the apartment tonight since your girls won't be coming until tomorrow?" I asked Sha as we made our way up the block to get to her Mom's apartment.

"Yes, I'm sure. My Mom has been trying to get rid of me since my father died when I was a year old. She gets a check from social security for me that she spends on my sisters and herself. She won't even provide for my basic needs. If not for me having a side hustle doing hair and all my girls and their Moms stepping in and buying me the necessities I'd be fucked. She makes me sleep on the couch and gave both my sisters the other two bedrooms in the apartment. I used to think that she did all this because Renard didn't want me there anymore, but he gets onto her about the way she treats me. I'm tired of living this way and after today I will no longer have to deal with her and her bullshit. The thing that drives me crazy is that I have a family that would have willingly taken me in, but my mom moved us away from them when I was 8 years old and I haven't seen them since." Sha told me letting me know we had a lot to talk about.

"Well let's go in there and get your shit. Do you need any boxes, because I have a few left in the back from when we moved Ray?" I asked as I parked and prepared to exit the SUV.

"Four boxes should be enough I don't have much. I just want to be sure to get my hair supplies and notebooks with my formula." Sha said as she climbed down from the passenger seat and met me at the rear of the SUV.

I noticed that we were at the same building that I picked them up from earlier today. Shamena walked up to the 4th door towards the end and knocked. A dark-skinned woman that could pass for Shamena's older sister opened the door for her with an attitude.

"I thought your ass was gone. What are you doing back?" is how she greeted Shamena at the door.

"I just came to get my few things and I'll be out your way." Shamena answered in a dry tone.

"Don't get smart with me, little girl. Hurry up and get your shit and don't come back." was her cruel response.

I could tell she was trying to get a reaction out of Shamena, but she paid her no mind and stepped in carrying the boxes. Shamena went into a closet off the living room where she began to pull clothes out and placed them in one box. The second box she placed all her shoes. The third box she placed gallon sized zip lock bags filled with various items and 4 composition notebooks. The fourth box she placed more zip lock bags and various styling items. When she finished, she placed each box by the door, and I helped her carry them back to the SUV and placed them in the backseat. I opened the passenger door and helped her into her seat, secured her seatbelt and closed the door. Then I got in and headed back to Ray's apartment.

I couldn't tell by her expression if she was happy or sad. She just looked drained, like she held the whole world on her shoulders. *"You wanna talk about it?"* I asked, knowing from experience it's better to vent than to hold that shit in.

"Not really, but everybody tells me it's better to let it out than to hold it all in," she replied while taking a deep breath.

"Where to start?" She sighed. *"When I was about 8 or 9 years old, my mom moved us over here away from the home my dad purchased for us. I started to realize that my mom started to treat me differently than she did my sisters after that. If I had something and they wanted it, she'd take it from me and give it to them. Then there were the beatings, she'd hit me for no reason out the blue. I didn't understand what was going on or what changed, but I knew it wasn't right. So, I began to stay off to myself and not really favor anything. The less I'd want the less they'd have to take."* She laughed and shook her head as if to clear it.

"Everything changed the summer I met Ray when I turned 10. Her mom had just moved in and I would go over and stay the night 4 to 5 times a week. She would share her clothes with me and take me shopping with her, Rod, and Winkie at Walmart and buy all my personal hygiene products. It started with Mrs. Sandra taking us every 3 months when Raylexia's uncles sent her the gift cards. Then over a span of 6 months Raylexia, Winkie, Johnya, Deana, and I all met and became closer than blood relatives. Then Mrs Johnny Mae, Ms Sandra, and Mrs Danelle all took turns taking us shopping for food and to get clothes using the gift cards that Raylexia's uncles sent every three months. Shit I practically lived with them from 10 years old til her mom moved them away

from the projects last year. The only thing that changed at home is that my mom knows not to put her hands on me ever again." She told me while looking out the window.

"We all made a pact to support each other's dreams, and because of our different talents we all make contributions in different ways. My contribution is fixing and keeping everyone's hair straight. Deana can sew and she can reproduce all the name brand clothes like Gucci or Chanel, so she makes the majority of our clothes. Winkie does interior design which is why all our parents' apartments in the projects are laid out with inexpensive furniture that looks professionally done. Both Raylexia and Johnya are smart as hell so they helped all of us pass the 11th grade equivalency test to skip 9th and 10th grade when we entered high school. If not for Deana making me clothes and Raylexia sharing her gift cards, I don't know where I would be now, nor what condition I'd be in."

"Damn Ma that's some crazy shit, but some families are fucked up that way. She tried to break your spirit, but you got too much heart for that. Let your success be your revenge. Show her that the shit she did only made you stronger. Opening your own business and getting your own place is just a start. I'ma get Myron to hire you at the dealership as a receptionist at $13 an hour so you can go down and get emancipated. Once the judge grants you your freedom go down to the social security office and report you have been on your own so you can get your own benefits yourself. I got a feeling the best way to hurt your mother is through her pockets. You should also look into finding your Pop's people as well. "I think your mom moved you away from them to be spiteful," I told her as we pulled up to the apartments.

I could see everybody was still here and half the fellas came over with the girls. I got out and went around to open the door and helped Shamena down. We then went to the back and got out her boxes and headed for the apartment. Shamena rang the doorbell and stood to the side. Ray opened the door and pulled Shamena in for a long hug.

"I'm sorry I forgot Shamena. I was so caught up in the bullshit going on with Zylar that I forgot to take you with me. It won't happen ever again." Ray told Shamena while holding her tight and crying.

"It's okay Ray. I know you had a lot going on so don't sweat it. I know you didn't do it on purpose, and we have no way of knowing if your Mom would have

let me come in the first place. I survived so it's all good." Shamena told Ray as they broke apart and hugged the other girls.

"Deana you Winkie and Johnya grab my boxes from Cree and bring them to the back room. Cree I'll be right back. Let me put this up right quick and holla at my girls." Shamena told me as they took the boxes and headed for the bedrooms.

"Okay. I'll be right here," I told her watching as she made her way to the back.

"What the fuck is going on C-Lo? Ray damn near took my head off when we got here, and you didn't pull up with Shamena. I thought something had happened to her. All the girls seemed to be on edge about her not coming straight here." Zylar asked while watching the hall to the bedrooms.

"No shit." Zaylar said, walking up, holding Johnya's son Tylan in his arms. *"Johnya amped out when she realized Shamena was not here. I thought she was all quiet, but she was extra heated worrying about Shamena."*

"Shit who you telling? Shayla wanted to leave and head for their apartment complex to look for her when she realized she wasn't here." K-O spoke up as he walked over to where we all stood next to the hall leading to the bedrooms.

"Y'all don't know the half. Deana was halfway out the door and calling for Ray to come on before I grabbed her up and brought her back inside. I don't know exactly what Shamena has going on, but Deana and her girls were worried as fuck until you guys got here." K-Boy said while watching the hallway.

It seems all Shamena's girls know how bad her situation is at home and tried to limit the amount of time she had to spend there. *"Its personal My Niggas and I can't tell y'all about it. Just know that I got her from here on out,"* I told them, having no intention of telling them or anybody else Shamena's personal business.

"Zy if you plan to move your stuff tomorrow, I think it's best if you move it after Ray gets the kids off and leaves for school. That way if you encounter trouble in the form of Chandra, Ray won't be there to get upset. Shamena moved all her things tonight, so we just have to get the other girls settled," I told him while reaching in my pocket to get my phone.

"Hold on Zy. Let me call Myron to check on something right quick," I told him and hit the button to call Myron.

He picked up on the 4th ring sounding agitated. *"Speak."* He barked into the phone.

"Say, My, have you filled that receptionist position down at the dealership yet? If not hire Shamena until they can get the salon up and running," I told that Nigga not worrying about his foul ass mood.

"Nigga this couldn't have waited until in the morning, I got all type shit going on right now?" He asked while talking to someone in the background.

"No, it couldn't wait until the morning. If you have already filled the position, I would be looking for something else. I just remember you talking about this earlier today, so I told her about it. Is the job still available or not?" I asked that Nigga not trying to play 20 questions with him.

"Yeah, it's still available. In fact, we have 5 positions open at the dealership. I had to fire all the ladies that were answering the phones and the females in the office. AnDro and Deuce been fuckin' all of them hoes and they thought that meant they didn't have to do their jobs. So I had to let all them hoes go and I need to let Zaylar know his boys need to do something different. The car lot practically runs itself and them Niggas be fuckin' up. I guess everybody ain't cut out to work in a legitimate setting. Them Niggas live for the fast life in them streets, but with the way we run things now I don't want them connected on that level anymore. I'm not sure if we can truly trust them Niggas because they were all a part of that crew that ran with Biz and Eric. I know Deuce got shot and liked to died and all, but my gut is telling me not to put him on with the other business." Myron said into the phone sounding conflicted.

"Myron if your gut is telling you not to put that Nigga in the mix of things follow that feeling. We have come too far to get caught slipping because grown ass men wanna play instead of make money. Leave them Niggas where they are at for the time being and hire Shamena and her girls to fill the positions in the office. It's 5 of them and they are all highly intelligent. I'm sure after a day or two they will get the hang of things and be running that whole dealership. If need be you can switch Jay and Shane over to the dealership and put AnDro and Deuce in the strip club," I told that Nigga letting him know we have people to step in and fill the positions that we can trust. The girls can even keep an eye on what them Niggas doing until we get their shop ready.

"I forgot all about them, C-Lo. Ask them if they can start tomorrow after we settle things for their shop. If so, I can train them for 3 hours on what's needed and cut them loose." Myron told me, sounding relieved.

"Hold on Nigga. Let me check with them," I told that Nigga as I made my way to Shamena's room. I could hear all the girls crying and started not to interrupt, but Shamena needs this change and I wanna make sure she gets it.

I knocked on the door and Shamena came to open it with red rimmed eyes. *"What's wrong Beast? Who I need to fuck up?"* I told her, making her smile wide.

"It's a good cry Cree. You don't need to fuck nobody up. What you need?" She asked me while grinning at what I said.

"I got a question for you and your girls if that's okay." I asked while looking into her red rimmed eyes. She backed up and I followed her.

"Sure, come on in. We were having a small cry, but we are good now," she said walking over to the bed to take a seat by Ray.

I stopped right in front of them and took them all in. They were all sitting on the bed in varying degrees of disarray. Shamena's eyes were puffy, but so were the rest of the girls. I'm glad she has such a tight knit group of friends. Seeing their bond I feel confident they will look after her when I'm not able to be there.

"I just got off the phone with Myron about that job I was telling you about earlier and it turns out we have 5 openings that I'm hoping you and your girls will take until we can get your shop open. You guys would be helping us out a bind and we'll pay $15 an hour to you all. If you guys are interested. Myron said, "You all can start tomorrow after you get moved and look at the location for the shop and choose the design for the contractor. He said you will only have to train with him for 3 hours to get the routine down." So, are you guys interested in filling the positions and starting tomorrow?" I asked them while looking into all their red puffy eyes. They really had a good cry from the looks of them. I'm just glad they truly care for my girl.

"Hell, yeah we're interested. Will they be able to work around our school schedule? We all get out at 11am Monday thru Friday and Ray said she gets out at 1pm Monday, Wednesday, and Friday. Her Tuesday-Thursday is open. Can they work around that?" Shamena asked forgetting that we own the business and make the schedules.

"I agree with Shamena. We definitely want the job as long as you can work around our schedules for school. This takes a load off my shoulders. I was worried about how we were gonna be able to pay the bills here at the apartment. With this job and splitting the bills 4 ways, we got it covered," Winkie said while smiling wide.

"Yes. I want the job. Like Winkie said, "with this job we can pay these bills with ease" and I will have more money to provide for me and Tylan. We won't be a burden on my parents anymore." Johnya said looking relieved.

"I'm in too. This job sounds great and the pay is well above the minimum wage. We can pay the bills at the apartment and start saving for the future. Getting the business opened is just the first step for us. We all had plans to travel and see the world, and to open salons in the different cities across the US. Hopefully with this chance we can make those dreams a reality." Deana spoke, making all the girls nod in agreement.

"Ray what about you? I know you have a job right now. Are you willing to work for us instead?" I asked Ray since she was the only one who hadn't said anything about taking the job.

"Yes C-Lo I want the job as well. I just have to quit Price-Lo Foods, but after the shit that happened yesterday, I'm ready to be done with that job anyway. I have school tomorrow until 1pm then we have to meet with Myron about the shop, after that I can start at the dealership. I just have to call Mrs. Chance and let her know about all the changes," Ray said while pulling out her phone and placing a call.

"Okay then. Let me tell Myron," I told them all and put the phone up to my ear.

"Yo, My. The girls all said they want the job and can start after they meet up with you about the shop," I told that Nigga hearing him sigh into the phone.

"That's a relief. I was trying to figure out how to juggle the dealership with my other responsibilities. I think it's time I have a sit down with Zaylar and his boys. Jay and Shane are doing fine at the strip club, but I'm not in the habit of schooling muthafuckers older than me. It's like they feel entitled to some shit like Zaylar gone pay them if they put in work or not. Deuce and AnDro don't have to do nothing but act as figure heads at the dealership and they can't even pull that off. I'm not cool with paying a grown ass man to do nothing." Myron said

and I agree with him. We worked hard to turn Zaylar's businesses around and holding on to them leeches he is dragging around ain't gone work for me.

"I hear you man and since he here now I'ma run the shit by him tonight before he heads in. I think we need to get a handle on that shit now before it gets out of control," I told My and ended the call.

Shamena was looking at me with a worried look on her face prompting me to take notice of where I was for the first time.

"My bad ladies. I didn't mean to start discussing business in front of you guys. Sha let me go holla at Zaylar right quick. Let me know when you all are done so we can talk," I told her as I walked up and kissed her on the lips and left back out to talk to Zaylar.

Shamena Greene

I watched as Cree left back out the room to go handle his business. I knew that he was in the game heavy because he was in Zylar's inner circle, but I'm beginning to see that he must be damn near running things like Zylar and Zaylar. If he is that connected that means I need to get my act together. He's a boss so he will definitely need a boss bitch on his arm. This opportunity he is giving me, and the girls will definitely help us get our shit together. We all needed something positive to happen after Raylexia went missing for 10 months without a word. Us all working together and being given the chance to live on our own is just that, a blessing.

"Guys this opportunity has to be our blessing from God. A job for all five of us at the same place is heaven sent, and with us all working together and living together it cuts out the need for us to find rides to and from work. "We can just all ride together," I told them while ear hustling on Ray's conversation with her sitter.

"Mrs. Chance I would really prefer it if you would move into the guesthouse behind our new place out past Ellerbe. I haven't had a chance to check it out yet, but it will eliminate your need to take in more kids to pay them high bills in your house. You can keep all your payments from the childcare and live rent free. You own your home so you could always rent it out or sell it. You helped take care of us when we had no one and you are the only person I trust outside of my friends to keep my son and siblings. In fact, we need to add Tylan to the mix since he will be here with Johnya. Just think about it and let me know when you get here in the morning. Okay, see you tomorrow. Bye." Ray ended her call and turned to find Johnya eyeballing her like crazy. Johnya knows Ray is short on tolerance for bullshit. So, she better move carefully.

"What's this about Tylan to the mix?" Johnya wasted no time asking Ray about her call letting me know I wasn't the only one ear hustling.

Ray tilted her head and looked at Johnya. She had the sense to look sheepish. Ray was cool, but not that cool.

"I was just letting my babysitter know that she will need to keep Tylan along with Zan, Reign, and Rod. She keeps them all here through the day and goes home after I come in at night. Since you will be staying here with Tylan it just makes sense that she keeps him along with the others so you can save on that high ass day care your parents have him in." Ray told Johnya.

Johnya just stared. I guess she was at a loss for words. Ray sighed.

"I am just telling her about him, Johnya. If you don't want her to keep Tylan it's fine. I know it's more convenient to have in-house childcare. Some days when I get off my feet hurt so bad; I can barely walk. Stopping to pick up kids then head home is no fun at all. There is no rush, I was just letting you know the option is there." Ray spoke and then gave Johnya an expectant look letting her know she better come better than she just did. The rest of us held our breath, waiting.

"That's great Ray. I was just wondering how I was going to be able to convince my parents that I'll be able to take care of Tylan on my own and you just solved one of the problems with reliable childcare in-home. You know how my parents are overprotective about us since that bullshit happened with Tyrone, so this and the job gives me the confidence I needed to tell them about the move tonight. Thanks a lot Ray. I really appreciate everything you're doing for us. You didn't have to give us this place, you could have just broken your lease and moved out. Giving us this place gives us all the opportunity to start our bid for independence off in a safe place." Johnya told Ray damn near in tears. She got off the bed and gave her a hug. We all released the breath we were holding.

"You guys are all welcome. Shit when I first moved out here around all these white folks I didn't know how to act, but I came to understand that living out here is no less than I deserve." Ray told us and then promptly changed the subject.

"I have been thinking hard about doing a half day tomorrow and emailing my last two professors so I can leave at 11am to take you guys by my bank before you all start moving your stuff. If we are going to start working making $15 an hour it's best if we do direct deposit instead of a paper check, and you guys need a bank account anyway. My check card is my new best friend. I never have to worry about getting robbed and it makes paying bills so easy. Besides, I wanna be

here when you guys move in." Ray told us all while grinning. My heart dropped because I know I probably don't have enough money.

"That sounds good to me, but how much will we need to open an account? You know money is tight for us until we start working and make our first check." I asked her, remembering I'm down to my last $30. I know Ray has good intentions, but I'm broke.

"It costs $50 to open the accounts and I am paying to set them up for all of you. I know how tight money is right now so I wouldn't have suggested it if I wasn't planning to pay the fee." Ray told us as she stood up to face us sitting on the bed.

"Guys look. I know how hard it is for all of you right now and you wouldn't believe how much growing up I have had to do over the past 10 months. I am all Rod, Reign and Zan have and I refuse to ever live like I did with my Mom ever again. Having a baby put everything into perspective for me. There is nothing more important to me than taking care of him and making sure he has everything he needs. Mrs. Chance taught me about paying bills, managing money, cooking, cleaning, and parenting so I can be the best me there is. She is a truly wonderful person that got fucked over by her husband. Based on what happened to her I will never depend on anybody but me ever again, because that shit can turn around and bite you in the ass. Don't get me wrong guys. I'm not preaching to you about how to live your life. I'm just passing on some knowledge that Mrs. Chance gave me while living with her. Once you guys get to know her, you'll see what I mean." Ray told us and headed towards the door continuing to talk.

"So, guys, have you all checked out the other rooms to decide which of you is taking which room, and what you're gonna bring from home, so we'll know what you need to toss out. I know everybody had their own bedroom furniture besides Shamena and she's set already. What are you guys gonna bring?" Ray asked while exiting my room to go check the other rooms.

We all followed her out of my room over to the other rooms until they all picked their rooms and decided what to have tossed out. Ray then made quick work of giving us all a set of keys to the apartment and the code to the alarm system. She then walked each of us through setting the alarm and deactivating it. Once she was convinced, we had it she hugged us all and went to get a sleeping Reign and Rod up to leave. Zan was with Zylar wide awake and cheesing at everybody around him. Once Ray had them all bundled up in their coats, they all sat down on the couch to wait for Zylar.

Deana helped K-Boy get up with his little girl Brea who was asleep with Reign and put on her coat. Then she put on her coat and walked him down to his 2012 Cadillac Escalade EXT truck. He kissed her goodbye and left after dapping up all his boys.

Winkie walked over to talk with K-O and they went off toward her room to talk.

Johnya started getting Tylan's things together to load in the car when Zaylar broke off from talking to Zylar and Cree to tell her to hold up before she heads out.

"Okay Zay, but it's getting late and we have a busy day ahead of us tomorrow. I'm just going to put on our coats and sit our stuff by the door." Johnya told that nigga letting him know not to take all day.

I was happy. Johnya used to let Tyrone get away with all kinds of foul shit. I guess it has a lot to do with age too. She was just too young to be dealing with adult things at that time. We all settled on the sectional to wait and Ray leaned over and touched my hand.

"Shamena I have something for you that I've been holding for the last 4 months. My uncles sent us $6000 in gift cards for Wal-Mart, Target, and J C Penny's after they found out about us going into foster care. I saved the ones that were in the mailbox at the apartment and what we had left over for you. You can go shopping and get whatever you need cause it's over $3000 left. You can even share it with the other girls, but this is your portion." Raylexia told me as she handed me 6 gift cards.

"I am really sorry that I forgot to take you with me when we moved, but I just wanted to put distance between me and Zylar as fast as I could. I was in survival mode and nothing else even registered until after I got emancipated and they gave me full custody of Rod and Reign. I think that's the first time I thought about you and wondered if you were okay." Ray told me letting me know that whatever happened between her and Zylar was no small matter, and she would go to great lengths to make sure he won't find her if he fucks up again. That's why we were so shocked that she agreed to take him back.

"Thanks Ray. I really appreciate you always looking out for me and making sure I'm straight. You are my sister in every sense of the word. I don't know what

I would have done without you all these years," I told her while giving her a hug. She just don't know how much she means to me, or how much I missed her over the past 10 months.

"I believe everything happens for a reason though, and like Cree said, "I need to get my check in my own name." Mom never gives me anything out of it so I most definitely need to fix that."* I told Ray. She nodded.

"You would have survived and prevailed to go back and show your Mom that even with all she did. It didn't do anything but make you stronger. She could never break your spirit, Shamena. Remember that because that's what makes you the beautiful person you are," Ray said with a devilish grin on her face.

I laughed at Ray and noticed that Cree and Zaylar were in a heated discussion and Zylar and Cree faced off against Zaylar. We all got up and walked closer to hear what was going on.

Zaylar looked frustrated, but he was calm. He nodded when needed and even said okay several times. Zylar and Cree were relentless though.

"Zaylar you have been carrying them niggas long enough. They act like you owe them something and are gone to pay them if they work are not. Me and Myron have worked hard to turn your businesses around and set you up with legitimate forms of income that will keep you going even if you stop dealing today, but you can't continue to carry around that dead weight. If them niggas don't want to work, they gotta go. I'm not finna be constantly scolding no niggas older than me about how to behave at work, and we don't feel comfortable letting them know anything about the other side of the business. It's just a gut feeling we have, but my gut has never steered me wrong before. We just need you to sit down with us to talk to them niggas. If after that they can't get right, you gotta cut them loose. If they have a problem with that, I'll handle them my way." Cree told Zaylar in a menacing tone that changed his whole facial expression. Further confirming my earlier suspicions that he was running things along with Zaylar, Zylar and Myron.

"I hear y'all. Set that shit up for when y'all bring the girls out to train tomorrow. I'll come out to talk to them then since I will be getting Johnya a car at that time. I hope they fall in line and make this money, but if not, I'll have to cut ties. I refuse to carry grown ass men on my back, and I for damn sure

don't have time to babysit." Zaylar said and headed over to where Johnya was waiting with Tylan.

Zylar and Cree came over to where we were sitting on the couch. *"You ready to head out Ray?"* Zylar asked and Ray turned around to give me another hug.

"I'll see you in the morning. Are you gonna be okay here by yourself?" Ray asked as she strapped Zan into his car seat and stood as Zylar grabbed Reign and shook Rod awake.

"Raylexia, you know how bad it was for me at home. I'd rather stay here by myself tonight than to deal with that woman's bullshit for even a minute more," I told her with feeling. Ray gave me a sympathetic look and nodded.

"My bad Sha. I must have confused you with that question. My mind is now working right. I forgot, we have deadbeat parents." Ray laughed and hugged me again on her way out the door.

Zylar dapped up Cree and headed out behind Ray carrying Reign, with Rod in tow.

"Are you staying the night with me tonight, or will I see you tomorrow?" I turned and asked Cree once I watched Ray drive off followed by Zylar. Then I saw three other cars pull out from different spots in the lot to trail behind them.

"I was planning to go home, but I don't like the idea of you staying here alone. Let me run down to the car and get my bag and I'll spend the night with you." Cree told me as he headed for the door. Just the thought of him staying the night has my pussy thumping.

"Say C-Lo are you heading out?" Zaylar asked as Winkie and K-O came out from the back room with Winkie looking a little flushed, smiling hard as hell. I could tell K-O really cared about my girl.

"Naw. I'm just going down to my ride. What's up?" Cree asked as he paused by the door to wait for Zaylar.

"Do you know if we still haeve the 2012 Audi Q7 that we got in last week. I know Quinn was looking at it. Do you know if we still have it in stock?" Zaylar asked, making Cree pause before answering.

Cree shook his head and looked at the door, then back at Zaylar.

"Yeah we still got it. That nigga wasn't willing to pay the price for it even with the $5000 discount the salesman offered him. Myron had to let the

salesmen know not to accept anything less than $5000 under market value without running it past us, cause some of the Fellas feel like they are supposed to be driving luxury vehicles for peanuts." Cree told Zaylar while giving him a strange look.

Zaylar grunted and nodded. *"You don't have to give me that look Nigga. I heard what you and Zylar said loud and clear. Tomorrow I will make sure everybody knows ain't no muthafucker finna be freeloading off me. They will either be doing the job I pay them for or getting the fuck on."* Zaylar said as he walked over to dap Cree and K-O up while toting Tylan down to the car.

Deana came out of her room smiling into the phone until she saw Winkie and Johnya giving me hugs and heading for the door.

"Kayden I'll call you when I get home, we are heading out now. Bye." Deana spoke into the phone while walking up to give me a hug.

"See you in the morning Sha. Lord knows if we didn't have tests in three of our classes tomorrow, I'd skip school. Today has been crazy as hell. Let me go get this talk with my parents over with. You be safe and call me if you need me." Deana told me as she put on her coat and grabbed her bags following Johnya and Winkie down to the car.

K-O put Winkie's bags in the car and hugged and kissed her before helping her into the back seat. Then he turned to dap up Zaylar and Cree and made his way to his 2012 Dodge Challenger and pulled off.

Deana put her bags in back and hopped in the front passenger seat to wait for Johnya.

Zaylar helped Johnya strap Tylan in and then gave her a heated kiss before tapping her on the ass so she could get in the car. I could tell by the way Johnya was looking at Zaylar she didn't want to leave. He leaned into the window and kissed her again before heading off to his 2012 Porsche Cayenne. He honked at Johnya so she could pull off and fell in behind her. As I watched them pull off, I saw 4 other cars parked in different areas of the complex slowly pull off behind Zaylar. Cree watched as they all left and then he grabbed a large duffle bag from the back of his SUV and headed back up the stairs.

I stood in the doorway and waited for Cree to walk in and then locked the door and set the alarm behind him. Then I followed him to the couch and hugged him from behind. I placed my head on his back and leaned into him for support.

"What's wrong Beast?" Cree asked as he turned around in my embrace and hugged me back. I rested my head on his chest rubbing my wet clammy hands over his muscular back. He had a well-defined torso with muscles equally proportioned to fit his build.

I sighed in relief, happy just being with him like this, *"nothing's wrong. I just felt the need to hold you right now. A lot has happened today and I'm still processing most of it, but the best thing by far was meeting you. You are the first guy I've met that I want to give myself to. When I talked to Ray and Johnya about what to expect their experiences were totally different, but I am experiencing some of the things that Ray described,"* I told him now feeling a little nervous.

"Word. What are you experiencing, Beast?" Cree asked while rubbing up and down my back. It felt so good my body was humming.

"I am short of breath, with wet clammy hands," I explained, rubbing my hands against his back. *"My nipples are sensitive in my bra, they almost hurt. I have butterflies in my stomach, my clit is throbbing, and my pussy juices are running down my legs. If you rub your hand between my thighs, you'll feel how wet I am. Since this morning riding next to you on the way here I have been having this reaction. Every time you come in my presence, I feel this way,"* I told him not feeling shy anymore. In fact, I felt the need to be a bit bold, so my hands began to roam.

"How many times have you felt this way?" Cree asked in a tight voice.

His hands now caressing me intimately. I could feel them slip under my sweater to touch my bare skin. His hands were cold against my heated back. My body shivered and I couldn't tell if it was from the cold or something else.

"This is the first time today with you. I told you, you make me wanna give myself to you and I've never felt like doing that before," I told him leaning back to stare up into his sexy hazel green eyes.

"Okay Beast. So, what do you want to do about these feelings?" Cree asked, as he pulled his hands from under my sweater to reach up into my hair. He tilted my head back so I could look him directly in the eyes. The sight was so hot I shivered from head to toe.

Licking my lips, I rasped, *"I want you to teach me how to please you and make me a woman,"* I told him, my eyes never leaving his smoldering gaze. The look promised pleasure and I wanted it all.

"You're all woman already now Sha, but I will gladly teach you how to please us both. Are you sure you're ready? There is no rush, you know. I'm not going anywhere," Cree asked as I grabbed his hand to lead him to my room.

"Yes. I'm ready. I want you more than anything. My inner Beast is calling your name, can't you hear it?" I asked him walking down the hall, holding his hand. This apartment is bigger than most, so it took forever to make it to my room. My anxiety builds with every step.

When we crossed the threshold to my room Cree grabbed me by my jaws and kissed me aggressively. I felt the ball on his tongue ring rubbing against my tongue and the roof of my mouth. I tried to keep up, but I've never kissed anyone before, so my teeth keep bumping into him and catching against the ball.

Cree pulled back without releasing my jaws. *"Sha follow my tongue with your tongue and when you open your mouth cover your teeth with your lips. Most importantly, breathe through your nose. The ball is just extra, you'll get used to it in no time."* He smiled as he began to explore my mouth again. I could feel his lips curl each time I got it right. That ball against the roof of my mouth caused me to gasp.

This time I was able to kiss him back without my teeth bumping against his teeth or ball. He thoroughly explored every crevice of my mouth, making love to my lips and tongue. It was so erotic, that ball adding extra sensations my body started trembling and I couldn't stop. Smiling, he gave my lips a last lingering lick and sucked hard on my tongue. Releasing my mouth, he turned my head and licked from the base of both sides of my neck to the crown of my ears, his ball providing a strong electrification. All the combined stimulation had my toes curling, the heat building in my core to inferno. It felt so good, I felt the heat increase in my cheeks to spread all over my body. Never had I been so happy about my dark ebony complexion.

"Let's get out of these clothes." Cree announced and proceeded to unbutton my jeans. As he slid the zipper down, he watched as each piece of skin was revealed. Rubbing and caressing igniting fire wherever he touched, the pleasure was so intense I could hardly breathe.

"You are fuckin' beautiful Beast, and your skin is silky soft." Cree told me as he continued to rub up and down my legs exploring all my exposed skin. Once he peeled off my jeans he dropped to his knees and removed my panties. I held my breath watching his reaction to my landing strip of hair on my kitty. His eyes darkened even more, almost a forest green as he purred, pulling the ball between his teeth.

"Beast you are dripping fuckin' wet." Cree said as he leaned in and licked between my folds, before wrapping his lips around my clit pushing the ball in and sucking hard making me shout out in ecstasy causing my knees to buckle.

Cree "C-Lo" Logan

The smell and taste of Sha is intoxicating as hell, making me damn near dizzy. I think I just found my new drug of choice. Just knowing she's never been with anyone else has my dick so hard it's about to burst through my jeans causing my dick piercing to simulate fucking. I rubbed my nose hard against her clit sliding against her hood, as I fucked her hard with my tongue and ball. Sha began to shake and grabbed my head to pull me closer to her dripping wet pussy. I licked and sucked my way back up to her clit rubbing my ball against her folds and pushing my ball under her hood and latched on sucking and flicking the ball back and forth alongside my tongue. Sha's thighs had a vice grip on my head as she trembled and squirted all over my face.

I tapped her legs for her to release my neck. Then made quick work of removing the rest of our clothes. Sha looked over my body from head to toe with a dreamy expression on her face taking in all the piercings and body art on display. I couldn't tell if she liked what she saw or if it was the aftermath of her orgasm. I didn't have long to wait because Sha reached out and ran her hand over my abs and up to my chest to pull on my nipple rings. I hissed and moaned in pleasure as she gave each a little tug.

"Cree, you are beautiful. Riding over here with you this morning I was fantasizing about running my hands all over this milk chocolate skin and exploring all these muscles I could see bulging through your shirt. Look at how it has me leaking and my clit is throbbing. My mouth is watering for you. Can I please taste you? Teach me how please? I really wanna suck your dick. That dick piercing looks painful. Is it?" Sha asked me as she reached down and began to stroke my dick rubbing tentatively over my dick piercing.

"No!" I hissed, barely able to speak.

I felt like the rest of the blood in my body all rushed to my dick and I had to struggle to keep from bursting. I looked down between Sha's legs and sure enough her juices were flowing down her legs and a fruity scent was coming off her body. There was no way I could handle teaching her how to suck my dick this first time around. I'll have to do that later. Sha's body is ridiculously sexy and calling my name. She has grapefruit sized breasts, a flat stomach and a wide 12-inch waistline with ass and thighs to match. Her dark ebony skin tone beckoned me to lick her from head to toe so I grabbed her up and laid her in the middle of her bed.

"Sha, I don't have the patience I need to teach you how to suck my dick this first time, but later I promise to teach you everything you need to know," I told her and then proceeded to lick every inch of her body before reaching down for my pants to retrieve a condom. Once I had my dick covered, I proceeded to lick her folds and suck on her clit, my tongue and ring ball fighting for dominance. Sha's juices flowed down her legs soaking the bed.

I kissed my way back up to her lips and kissed her lips giving her a taste of herself on my lips. She shocked me when she bit down on my ball as I guided my dick to her opening and started to ease in encountering resistance. *"Sha let me in baby. Bring your legs up and open them wider for me. It's gonna sting a little with my dick piercing, but I promise you'll learn to love it,"* I told her as I reached between us to play with her clit. Sha released more juices and I slid in a little farther.

"Shit Cree it hurts." Sha exclaimed, gripping my forearms.

"You want me to stop Beast?" I asked, knowing it would kill me to stop now, but I would if she can't continue.

"NO!" Sha shouted as she quickly wrapped her legs around my waist and surged up taking more of me inside causing me to push through her barrier. I could hear her hiss as the piercing pushed through her barrier. I grabbed her hips to stop her from moving and to give her time to adjust to my size.

"Just breathe Sha," I told her as she started to wiggle in my grasp.

"I need you to move Cree. I'm on fire and there's a thumping in my clit. If you don't move, I'll go crazy." Sha told me and I realized she gets off on the pain.

I moved forward, giving her all 10½ inches at once. *"Fuck Cree, it hurts so good."* Sha told me as she began to swivel her hips round causing my dick piercing and dick to caress all her pussy walls. I started off slowly stretching out her walls and giving her time to better adjust to my size. Once she started to meet each thrust, I raised her left leg over my arm and went in deep. Sha's pussy juices were running down her legs and flowing all over my dick making me stroke her even harder. The added stimulation on my dick piercing makes my toes flex.

"Fuck Cree. Fuck me harder." Sha screamed, making me throw her other leg over my shoulder and take a firmer grip on her hips while doing pushups in her pussy. The harder I pounded the wetter Sha's pussy got causing me to grind my back teeth in an effort not to nut prematurely.

"Damn Sha this pussy soaking wet," I told her as I concentrated on trying not to cum. I dropped her right leg and threw my left leg over her leg sliding up to pound from a different angle. This made me stroke even deeper.

"Yes! Right there Creeee." Sha came screaming on a keening moan, legs shaking, and pussy gripping me impossibly tight. I had to switch positions again. I stopped, dropped her other leg and flipped her on her stomach. I slid in from behind with both my legs on either side of hers. The fit was so tight my head damn near exploded.

"Ohh Ahhhh! Cree. Fuck me good Cree, Fuck me goooddddd!" Sha muttered as I went back in pounding her relentlessly.

"Right there Cree. I'm cuming again. Yes, fuck your pussy harder Cree. Fuck it good." Sha continued telling me how good I am making her feel.

"Shit Sha." I hissed as Sha's pussy clamped down on my dick with a vise grip. I could feel her pussy muscles clenching as she came with her legs shaking. Not giving her time to recover. I pulled her hips up, opened her legs, slid between them while pressing my hand on her back to keep her face down in the pillow, and went back in.

"Ahh Cree!" Sha yelled at having to take the full force of each stroke. I didn't let up. I pounded harder, causing Sha's pussy to flow like a river. All you could hear in the room was her ass clapping and her gushy pussy.

"This my pussy right Beast?" I asked Sha as I slammed into her while circling my hips.

"Yesssss. It's your pussy Creeeeeeeee!" Sha shrieked on a hoarse moan.

"So, take your dick. Am I deep enough now Sha? Can I tame that Beast?" I asked as that familiar tingling started at the base of my spine.

"Ahhh!" Sha screamed and squirted all over the bed letting me know I was pounding on her g-spot.

I backed up to watch my dick sliding in and out of Sha. Big mistake. Her pussy lips were glistening with her juices running down her legs and dripping on the bed. The sight was so erotic, just watching her soft ass jiggle caused me to slam in as hard as I could. I felt Sha stop and her pussy muscles locked up around me pulling my seeds and my sense straight out through my dick. I couldn't see or breathe as my back bowed and my knees locked, leaving me feeling lightheaded.

I came back to my senses to find I was laying across Sha's back breathing hard as hell. *"You okay Beast? Am I now qualified as your Beast tamer?"* I asked as I slowly pulled out of her while making sure my dick piercing didn't break the condom and it was still secure. I moved her out of the wet spot and stood to my feet headed to the bathroom to dispose of the condom.

"Yes, Cree I am fine and thoroughly tamed. Take me with you so I can soak while you strip the bed." Sha told me in a sleepy voice. I stopped and turned to get her off the bed.

"Are you sure you're alright Sha? It was very rough, and it was your first time." I asked trying to make sure she's okay after such a hard fuckin'. She doesn't know it yet, but she's stuck with me forever. Her pussy is grade-A and all mines.

"I'm fine Cree. I just need a little soak my body is aching all over, but I feel amazing." Sha told me as I picked her up and headed back to the bathroom.

I sat her down on the toilet while I tied off and threw the condom in the trash. *"Shit it burns."* Sha said as she began to relieve her bladder.

"That's to be expected, Sha. It was your first time and I have a dick piercing shaped like a half-moon with two balls on either end. Not to mention it was a hard fucking. Let me check under the cabinet to see if Ray has Epsom salt," I told her as I searched under the sink.

I found the Epsom salt and started her a hot bath using a generous amount of the bath salt. Sha sat on the toilet until the water was ready then wiped herself, flushed and got in the water.

"Shsss." She hissed as she eased down into the water and let out a contented sigh.

"Feel better?" I asked, preparing to go shower in the other bathroom and change the sheets.

"Yes. This water feels so good, but I'm sleepy so don't let me drown." Sha said while smiling up at me sleepily.

"I got you Beast. You soak and I'm gonna go shower in the other bathroom," I told her after giving her a kiss on the lips and heading for the second bathroom.

I made quick work of my shower, dressed and made the bed with the spare bedding I found in the hall closet. By the time I went to check on Sha, she was fast asleep. I stood in the doorway and watched her sleep taking in her flawless ebony skin, big round breast, and oval shaped face. This girl has me feeling things I've never felt before, and the sex is fuckin' phenomenal. I think I found my forever. I thought as I walked over to the tub to check the water. Sure enough, it was barely warm.

"Sha wakeup so you can bathe and get out. You're starting to prune," I told her as I rubbed my hand across her thigh. She slightly shivered.

"Creee." She moaned and opened her eyes. *"That feels so good,"* she purred. "I need my bath gel from the dresser and the bath sponge."

I took Sha the bath gel and sponge then I went and started her sheets to wash. There is no saving the comforter Sha bled all over it. I'll just have to get her a replacement tomorrow. Returning from the washroom I found Sha standing in the hall closet pulling out an extra blanket. My dick bricked up immediately.

"I get cold at night, so I need extra cover." Sha told me while looking at me like I'm a snack licking her lips.

"Sha stop eye fuckin' me before I pin your ass up against this wall. I'm trying to give your body a chance to recover so we can play tomorrow," I told her as I took in her shorts and muscle shirt that in no way concealed her body. My thoughts instantly turned dark. I was jealous, so I spoke without thinking.

"Sha what the hell do you have on? I know you weren't sleeping in this shit when you lived at home?" I asked her madder than a muthafucker. I had murder on my mind. Another first.

Shamena looked startled, then hurt. *"NO! I slept in pajama pants and shirts at home. I didn't have a room, remember, so I had to be fully clothed."* Sha told me, now sounding offended.

"My bad Beast, but just the thought of another Nigga seeing what's mine has me hot. This is a first for me, so you're gonna have to help me adjust to this shit.

I'm the only muthafucker I want to have glimpses of what you look like without clothes. You feel me?" I told Sha serious as a heart attack.

"Yeah, whatever, nigga." She snapped back showing her spunk.

I chuckled, *"I'm serious though. This is all new."*

She grunted, *"I understand Cree. This is new for me too. We will just have to learn and adjust together as you say. I am only interested in you, and if that happens to change, I'll let you know before I'd ever cheat."* Sha said to me, and I had a visceral reaction as if she struck me.

Not trying to read too much into my reaction to what she said, I went to the living room to grab my bag and followed Sha back to her room. After taking care of my hygiene, I joined Sha in bed. I reached out and grabbed Sha's hand pulling her into the spoon position.

"Goodnight Cree. Thanks for making my first time special." Sha told me as I closed my eyes.

"Thank you for giving me such a precious gift. I will cherish it forever. Now get some rest, you have a busy day tomorrow," I told her and cradled her to my chest and drifted off to sleep.

CHAPTER THIRTEEN
Cree "C-Lo" Logan

January 20, 2012

"Sha, your cell is ringing." I shook Sha awake because her cell kept ringing and its 5am. *"Who in the hell is calling her this early in the morning?" I questioned.*

"I'm up." she said and reached out to grab her phone, stopping the ringing. That's when I realized it was her alarm.

"Why are you getting up so early Sha? You don't have to leave for school until 6:30am." I questioned wanting some more cuddle time. My phone rang all night with bullshit that coulda' waited until this morning. I was in no way ready to get up this early.

"I'm getting up early so I can start breakfast. When Ray still lived in the apartments, we all ate breakfast together before we headed to school. Hopefully, they will come early to eat." Sha told me while heading to the bathroom.

Seeing there would be no cuddling this morning I decided to grab my bag and wash up in the other bathroom. After taking care of my hygiene, I dressed in black, white and gray Nike joggers, with a white Nike tee, and all black gangsta Nikes. Keeping it simple, I put on my platinum diamond C chain and white gold Tag Heuer watch before heading back to Sha's room. I made the bed and went to the washroom to start drying her sheets. As I headed back to check on Sha in the kitchen the doorbell rang.

Headed to answer the door, I saw Sha coming from the kitchen headed in the same direction. *"I got it. Do you need some help with the food?"* I asked her as we both made our way to the door. Sha's ass cheeks hanging out, jiggling in the bootie shorts she slept in.

"The food is ready, Cree. I just have to get dressed, but thanks for asking." Sha told me as she put the alarm code in to deactivate it and waited for me to open the door.

Before that I looked at her and shook my head. *"Look Sha, I'ma need you to go get changed now. I'm territorial as fuck and I'm not feelin' you opening the door while wearing that."*

She nodded, *"I'll go right after."*

I looked at her again and I was angry. We were at an impasse, so I just nodded.

I opened the door to reveal an older black lady with a pleasant smile. *"Can we help you?"* I asked, not knowing who she was.

"Hi I'm Anna Chance. I babysit for Raylexia. She told me to come over early today because she had some people, she wants me to meet." She answered while giving us an assessing once over.

"Ray's not here yet Mrs. Chance but she told me you would be here this morning. I'm Shamena Green and this is Cree Logan. It's nice to meet you. Come on in and make yourself comfortable." Sha replied to the woman and moved back to let her in. She was careful not to let anyone outside see her as she blocked her body with the door.

I was still pissed, but I relaxed somewhat and paid attention to our guest.

"Thank you, baby. It's cold out there. You got it smelling good up in here. Did you fix the famous breakfast Raylexia has been telling me about?" Mrs. Chance asked as she walked over to the closet and began to remove her coat. Making herself comfortable.

She was a nice looking middle aged woman with skin the color of toffee. She had her hair in a neat bun to the back and minimal makeup.

"Yes, I made breakfast. I don't know about famous, but it will hold us until we get out of school. I'm going to go get dressed so I'll be ready to leave after we eat." Sha laughed as she closed the door and headed back to her room to get dressed.

Just as Sha hit the corner the doorbell rang so I walked back over and opened the door. Ray was on the other side. *"What's up Ray? Why are you ringing the bell? Where is your key?"* I asked her as I grabbed Zan's car seat out of her hand and sat him on the couch.

"Hey C-Lo. This is not my apartment anymore so I can't be walking up in here without knocking. Can you help Zyler get the rest of the bags out of the car?" She asked and walked over to the couch to sit Zan's diaper bag down.

"Hey Mrs. Chance, I'm glad you came early." I heard Ray say as I opened the door to see Reign and Rod coming in with their backpacks and bags.

"What's up Rod? Hi Reign." I spoke and dapped Rod off as I went down to the car to help Zyler get the rest of the bags.

"What's good Nigga? What's all this?" I asked as I saw Zy take out five bags full of food.

"Man, Ray went to the store this morning to get groceries for the girls. She said she has food over here but not enough to hold them until they get their first paycheck." Zy told me as I helped him take the rest of the bags out the back of Ray's SUV.

As we reached the stairs Johnya pulled up followed by three other vehicles I didn't recognize. They all exited their cars and walked over to the girls. Judging by the look of them and the fact that they all walked over to help the girls unload their bags. I'd say these are their parents.

When we made it upstairs and put the bags in the kitchen, the girls and their parents came through the door. Shamena came from the back fully dressed in a pair of tight black jeans, a white sweatshirt, and black ankle boots. Shamena's shape is sexy as hell, so covering up does little to hide it, but I let out a sigh of relief. I'm not trying to put too much thought into my possessiveness where Sha is concerned. I'll figure it out later.

Sha and all her girls hugged and talked in the middle of the living room area. You couldn't tell they'd just been together the night before. Everyone else was just standing there looking around the apartment. Ray broke off and turned around to face them.

"Let's get your groceries put away and then I can make introductions." Ray told everybody as her, the girls, and Mrs. Chance made quick work of putting up the food and coming back out to the living room.

Ray stepped forward and took the lead. *"Okay everybody I'd like you all to meet Mrs. Chance. She is the Foster Mother they placed us with when we were placed in state custody. She allowed me, Rod, and Reign to all stay together and helped me get situated when we moved in here. She has truly been a blessing from God to us."* Ray finished while smiling at Mrs. Chance.

"Mrs. Chance this is Mrs. Sandra Harris Winkie's Mother and her Uncle Sammy Harris, but we all call him Slim." Ray introduced and they nodded.

Winkie's mother was her look-a-like only shorter with grown woman curves. Her uncle looked like the male version of his sister, only his 6'2" height and skinny muscular frame being the difference. He was much older than her, making me think Ms Harris was a late pregnancy for their parents.

Ray continued gesturing towards the other two couples, *"this is Mr. and Mrs. John and Danelle Wade Deana's parents and Mr. and Mrs. Carl and Johnny Mae West Johnya's parents."* Ray finished the introductions while they all exchanged greetings.

Just looking at Johnya's and Deana's parents, I could tell that both of them were an equal mix of both their mothers and fathers. Johyna was her father's twin with her mother's sexy body. While Deana had her father's eyes and mouth, her heart shaped facial structure and curvy body type were all her mother's.

"I know you all have mixed emotions about the girls being on their own, but they all would have been leaving for college in the summer anyway. This just gets them ready for the change earlier. This apartment is in a safe environment, and their rent is paid up for the year. We all just got a new job that we start today, so they can handle the bills. Mrs. Chance made me install an alarm system that my uncles paid for when we moved in, so they are as secure as possible living here." Ray told them while making eye contact with each set of parents.

"I know that they are only 16 years old, but all of my sisters are sensible with a good head on their shoulders. We don't drink or do drugs, and you have never had to worry about us being out in the streets acting wild. It has just never been our thing. Do you guys have any questions you want to ask us before we eat and get ready to head out for school?" Ray asked after she seemed to touch on every objection the parents could have had.

I'm not gonna lie. Ray is intelligent as hell, but more than that she has some street smarts. I guess you can't grow up living in the Projects without learning a thing or two to help you survive. Zylar had to be a fool to fuck up things with her. I thought looking over at that nigga holding Zan while watching Ray's every move.

"Ray, my biggest concern was about daycare and the overall safety of the environment that Johnya and Tylan would be living in. But after seeing this

place I'm sure they would be safer living here then they would be living with us back in the jets. The only other concern we have is Tylan. Johnya told us that Mrs. Chance would be keeping him here at the apartment. Is that true?" Mr. West asked while looking at Ray expectantly.

Ray gestured at Mrs. Chance and spoke, *"yes. As I told you all before, Mrs. Chance is the foster parent that they placed us with when we were taken into state custody. She allowed us all to stay together until I got emancipated and received full guardianship of Reign and Rod. She also taught me how to take better care of myself and my siblings. She now keeps them here at home for me to be able to go to school and work."* Ray told Mr. and Mrs. West making sure to make eye contact and speak clearly. You would never believe she is only 16 years old. Johnya's parents exchanged a glance and nodded. I could see Johnya sigh and relief spread across her face. Ray had just helped her convince her parents.

I respect the shit out of Ray and I am happy Shamena has her as a friend.

"Shayla has told me that you all will be starting a new job today that pays $15 an hour and they are willing to work around your school schedule. Is this true as well? I know that you guys are close and enjoy being together, but I don't want you all lying to stay together and you all won't be able to pay your bills. More than that I don't want you all messing up school just to work and be on your own." The one introduced as Ms Sandra Harris asked.

Ray frowned and looked at Winkie, then back at her mother. *"Yes. Ms. Sandra, we have a job that we start today and yes. It pays $15 an hour. We are going to open them all bank accounts at Capital One Bank today so they can do direct deposit. I'm surprised you would ask if Winkie would lie about that since she has never lied to you about anything else."* Ray told Ms Sandra while looking slightly hurt for some reason.

"Believe me when I say I questioned her thoroughly last night and she said the same thing over and over again. It's just that jobs paying $15 an hour are hard to come by and rarely are they given to 16-year-olds. I trust my daughter and we have a wonderful bond. I just wanna make sure she'll be good on her own. Having freedom and living on her own sounds wonderful. I just wanna make sure she'll be alright and safe." Ms Sandra said and Ray visibly relaxed.

I could tell from their interactions that Raylexia was close to each of these families. They all respect her and seem to trust her and her judgment. That's rare to find in one so young.

Ray nodded her head as if in agreement and spoke, *"that's understandable Ms Sandra, and I understand your skepticism, but we all truly have a job that we start today. In fact, I have to quit my job at Price-Lo Foods so I can work the new one."* Ray told Ms Sandra while they all smiled.

The only people yet to speak were Deanna's parents. Ray turned to face them and asked. *"Mr. John and Mrs. Danelle do you guys have any questions for us?"* They were just quietly observing the girls and Mrs. Chance.

"Ray Deana explained everything to us and just looking at the environment she will be living in and the safety features you have added to the apartment has put both our minds at ease. We are working hard to save enough to move out of those apartments to something better, and just knowing our baby won't have to come back there to stay is a comfort. Hopefully we'll be getting us a house as soon as we clear up the last 2 items on our credit. Deana leaving helps take a weight off our minds. So, thank you Ray for allowing them to stay here. We're really grateful." Mr. John said while smiling down at Deana. The whole little scene just made me think about putting them in touch with Myron to help them get a home in a safer area.

They all seem to be good people who do what they can to survive. It's just sad that Shamena's mom didn't come and not one of them seemed to have found it strange. Her mom is truly a piece of work.

"Okay then you guys can walk around and take a look at the apartment. It has four bedrooms, so all the girls have already chosen their rooms and what they want to throw out and bring from y'alls place. I'm gonna go eat and feed the kids so we can get ready to head out. It's really good to see you all. I have missed you all these last 9 and a half months." Ray told the parents as she walked up and hugged each one before heading to the kitchen with Rod and Reign in tow.

The girl's parents walked around and checked out each of the girl's bedrooms and the rest of the apartment while Ray fed Reign and Rod. Soon after the parents all left with promises to come back for Sunday dinner. I took that time to gather up the trash that included Sha's comforter and grabbed my duffle bag to drop on top of my hood on my way to the trash dumpster.

On my way back up to the apartment I saw Zylar standing outside by his car waiting for me looking stressed as hell.

"What up My G? Why are you standing out here in the cold looking all crazy?" I asked that Nigga when I walked over to my SUV to put my duffle bag in the back.

"I don't know what to do bruh and this shit is driving me crazy," Zylar said and I knew whatever was going on with him had to involve Ray in some way That nigga looked nervous as hell. If Ray didn't know something was wrong, he'd give it away with all his nervous tension.

"What the hell are you going on about?" I asked him. Not in the mood to play 20 questions with his ass.

Zylar was a completely different person since Ray upped and left his ass. No way would a nigga believe he helps run a thriving drug ring as scared as he's been acting. His ass bet not never try to cheat again cause he got a woman who will make his ass feel it.

Zylar rubbed across his braids in frustration. *"Man, that bitch Chandra talking about she is pregnant with my Jit, and if she is it had to happen that night she hopped on my dick when I was passed out on the couch over at Jayce's house when we had the kickback before Christmas. I thought I was dreaming about Ray when I woke up fuckin' that hoe. I tried to knock that hoe head off because I ain't touched that hoe since Ray left me, and I definitely have never fucked her raw,"* he said as he started to pace.

I remember that night clearly. We all thought he was gonna kill her ass that night. She straight violated that man and not one person in the room spoke against him beating her ass. That happened while Ray was gone though. So, I didn't see the problem.

"That's an easy fix if you don't want the kid. Murk that hoe and move on with your life. Chandra is a bird and all she wants is hood celebrity. You have been messy allowing that hoe to move around the spots and she got comfortable. She thinks she's your girl. Shit until you flipped out after Ray disappeared, I thought she was your bitch too. Get Kahmala to tail that hoe and knock her off before she causes you to lose your family. Because let's be real. Ray will leave your ass and never look back," I told him not seeing the issue. He knows he doesn't want no kids with that birdbrain hoe anyway.

"That's just it though Bruh. I haven't been fuckin' with that hoe at all over the past nine months. She was still popping up, but that had nothing to do with me. From what Jayce said, he found out Derricka was telling that hoe when I was around. That's why he cut Derricka off after what Chandra did at his party. I don't want no kids with that hoe, but I still don't want the shit getting back to Ray either. I just told her I haven't been with anybody else since she's been gone and I haven't. At least not willingly." That Nigga told me making me shake my head at his stupid ass.

"You better kill that hoe and keep it moving, but to be honest with you. Why not just tell Ray about the situation? She's been gone for damn near a year. I'm sure she wouldn't hold this against you if you explained to her what really happened, and that you were afraid to tell her about the shit cause you were trying to get her back. The worst thing that can happen is Ray finding out from that hoe Chandra. That will set up a whole other narrative that she will control," I told him as I made my way back into the apartment to let Sha know I'm heading out.

I got skeletons in my own closet I need to take care of. Just watching Zylar stress over this bullshit, makes me wonder if I should tell Shamena about Adrianna.

Zylar Crewens

I stood outside thinking about what C-Lo just told me, and he has a point. We have been apart for damn near a year and this shit happened before we got back together. I would rather tell Ray what happened, and we fight about it over Chandra telling her about the shit and she leaves me for good. After going back and forth about the shit in my head. I decided I'll tell her about it tonight after we get home. I have definitely learned my lesson about keeping shit from Ray. I never want to experience being separated from her like that again, so I'll take my chances by coming clean about the shit.

Just as I was about to head back up the stairs to the apartment, I saw Buck pulling into the complex. So, I leaned up against Cree's SUV and waited for him to pull up and get out of the car. *"What's good?"* I asked and dapped him up.

Buck was in his 30's and was more straight laced than most of the guys working for Black. He has a military background so he has seen more than most. I am confident that I don't need to worry about Ray and the kid's safety with him in charge of our security.

"Zy I think we are going to have a real problem with the lil nigga from your girl's job." Buck told me while rubbing the back of his neck. Letting me know he's agitated.

"What do you mean?" I asked not wanting to hear any more bad news right now. What the fuck else can go wrong?

"He came back out here last night and stayed until about three this morning. Of course, your girl wasn't here, but what if he turns out to be mentally unstable? I have a detail in place for her and the kids, but crazy people tend to do crazy shit. That little ass whipping the fellas put on him yesterday ain't do shit." Buck told me, looking worried.

I nodded thinking about what he just said. Crazy people are unpredictable and never do normal shit. I'm not trying to let Raylexia and the kids get caught up in whatever the fuck that nigga got going on. I got enough problems on my hands trying to get rid of Chandra's stalking ass. Ray's new stalker is one stalker too many. I squeezed the back of my head and let out a long tired breath. Buck waited patiently as I paced in front of him trying to organize my thoughts. Shaking my head I looked over at him.

"Keep eyes on him and I'll have to get Killian to see to him. Get me a routine schedule for him so I can give it to Killian. He'll take care of the rest. Just make sure our guys keep Ray and the kids safe until Killian can handle him," I told him and headed for the stairs to go back inside, passing by Rod headed for his bus.

"See you later Zy. You wanna play NBA2K when I get home? I wanna try out my new Joystick. That shit is sweetttt!" He exclaimed, excitedly acting like the teenager he is for once, and not some old man.

"Sure, thing Lil Nigga I'll bring mine over to your room or do you wanna hit up the man cave?" I smirked at his shocked expression when I invited him into the grown-up room. Rod would be 13 soon and I wanted to make sure he knows he can depend on me too. Not just Ray, and there are things Ray won't be able to help him with that I want him to be comfortable coming to me about. I know I'm young, but I had some hella good role models coming up. Just looking at their situation. Rod has never had that, so I plan to step up and be that for him.

Grinning, he nodded, *'yeah, we can do that. Hit me up when you get in so we can hook everything up and get Ray to fix us some snacks. Let me get to this stop, before I miss the bus. See you later Zy,"* he told me and dapped me up as he headed to the front of the apartments.

I stood there and watched Rod as he made it to the bus stop and dapped up a couple of youngsters close by and hit others with a head nod. All the kids then moved closer to him and started talking animatedly. Just watching their interaction, I could tell Rod is one of the popular guys around here and all the youngsters look up to him. The bus pulled up 5 min later and they all ran up the stairs and rushed to the back. I then watched as his security detail pulled off behind the bus letting me know Buck had them covered. Making my way to the stairs I saw C-Lo coming back out and met him midway up.

"You got anything going on right now, or can we go get my shit moved in now before you get into anything heavy? I wanna get my shit moved in before we have to deal with the girls." I asked that Nigga so I can get all moved in before I have that talk with Ray tonight. If I'm not moved in, Ray might not let me stay after hearing this shit.

"Nah., I don't have anything pressing, but I wasn't planning on helping yo ass pack neither Nigga. Who the hell do I look like to you? You want me to see if we have two of the packers and movers available to get your shit together? Cause I ain't packing shit. Your Moms is the one who got my house and the house I got for my Ma ready. What I look like helping you pack your shit, and I didn't pack my own." That Nigga ranted at me with his face all screwed up making me laugh.

Chuckling I pressed, *"yeah, C-Lo come on Bruh. You know I'm trying to get this shit out the way just in case some shit pops off that can't wait. My phone rang all night, and it was mostly bullshit that could've waited until this morning. I'm used to the shit, but when Zan wakes up he's cranky as hell. I had to wake Ray up to put him back to sleep. So, can you get the shit setup and come with me to handle the shit? If anything pops off with Chandra, I'll at least have you to make sure I don't murk that hoe in broad daylight,"* I told him hoping he'll do me this solid. I hate moving and I have a room full of shit I don't even wear, so I know it's going to take some time getting everything moved.

"Okay Nigga. Go inside and make sure Ray is good and come on. I see you brought your car, so follow me to Stone's to get the movers and packers setup and then I need to check on the warehouse to verify yesterday's count. I was planning to head to my crib before I went to check on the businesses and pick up my drops, but I guess your ass is doing half of my pickups today since you want me to help you get your shit," he told me while waiting like he thought I would disagree. Hell, I'll do pickups and whatever else, for him to help me straighten this shit out.

"I'll do that. Let me call Killian and get him and Kahmala to meet us at Ma's old place so I can tell him about this lil nigga that's been stalking Ray and get Kahmala on Chandra and Derricka. Buck thinks the nigga is gonna be a problem and I wanna nip that shit quick. You already know what time I'm on with Chandra," I told him and walked inside to let Ray know I was heading out.

It took no time saying bye to Ray because she was distracted talking to Mrs. Chance about moving into the pool house on our property. If Ray could pull it off that would be great. That would make it easier to put a detail on her and keep her safe while she has the kids.

IT TOOK US NO TIME to verify everything at the warehouse and C-Lo set up packers and movers to follow us over to Ma's old crib. They made quick work of packing everything and loading the truck up. Killian and Kahmala showed up just as we were heading out to drop my shit off at the crib, so I had them follow us because what I needed to discuss with them was too sensitive to discuss in mixed company. As we were headed out the gate, I peeped Chandra trying to follow us and my security blocked her path while we continued on our way. That shit right there further confirmed I need to handle that hoe with the quickness. Once we made it to the crib the packers got everything put away and the movers retrieved and discarded all the boxes and packing supplies back onto the truck. Since they all finished and got everything situated so quickly, I gave them all a $100 tip and escorted them down to the main gate and off the premises.

When I made it back to the crib, Killian and C-Lo had made themselves at home in the mancave watching "Heat" and Kahmala was looking through the rest of the DVD collection. I wasted no time getting to the point.

"Thanks for coming out so early you guys, but this shit can't wait. I found my girl and we just moved in here together with my son and her brother and sister. The problem is she has a nigga that's been stalking her that I need you to handle as soon as possible. I know you guys have been trying to find Biz and Eric, but we're gonna have to put that on hold until we get this taken care of first. Buck seems to think the lil nigga maybe unstable because he has pending charges concerning him stalking Ray and that hasn't discouraged him in the least. He followed us back to her apartment 2 nights ago and he has been at her apartment overnight the last 2 nights trying to catch her at home. She let her girls keep her SUV to get around, so it wasn't at the apartment last night, but he still camped out there until 3am lurking. Killian, I need you to take care of him for me before he gets the chance to hurt my girl," I told him as he leaned

forward taking it all in. Killian is a 20-year-old hitta that's been working for Zaylar since before he took over for dad.

Him, Kahmala, Khiershan, and Kilayla are a team of brothers and sisters that handles all the contracts for Zaylar. He's quiet and stays to himself. Other than the occasional gathering Zaylar demands he attend. He never really kicks it with any of the guys. I guess I can understand that since sometimes he ends up having to kill the very guys he'd be kicking it with.

"Do we have an address and name on this nigga? I can do my own research, but it would help if you can give me some basic information," he told me as he pulled out his phone and went to tapping.

"Sorry My G. I don't know where my head is at. Let me call Buck so he can shoot me his info and I'll shoot it to you. You want it in the dummy email, right?" I asked as I pulled out my phone and called Buck.

The phone started to ring as Killian answered.

"Yes. The BlackSlate.org email is the one we use because it's not tied to anybody and can't be traced back to any of us. Make sure you send it from your dummy email nigga," he told me while continuing to tap on the screen of his phone.

"Buck, send me everything you have on ole boy so I can get it to Killian. Bet," I told him and hung up as my phone dinged with an email notification. I then forwarded it to Killian and turned to Kahmala.

Kahmala is a 22-year-old lethal beauty with her coffee-colored skin tone, slanted caramel brown eyes with exotic facial features. She reminds me of a young Stacy Dash. Don't let her pretty face fool you though. Kahmala is as deadly as she is beautiful.

"Hey Kahmala. Thanks for coming. I need you to take care of Chandra and her friend Derricka. That hoe is getting out of control. She showed up with Derricka to Ma's old crib yesterday causing problems at the gate to the property. When I went down to the gate to make them leave, she started talking crazy about us being drug dealers in front of all of them folks outside our gated community. Zaylar is pissed and wants her and Derricka handled as soon as possible. The only problem is she claims she's pregnant," I told her not knowing how she'll feel about knocking off a pregnant woman.

I don't give a fuck either way, but I don't want to cause no problems for her morally.

"Why is her being pregnant a problem? Is the baby yours and do you want to keep it?" Kahmala said with no emotion.

"Yes. Zylar is the baby yours and do you want to keep it?" Ray said while coming into the mancave wearing a blank expression.

She startled me so much that I almost leaped up from my seat, I didn't realize she was present at all. Killian and Kahmala appeared undisturbed, implying they knew she was around. C-Lo remained still, indicating that he also sensed her presence. Looking at her, the lack of emotion on her face doesn't overshadow her striking and seductive appearance at all. Immediately after she joined me at the sectional, I stood and delicately touched her back, then shifted my attention to Killian, Kahmala, and C-Lo.

"Guys give me a moment to talk to Ray." I turned to face Ray. *"Let me talk to you down the hall,"* I told her and waited for her to exit the room.

She stared at me without saying a word, and nodded, walking out of the room. I could see everyone exchanging glances as me and Ray left. I followed her down to the formal living room where she stood next to the couch with her right hip cocked up and her arms crossed looking at me with a nigga start talking expression. I decided to just get the shit over with.

"Yes, Ray, Chandra insists she's expecting my child, but I'm skeptical about both her pregnancy and my supposed paternity. I truly meant it when I told you I hadn't been with anyone since you left me. Jayce hosted a Christmas kickback that we all attended. I drank too much and ended up unconscious on his sofa. I woke up to that hoe riding my dick and damn near beat that hoe to death." I paused to take a deep breath. Looking in Ray's eyes I couldn't read her expression. So, I continued.

"I wasn't fuckin' around with her and I have never had sex with that hoe without protection. I don't think I even released because I instantly went soft when I realized it wasn't you ridin' my dick. So, when I told you I haven't been with anyone since you left, I meant that shit. I haven't touched another girl willingly since you left me. I was just afraid to tell you about that shit and you not wanting anything to do with me afterwards. You and Zan mean the world to me, and I have learned my lesson about cheating. From here on out, it's all about you. I told Kahmala about Chandra being pregnant because I'm not sure if she'll want to do the hit with her being pregnant. Some people have religious

beliefs, and I don't want to offend her with the request," I explained to Ray, not leaving anything out.

Ray didn't say anything for a long while. She just stared at me as I stared back at her. Finally, she took a deep breath and spoke. *"I know we have been apart for a long time and I never expected you to be celibate for all that time. You're a man and you have needs so I thought you might have been with many girls since then. I was too busy trying to survive to be worried about a man, and after we got settled there has been no one other than you who makes me want to give them my body. So, I wasn't upset about you having sex with her or anyone else while we were apart. My problem came with thinking you might have a baby coming with that girl. I don't know if I want to deal with the baby mama drama Zylar. My life has just started to be somewhat normal and I don't want to deal with more bullshit from anybody."* Ray told me and I could tell she has no plans on dealing with Chandra or any of her bullshit.

That strengthened my resolve to do what needs to be done. I walked over to Ray and wrapped her up in my arms. *"I understand Ray and I'm trying to get the shit with Chandra and Derricka handled as soon as possible. Zaylar wants them taken care of as well. That's why I have Killian and Kahmala here so I could give them the details to handle them hoes. I just don't like discussing this type of business around you, because I don't want you connected with this type shit,"* I told her as she leaned back from me looking crazy.

"Who the fuck is Derricka?" Ray asked, face a stoney glare, and I realized that I never told her about anything that went on last night. C-Lo was right. I have to tell Ray about all this shit, so she won't be out here caught unawares if they decide to jump stupid.

"Sorry baby I forgot I didn't tell you about all the bullshit that went on at the gathering yesterday. So, peep this. Jayce was fuckin' with the hoe Derricka who is friends with Chandra. He stopped fuckin' with her after he found out she was telling Chandra my whereabouts so she could pop-up on the scene. Last night she followed Jayce to Ma's old place and walked into the door like she was with Jayce. I snatched his ass up and told him to get that hoe out of there before she tried to start some shit. He pulled her out the house and she tried to make noise on her way out the door. Then she went got Chandra and brought her back over there causing a commotion down at the property gate. That's what I went to handle after I escorted Stephanie's dude out, and that's when she told me about

her being pregnant," I told her everything that happened trying to make sure I didn't leave anything out.

She started to shake her head, chuckling to herself.

'This shit is crazy. So, what are you gonna do to get this hoe in check, because I don't see her bowing out gracefully? If you take into consideration that you have been dealing with this girl ever since I left. I can't see it happening. If she hasn't given up in all this time. She's not." Ray said, still shaking her head.

"That's what you walked in on us discussing. Killian is gonna handle the dude from your job and Kahmala is gonna handle Chandra and Derricka. Normally we wouldn't bother with them for just stalking us because we have security, but since Chandra used to come get fucked at one of my brother's trap houses. She knows what we do, and we can't have her talking reckless about us being drug dealers. That shit could get to the wrong person and we all end up in jail. We still haven't found Eric and Biz, so this is some extra bullshit we don't need," I told Ray while rubbing my hand over my braids, getting more frustrated by the minute having to deal with this unnecessary bullshit.

"Wait. What do you mean by handling the dude from my job, and I thought Biz and Eric were your brother's boys? What happened?" She asked and I see now that I need to tell her everything, not just bits and pieces.

"It was around three months after you moved away that we found out that them niggas have been stealing from Zaylar. So Zaylar changed things up and cut them niggas off from all aspects of the business without telling them shit, but by the time we had everything moved around so we could make a move on them. They upped and disappeared. We have been looking for them all this time, but them niggas seems to have fallen off the face of the earth. We have eyes on most of their family members and we got rid of almost all the niggas that were a part of the crew back then, and that nigga that's been stalking you has been posted up outside of your apartment the last two nights until about 3 to 4am," I told Ray and waited for her reaction. Which didn't take long.

"What the fuck Zylar. That nigga has been out in the parking lot of my apartment building and you didn't say anything? I need to call and tell Mr. Gains so he can let Mrs. Coleman know to add it to my file, and I'm going to check about filing a restraining order on his ass. That nigga has a real problem with the word no. It's like he's never had a girl not be interested in his lame ass

before. These spoiled rich boys are truly a trip," she said and pulled her phone out to make a call.

Judging by the way she looked at me when she said *"these spoiled rich boys,"* makes me think she's lumping me in with that nigga stalking her. I don't know quite how to feel about her suggesting I'm a spoiled rich boy. So, I just stood back and watched as her face contorted into a frown the longer she listened to what was being said on the other end of the line. *"Okay Mr. Gains thanks for letting me know and give me your personal cell so I can contact you about a job. Let me talk to my new boss. He may have a job that's perfect for you, and I'm sorry you're being put in this position simply because you were doing your job. Wait let me key it in,"* Ray said as she took the phone from her ear, repeated the number back and ended her call.

"Well, I'll be damned. The Lord works in mysterious ways," Ray said while shaking her head.

"What do you mean, and what's going on?" I asked because she seemed to be extremely upset about the phone call.

"Mr. Gains just told me Mrs. Coleman was transferred to another district on Thursday, and the new district manager said there's not enough evidence to file a claim and get the police involved so they're dropping the case. He told me he gave his two weeks' notice and is looking for another job because he can no longer work for Mr. Wells with him trying to pull this shit. I'm going to ask Myron if the dealership can use a highly qualified license to carry top quality security guard. Mr. Gains said he can no longer work there since Mr. Wells is trying to sweep what his son was doing to me under the rug. I hope Myron can give him a job because Mr. Gains is the sole reason I'm not in jail right now for fucking Maine up," she told me and I pulled my phone out to call Myron.

"Yo My I need you to add security out at the dealership since the girls will be there and they handle large sums of money daily. I wanna make sure Ray and the girls are protected and her security detail can't protect her and stay invisible if they are posted up inside her job," I told that nigga and he surprised me with what he said next.

"I already know Zy, but it's going to take some time. I put in a call to the different security companies around town to get some resumes' to look over, but they all said they'll send me over something later today. I don't feel too good about them not having security there when they start, and it will take time to

vet somebody for the position and do the background checks. We can't just have anybody working at one of our businesses with all we have going on," he told me letting me know he was worried about the girl's well being too.

"Ray has someone who's licensed to carry and can start today. You want me to have him meet y'all out there today? In fact, let me let you talk to Ray so she can give you all the information while I go take care of some shit with Killian and Kahmala," I told him and passed Ray my phone as I headed back to the mancave to let them know they can handle the situation however they see fit.

When I walked in all three of them seemed to be engrossed in the movie. Once again, the movie was at the part where they were laying muthafuckas down wearing all black with big bags on their backs. I couldn't wait to take some time out and watch this shit. Just from the little bit I've seen I know it's gone be good as hell.

"Killian it's for sure a go on that little nigga. His people must have some pull around here because they got Ray's whole case thrown out and transferred the district manager out and put one in place to cover the shit up," I told him and then I looked over at Kahmala.

"No, Kahmala, I don't care about you killing that hoe with her being pregnant. I just didn't want to offend you by asking you to do something that went against your beliefs. If you're fine with it, I'm for sure fine with it. I want that hoe gone like yesterday," I told her as she stared at me with an intensity I couldn't understand until she spoke.

"You found your one. I can tell, because your energy is different. You seem more balanced. Good for you, because the way you used to act was gonna have you sad and lonely until you were in your 50's." She laughed as Ray came back into the room.

"Ray come here and let me introduce you to Kahmala and Killian," I told her and she came and stood between my legs waiting.

"Kahmala this is Raylexia and she's my world, and Ray this is who you call when you want a bitch taken care of," I told them and Ray rolled her eyes like I was joking.

"Nice to meet you Kahmala. Sorry it's under these circumstances. Are you busy tomorrow at noon? We are all meeting at the Pierre Bossier Mall to do some retail therapy and you're welcome to come. That way I can introduce you to all my girls and let them know we got back up when we need to fuck somebody up."

Ray laughed as her and Kahmala exchanged contact info and kept right on talking like we weren't there.

"Well damn. Am I invisible in this bitch?" Killian laughed, liking the fact that Kahmala seemed to be comfortable talking with Ray. She didn't fool around with females other than her sister Kilayla, so I know Killian is just happy about her being so cool with talking to Ray.

C-Lo answered his phone and then started smiling. I knew instantly he was talking to Shamena. That's when it dawned on me that Ray was supposed to be at school, but here she was at home. I waited for her and Kahmala to have a break in their conversation and asked, *"Ray why are you not at school?"*

"Oh, I forgot to tell you when I first came in since I got sidetracked by the discussion you were having. All my classes for today were canceled because there was a big commotion at the school involving one of their major alumnus that contributes thousands to the school each year. I'm just waiting for the girls to call me so we can head to the bank and open their accounts. I can't wait to see the properties where we will have the shop. I have all types of ideas for promotion and advertisement that I want to try. Thank you so much Zylar for helping us make our dream come true." Ray told me while smiling hard.

"Aye Zylar the girls are done with class, so they are headed back to the apartment to wait for Ray. I'm about to go get the truck with three movers and another supply of boxes setup while I do some of my pickups. You wanna handle the ones in Bossier and Benton while I head to the northside? That way we'll be done by time they finish at the bank and seeing the property with Myron and the contractor." That nigga told me like I forgot I was gone help him do his pickups since he helped me get my shit moved in this morning.

"Alright just tell me which stops I need to make, and I'll head that way. Ray, I'll meet you at the dealership because I wanna meet the new security guy and show him some photos of muthafuckas to look out for," I told Ray and gave her a kiss while grabbing a handful of her ass. We all headed out together and just as Ray set the house alarm and we closed and locked the door; I got a call from Jayce.

"What's up nigga? That babysitting job too much for you. You need some help?" I asked that nigga as I popped the locks on my car and slid in behind the wheel.

"Zy man y'alls cousin is gone. I don't know where she went but she hasn't been in her room all morning. The last time I checked on her was 12am and she was up crying. So, I have no idea where she can be. At first, I thought she went down for the morning buffet, but when 10am hit and she still hadn't returned to her room I got worried and called you. Oh, and another thing, there's no forced entry or anything out of place. She left here of her own free will. So, what do you want me to do?" Jayce asked me, sounding frustrated as hell.

"You stay put for the moment. Let me holla at Zaylar and Nico to see what they want us to do. You can't go back to your crib until Myron finds you something new anyway, so just check on your pickups and sit tight. It may not be nothing or she can be on some fuck shit," I told that Nigga and hung-up to call Zaylar.

I don't know what Stephanie has going on, but I don't like the way she's moving. Everything about her sudden appearance around Ma seems odd, and I'm getting a funny feeling about it all. Why the fuck would she leave the hotel where she was safe with Jayce? It doesn't make any sense.

CHAPTER FOURTEEN
Zaylar "Stone" Crewens

After getting off the phone with Nico and Zylar we all decided to make our way over to Ma's house to make sure she didn't give Stephanie her new address or help her out in any way. If she wanted our help she would've stayed at the hotel with Jayce. Since she left, that lets me know she's on some other bullshit. We all know Ma has a good heart by nature, but we don't know what Stephanie's trying to do. If she's trying to set Ma up, her parents are gonna be one daughter short around this bitch.

It took me 15 min to get to Ma's place from Zander's Realty on Fern Ave where I have set up my base of operation for the legitimate side of the business. After taking the online business class suggested by Myron and C-Lo I found out that starting up new businesses and helping hardworking black people that are highly skilled, but less fortunate start their own business can be very rewarding. After putting all the drugs on the streets that I have over the years this is my way of giving back to the community. The added bonus is the tax write-off I get.

With the help of C-Lo and Myron my family now own Stone's Movers & Trucking Warehouse & Storage, Indigo Strip Club, Zan's Exotic Cars, 3 Della's Dry Cleaners and Laundry, 2 Zay's Automotive & Detail, 5 Zy's Premium Cuts Barber Shops, Zander's Realty, Stone Condominiums, and Key Stone Construction Company with plans of purchasing foreclosed businesses downtown to renovate to make upscale apartments. Nico has even purchased a building downtown and started to renovate it into his personal law firm that he plans to co-own with Josie. In just a little over 6 months C-Lo and Myron have helped us more than tripled the money we have made on the streets through completely legitimate means. If I wanted to stop dealing today I could and still live the same without it putting a dent in my incoming income.

When I pulled up at Ma's house, I saw that Zylar and Nico were already there and waiting out front puffing on a blunt. For Nico to be smoking knowing he has to go back to work is telling. I wasted no time exiting my car and walking up to them niggas.

"What's good?" I asked and dapped up both Zy and Nico while reaching for the blunt and taking a long deep pull.

"Ain't shit." Nico said, but I could tell he was agitated.

"Yeah, ain't shit." Zylar replied looking even more upset than Nico.

"Okay what the fuck is going on?" I asked both of them niggas because they seemed to be holding on by a thread.

"Where to start?" Nico replied and went on to tell me that Stephanie showed up at the courthouse this morning beat the fuck up and the judge granted her the restraining order and put out a warrant for the nigga Tyrone's arrest. He tricked Stephanie's stupid ass into coming out the hotel and beat her damn near to death. She called her parents, and they came to take her to the hospital and went to court with her this morning. They also let her come back home until she could get herself together.

"The reason I want you guys to talk to Ma with me is I feel that Stephanie has a hidden agenda. That nigga didn't just start to whippin her as and she could have been got her parents involved. So why now? To be safe I don't want Ma letting anybody on y'alls daddy side of the family know where she lays her head. I can't place it, but something feels off." Nico said looking distressed.

Today he was dressed in a custom made charcoal grey Armani suit with a white silk button up shirt, silk light purple tie, and matching purple Mezlan men's crocodile dress shoes. With his 6'6½" frame all of his clothes were customer made and expensive as hell. In my opinion our father's family has caused him too much grief for him to even be involved in trying to help Stephanie in the first place. Ma over looks all the shit they do because she's never been subjected to the negative treatment, and she has no idea about the ill treatment Nico has suffered. I keep telling him he needs to let Ma know so she can cut ties with them for good. Pops is gone now and we're all grown. Our grandparents will definitely understand.

"I agree with you on that Nico. We don't really fuck with none of them folks anyway. I still can't believe they had the audacity to try and take the insurance from us when Pops passed. He helped most of them muthafuckas start businesses and purchase their homes and they tried to handle us like we didn't deserve to get our share of the money from the insurance Ma had him in." Zylar ranted, making me look over at Nico. He and I both know that what Zylar really means is they had a problem with Nico getting his share of the insurance as stated in Pop's will.

He left everything he owned to Ma, me, Nico, and Zylar. He had already set his parents up nicely so they will be good until they passed on, but he didn't leave his brothers and sisters nothing. The crazy thing that everyone in that family tends to forget is Nico is set for life. He gets an automatic deposit of $10,000 every month and has been since he was born. That Nigga has never wanted for nothing.

"We still have the PI looking into their situation so hopefully he'll get back to us soon. We just have to have James tighten up Ma's security until we get it handled," I told both of them and took one last pull on the blunt before handing it back over to Nico.

"I got Kahmala on that situation with Chandra and Derricka, and Killian is handling the situation with the Nigga that's been stalking Ray," Zylar said getting both Nico's and my attention.

"What do you mean stalking Ray?" Nico asked looking at Zylar with a mean mug so deadly I had to step forward worried he'd attack Zy.

"Shit man I forgot I didn't tell you guys about it with all the other shit we have going on. My bad." Then Zylar went on to tell us about what the lil nigga been doing over the last few days and the fact her job dropped the investigation and never filed an official report with the police on Ray's behalf.

"Okay Zylar this is what I need you and Ray to do. If the security guard and the district manager are willing to give a statement, have them come talk to me on Monday. Get Ray to come down to the courthouse once you're done getting the girls settled today so she can file a restraining order and file stalking charges. I don't like the fact that his family had enough pull to get the company she works for to just drop the case with clear proof of the violation. They either have a stake in the company or they are wealthy enough to let their money make it disappear. Getting the paperwork filed will help us just in case Zylar ends up

having to protect her and goes to jail." Nico told us both and jumped on his phone to call the judge.

"Damn when it rains it pours around this bitch. The last thing we want is to have to deal with the police, but I'd rather Ray be safe than hurt because we don't fuck with them pigs." Zylar expressed while rubbing a hand over his braids. A sure sign of his distress.

Nico ended his call and placed his phone in his pocket while approaching us. *"Zylar I need you to have Raylexia drop by my office so I can get all the information we have available in the system on Mr Wells, because if he is doing this shit and his family is making the charges disappear this swiftly. I have a feeling it's not the first time this has happened involving him and a female worker at that job. If that's the case, Ray has a good chance of suing the company in a civil suit. The contractor is almost finished with our building downtown so Josie will be opening our law offices in a couple of months. Raylexia can be our first civil case,"* he nodded. *'Let's get this over with,"* he said and walked up to Ma's door and rang the bell. We all had keys, but we would never invade Ma's privacy by just barging in unannounced.

It took Ma a minute to answer and when she saw it was us her face broke into a huge smile. *"I get to see all my babies two days in a row, let me see if the sky is falling outside."* Ma made jokes while looking up and around at the sky.

"I see you got jokes old lady." Nico told Ma while giving her a hug and kiss to the forehead and continuing on to the sitting room off the foyer. Zy and I hugged Ma and waited until she locked the door and we all headed in after Nico.

Zylar and I walked on either side of Ma into the family room. Ma had it decked out with two oversized sectionals positioned to face each other with a functional coffee table in the middle. Everything was of high quality and durable enough to handle the kids playing in the room. Ma truly created a place to enjoy her grandkids.

"What's wrong? Did something happen? Is my daughters-in-law, okay?" Ma asked question after question while getting all worked up.

"Sorry to worry you Ma. The girls are ok, but we came to talk to you about Stephanie." Nico said as he got up and guided Ma over to the sectional so we all could sit around her as we talked.

"Oh, you guys had me worried something had happened to my girls. I talked to Stephanie and her parents this morning after they left the courthouse. Joyce called me to see if Stephanie could stay with me until they got the issue settled with that boy. Sadly, I had to let them know that I don't know Stephanie well enough to have her staying in my home. I offered to let her keep staying at the hotel until y'all were able to catch that Tyrone boy, and we'd pay the bill, but they wanted her to stay with me. We still have everyone thinking I still live in the old place and until it has been sold. I wanna keep it that way. They turned down my offer because Joyce claims the boy has been out to the hotel and he knows which one she was staying at. So they want her to live with me because I have my own security, and they feel she would be safe with me. I told them she was safe last night with Jayce until she left the hotel to meet with her boyfriend. I don't know what they have going on, and I'm sorry for Stephanie being in that situation, but I don't fuck with them like that to have that child staying with me." Ma shocked us all by saying.

We all burst out laughing and got up hugging Ma tight. Ma looked at us all like we were crazy and then sat back on the sectional and gave us the side eye. *"What did you all think that I was gone be stupid enough to let that little girl that I have not seen nor heard from in over 3 years just come lay up in my home? I keep telling y'all I ain't new to this life. I'm true to this. All the new games you youngsters are playing have already been played. They just changed the name, not the game."* Ma told us, leaving us all stunned.

We all talked to Ma a while longer and expressed our concern that something was going on with Pop's people and for her to keep her distance from them. Nico headed to his crib to shower and change so he could head back to the courthouse. Zylar took off to complete some runs for C-Lo. Since I have some time before I have to meet up with them all at the dealership, I decided to go break things off with Nisha and Alania. No time like the present to get the shit over with. Pulling out my phone I hit up Alania to see if she was at work. If so, I can stop by when I leave here since her job is only 20 min away.

She picked up on the third ring all agitated like I was disturbing her by calling. *"Yes. What can I do for you Zay?"* She said in a dry ass tone pissing me the fuck off.

Alania has some good pussy and fire head, but she's looking for a commitment and too bad for her I'm not interested in her ass that way. I shoulda dropped her ass a while ago after she started with this dry ass attitude, but I kept her on my roster because she's convenient and I'm lazy. One-night stands are fine for the occasional hook-up, but I rarely feel like putting in that type of effort so that's why I kept Alania around. After hearing how she's trying to handle me I decided not to trouble myself by giving her the courtesy of cutting her off in person.

"You know what Alania? You can't do shit for me anymore. Lose my fuckin' number. We're done," I told that hoe as I hung up the phone and blocked her number. I hate to disrespect women, but some of these hoes will take you there.

I called Nisha and she answered on the first ring like always. *"Yo. What's up sexy?"* She said making me laugh. Nisha is ghetto as fuck but cool people. We were friends before we started fuckin' and I hate it's come to this, but I know it's better to cut her off completely then to still be friends and Johnya find out we use to fuck.

"Aye, are you busy right now, or can I drop by the salon and holla at you right quick?" I asked her to see if she's with a client.

"You know I'm never too busy for you Zay, but I don't have a client and my next one won't be here for an hour. See you when you get here," she told me, sounding all happy.

"Alright bet. See you in 20 min," I told her and hung up the phone.

I checked my caller id to see how much time I got before I have to meet up and handle that business at the dealership. Seeing I'm good on time, I relax and make my way to Nisha. I pulled in from the back of the lot and I can see Nisha outside arguing with some tall buff light skinned nigga with dreads. I saw him snatch her up and prepared to jump out and handle his ass until I saw her hug that Nigga and give him a heated kiss. Well, I'll be damned. It looks like Nisha is gone be good. I smiled as I pulled up right next to them and exited my car.

Nisha noticed me and pulled out of the embrace while continuing to hold that Nigga's hand and leading him over to me. *"Hey Zay. I want you to meet Axel, and Axel this is my A1 from day one Zay."* She introduced us while grinning hard as hell.

"What's up?" I hit him with a head nod, and he did the same. I could tell the Nigga was sizing me up and I was doing the same with him. He looked familiar but I couldn't remember him or place his face. Then it registered what she said the Nigga's name was.

"Aye your name Axel "Blade" Greene?" I asked that Nigga and saw him still while looking at me with a hard expression.

"Yeah. That's me. How do you know my government name?" He said and I saw that Nigga whole demeanor change. He went from cautious to deadly in one point two seconds. I most definitely got to get this Nigga on my team.

"I know your government because your Pop's Switchblade used to be a hitta for my Pops Zander. Last I heard he left town after Pops got hit-up. We need to talk asap," I told that Nigga while giving him the same energy he's giving me. I want him on the team but ain't no hoe in my blood. Stone is always ready to come out and play.

He looked at me hard and then relaxed. *"I don't remember your face, but you do seem familiar. My Pops was never the same after your Pops was killed. He kept saying he knew something bad was gonna happen that day he just couldn't put his finger on where the shit was coming from. After he took care of the niggas that did the hit, he kept saying them young niggas couldn't be the head. I never figured out what he meant by that, and he hasn't been the same since,"* he said while looking off in the distance.

"Well, I came to let Nisha know I found my one, but I see I don't have to worry about her anymore. Take good care of her, she's one of a kind. Fuck up and you'll have to see me," I told him while looking over at Nisha still holding that Nigga's hand and grinning hard as hell.

"Aye Nigga I don't do threats, and I got her. She told me about you, and that y'alls friendship means the world to her. She said y'all had sex but your more of a brother to her than anything else, and she hates that y'all even took it there because whoever y'all got with would probably never be okay with y'alls friendship," he told me letting me know that Nisha feels the same way I do about the situation.

"I feel the same. Nisha has been my ace since middle school, and it's gonna be hard not being able to tell her about the bullshit I have going on and getting her unbiased opinion. Talking to Nisha is just like kicking it with the fellas from a girl's point of view," I told him I was already feeling the loss of my ace.

"I have no problem with y'alls friendship because I know she belongs to me. If you can take her or make her stray, that just means she was never mine in the first place," he said with confidence while devouring Nisha with his eyes.

"Bet. That's good to hear. Now I just gotta get my girl to see it that way," I told that nigga as Nisha cut her eye's over at me.

"You have a girl. Since when?" Nisha asked me while placing her hands on her hips and giving me her full attention.

"Yo Nisha, don't get fucked up out here." Blade told her while smirking. I could tell he truly had no fear that she wanted anybody but him.

"Since yesterday. I told you Zylar was having a get together for us to meet his girl, and I met my one. You'll love her Nisha. She seems quiet, but I know for a fact she's all fire," I said and Nisha gave me the skew face.

"TMI Nigga. I love you but we don't need to know all that," she said while laughing and hugging Blade.

"After we get some things settled and I make sure she's cool with us continuing to kick it, I want to introduce you to her and her girls. She's one of Zy's girl Ray's best friends, and I feel you and them will really hit it off. They're nothing like the other girls that we used to have around so I know you guys will be cool," I said to her, making plans to sit down and talk to Johnya about her tonight.

"Blade I need to holla at you about some work if you're interested. I know your dad was the best hitta in the business, but he left town after Pops was killed and he handled them Niggas that killed him. I have some shit to handle later today, but if you're in the same line of work as your Pops I'd like to put you on my team. Give me your contact info and meet me over at Zan's Exotic Cars on Bert Kouns in the Auto Mall at 4pm. I have a job that I feel is tailor made for you. Is your younger brother Steel in the business as well?" I asked that Nigga ready to put him to work. If we can use this Nigga and his brother to find Biz and Eric, I feel we can all finally relax and start living without having to look over our shoulders.

"Yeah. We both are in the business and we work as a team on most jobs. We just moved back to town a little over a year ago. Pops missed his people and Miami was too fake for us. I had to come home and find me a girl with cornbread fed hips, ass, and tits. All of them hoes out there are store bought. Nothing is real

all the way down to their feelings." Blade told me looking like he sucked on a lemon.

I couldn't help but laugh at him, because these bitches were truly on that build a body tip right now. *"Alright, I hear you Bruh. Bring your brother with you if y'all or interested in the job and I'll see y'all later on."* I gave him a dap and hugged Nisha before I jumped in my ride and headed out to the dealership. I wanted to make sure the little surprise I had setup for Johnya was ready.

When I pulled up to the dealership, I made a full circle around the lot just checking out how things were running. The service & parts center and detail shop were both packed. After we bought the business from Shortie Myron and C-Lo had the lot renovated and brought the adjoining two properties so we could expand the services we offer. So far as I know we have eight licensed mechanics and five certified detailers on staff, with a fully operational parts division to service all makes and models. Connected to the back over by the sales department is the full service detail shop where we do custom paint jobs and corrections, body work with ceramic coating, and full-service auto detailing car wash. All combined to provide the perfect cover for the chop shop in the back where we destroy the cars, we have to get rid of. Seeing that everything looks to be running correctly on the lot I decided to get out and walk around to the sales floor.

Coming in from the back I was able to peep Deuce trying to make the Manager we hired to run the business sell a car for more of a discount then we approved. *"Nigga if I say he can have the car for more than the $5,000 discount that Myron and Cree approved all you need to do is make it happen."*

"I can't and won't approve that and I'll be letting Mr. Dax know that you have been trying to make me do other things that they have not approved as well. I don't work for you. I work for Mr. Crewens and until I hear something different from him, all the new things you're trying to get us to do will not be happening, and the sales floor is no place for this discussion. If you want to talk to me about anything else, you can come to my office, but this matter is closed. No extra discount unless Mr. Dax or Mr. Logan approves it." Mr. Smith told him and walked off toward his office behind the glass doors.

Just hearing this shit has me heated. No wonder C-Lo and Myron want to get rid of this Nigga, he ain't nothing but another snake. I decided to test him and Mr. Smith. I walked in like I had just arrived and heard nothing.

One of the salesmen on the floor spotted me first and rushed over to greet me.

"Hey Mr. Crewens, we have the Audi Q7 in the detail shop getting cleaned up. If you want to test drive it before Mrs. West picks it up the carpet should already be dry. Mr. Smith said you wanted to add the ceramic coating to the finish and do a full-service check on the vehicle, so they took it back first thing this morning. I can have them bring it around so you can inspect it." John Lewis told me as he made his way back over to his desk and grabbed the phone.

I noticed Mr. Smith making his way to me and Deuce trying to cut him off, but Mr. Smith was determined and stepped around Deuce to greet me. *"Hi Mr. Crewens. We have added the changes to the SUV that you requested so the car will be out soon. Do you have a moment, I need to speak with you in private?"* He said all in one breath like he was afraid Deuce would stop me from hearing him out.

"Sure, let's step into your office," I told Mr. Smith and then I turned to Deuce and called him by his government.

"Steve I'll talk to you when I'm done," I said to that Nigga while giving him the death stare and followed Mr. Smith to his office.

We barely had the door shut before Mr. Smith started. Just listening to all the shit that Deuce had going on farther confirmed that I really should have gotten rid of all of them Niggas from that old crew when I found out about Biz and Eric. I'll be correcting that shit today.

"Mr. Smith I hired you to run my business because you are highly qualified and came highly recommended. Other than the things I have relayed to you through Mr. Dax and Mr. Logan, no one else has the authority to question what you do here. You are the Head Nigga In Charge at this dealership. Steve don't run nothing but his mouth, and after today he won't be working here anymore or be allowed on the premises. Not even to purchase an automobile. Do I make myself clear?" I asked Mr. Smith in all seriousness. I need him to run this business properly because this is one of our top money makers.

Mr Smith was a 36 year old car salesman that I poached from the Ford Dealership. He has an athletic build and strong facial features. He won me over with his smile and outgoing personality. But best of all, he knows everything there is to know about selling cars, so I had Myron recruit him. Ever since he took over the dealership has been prospering.

"Yes, Mr. Crewens, I understand and thank you for taking care of that situation. Once he's gone, I feel Mr. Tate will start to perform better. He has a knack for selling cars especially to older women. Mr. McCray has no interest in learning the business or helping to sell cars. His only interest was in sleeping with the office staff in the restrooms and sleeping in the office." Mr. Smith answered my next question about how well David "AnDro" Tate was doing. I'd hate to think that my whole crew was made up of nothing but snakes before I put Zylar's crew on, but that's what it's shaping up to be.

"Steve McCray is terminated as of right now. Call in a locksmith now to change all the locks and reset the alarm codes. Also change out the safe codes and deposit drop times. We are adding armed security today so that should put your mind at ease. You take care of all that and I'll go give Mr. McCray his walking papers," I told Mr. Smith and headed out front to see Myron, C-Lo, AnDro and an older gentleman I don't recognize standing up front talking to Deuce.

I walked up to that Nigga Deuce and snatched him up by the neck. I dragged his ass to Myron's office and waited for Myron to unlock the door. I pushed that Nigga into one of the chairs in front of Myron's desk as Myron, AnDro and C-Lo piled into the office and closed the door. Myron's office is the only one in the building that has walls instead of glass so no one can see what's going on.

"So, you think it's okay to steal from me Nigga? Since when do you have the authority to give extra discounts on the cars we sell? Did you go to auction and purchase some merchandise I have no knowledge of? Do you have a major contract with the various model distributors to sell their product? NO, you don't. This is my shit. You worked for me. Now I want you to tell me why I shouldn't put a bullet in your brain for stealing my money," I said in a low deadly tone and whipped my nine out, placing it under his chin.

"W-What do you mean steal from you? I haven't stolen anything." That Nigga said trying to take a deep breath around my hand crushing his windpipe.

"Oh, so when did it become okay for you to give customers $10,000 to $15,000 off the market price of a car? Why have the deposits for the dealership been coming up more than $15,000 to $20,000 short when you handle the drop off? Since when is it okay for you to bring people in to get custom work done for free? If you ain't stealing, then where is my money for all that shit Nigga?"

I asked that Nigga while squeezing his throat even tighter. I had the urge to snatch that Nigga's throat out with my bare hands for playing with me like I'm a joke.

"I-I.." He started but stopped when I snapped and went to bashing that Nigga across his head with my gun.

I had so much pent up animosity towards this nigga after all I'd done for him and he shitty on my efforts. *"Is this what being nice or cool with these niggas is leading too?"*

"Zay man you buggin. You can't be up in here beating this Nigga down in broad daylight. Let us call Killian and Kahmala to come pick this Nigga up. It's too many eyes here to deal with him like this." Myron preached as him, C-Lo, and AnDro struggled to pull me up off that Nigga.

I snapped out of my trance to see I had fucked that Nigga up along with having sprayed blood all over the desk and chairs in the office. I released that Nigga and stood up breathing hard as hell. *"C-Lo get Killian and Kahmala to come pick this Nigga up. Check his pockets and get his phone. Have Pete check on who this Nigga been in contact with. I wanna know the full extent of what he has been doing. Something ain't right in the water. Myron, get Khiershan and Kilayla in here to clean up this mess."* I told them Niggas and turned to AnDro.

"AnDro is there a reason Deuce had all this shit going on at my place of business and you neglected to tell me about it?" I asked that Nigga in a soft deadly tone. Everybody in the office knew that Stone had taken over and there wasn't gonna be no mercy given.

I went to school with AnDro, Deuce, Stacy, Eric, Jay, and Red. We all grew up together so I put them on when I got the chance. AnDro was a skinny nigga with light skin and a pretty boy smile. He'd worked hard to help support his family, so I hope I won't end up having to kill his ass.

"I had no idea he had all this going on, Zay. Shit the most I knew we both fucked a couple of the workers in the restroom. I knew nothing about him stealing from you, shit had I known about it I woulda murked his ass myself. This is the first time I have ever been able to make decent money from legitimate work, and I appreciate you setting me up with this job. I am no longer throwing bricks at the penitentiary just to make ends meet, and my mom is happy I'm no

longer in the streets." AnDro told me while looking me straight in the eye. I knew he was being sincere because I could see it in his eyes.

"*Alright AnDro that's good to hear, because Mr. Smith said he thinks he can make you a good salesman and teach you more about the business. You play your cards right and you'll be running this bitch. That was my soul purpose for putting you and Deuce over here, to have somebody I know and trust running my shit. It's sad this Nigga finna loose his life behind stealing money I woulda' gave him if he asked,*" I told that Nigga while heading to the restroom connected to Myron's office to see how much blood I got in my clothes. It's a good thing I keep a change of clothes in my ride.

I washed the blood off my hands and took off my sweater and coat. I'll just have to rock my wife beater until I get my change of clothes out the car. I pulled everything out of my coat pockets and stuffed them in my jeans. Then I turned the coat inside out and put my sweater inside. Confident I didn't have any blood visible left on my clothes and shoes, I exited the restroom to find AnDro, C-Lo, and Myron in the office with shop towels, bleach, and trash bags wiping up the blood off the surfaces. They zip tided that Nigga Deuce hands and feet and had him balled up in the corner sitting on plastic. I grabbed a trash bag and stuffed my coat inside to give to Kilaya to burn.

"*How long will it be before Killian and Kahmala get here?*" I asked no one in particular.

"*They're on their way. They had to pick up the van and change into a jumpsuit. Killian, Kahmala, Khiershan, and Kilayla will be here in 20 min.*" Myron answered while wiping down the chair in front of his desk.

"*Good. Give this bag to Kilaya so she can get rid of it. I'll be right back. Let me go get my bag out of the car so I can change my clothes,*" I told them and headed out the back exit to my ride.

Cree "C-Lo" Logan

I can't believe Zaylar snapped and damn near murked this Nigga in the office with all these witnesses around. That Nigga was not thinking at all. I know how he feels after hearing about all the shit Deuce was doing, but damn. That Nigga Stone took over and Zay had no control. I keep telling these Niggas we work with, that just because Zay is cool, don't mean he's soft. He's been in the game since he was in his early teens getting it out the mud, so we all know he has earned his spot. I guess he needs to let that Nigga Stone come out to play with these muthafuckas who have forgotten who the fuck he is.

It didn't take long for Killian and Kahmala to show up to pick up Deuce and Khiershan and Kilayla cleaned out the office. Once they were all done, the rest of us all went back out front to see the older dude from earlier still standing there waiting. I walked over to find out if I could help him. *"Hi. How can I help you?"* I asked while extending my hand for a shake.

"Hello. My name is Gerald Gains and I'm here to see Myron Dax about the security position," he said as he introduced himself and shook my hand.

"I'm sorry about the wait Mr. Gains. I'm Cree Logan. Let me get Myron, Zay, and Mr. Smith over here to meet you," I told him and signaled for Zay to come over.

Mr Gains was a middle aged black man, with a medium stocky build and a friendly disposition. Just looking at him I could tell he was easy going and would blend into the background at the dealership.

"What's up?" Zay said as he walked up. This Nigga changed into an all-black Nike hoodie, black Gucci jeans, and black Timbs. If it wasn't for the iced-out Z platinum chain around his neck, and the platinum Rolex watch he was sporting. His ass would look like he's going on a hit. He just letting all his thuggish ways hang out on display.

"Mr. Crewens this is Mr. Gains. He's here for the security position at the lot. He was told to come see Myron today. Mr. Gains, this is Mr. Crewens the owner of the dealership," I told them and they both shook hands.

"Yo My come here for a second and bring Mr. Smith with you." Zay called out and Myron's head snapped up from talking to Mr. Smith, and they both headed our way.

Myron and Mr. Smith walked up and I made quick introductions. We all talked about the job particulars and had Mr. Gains fill out his paperwork. Zaylar asked him what his salary was at his previous job and tripled it and made him head of security for the dealership. Afterwards we all walked around the property and Mr. Gains showed us hot spots and additional places where we need to install more video surveillance cameras. He also let Zay know that he needs at least three additional security guards to adequately protect the property. By the time we finished working out the particulars and showed Mr. Gains to the office he would be using, Zylar and the girls showed up.

They all met Mr. Smith and filled out their paperwork. Then Myron and Mr. Smith showed them to their desk and started training them in their positions. Since all their jobs were slightly different, they all wanted to learn each position so they can fill in if one of them needs to be out. Mr. Smith was pleasantly surprised and impressed by them and told them so. Me, Zylar and Zaylar were just following them around, serving no purpose, so Zaylar asked us if we wanted to go out back and take a smoke. As we headed for the back of the lot, I saw Zaylar stop and turn towards two giant light skinned Niggas with dreads and a menacing presence heading for the entrance to the building.

"Aye yo Blade. Over here." Zay called out and the guys looked up and headed in our direction.

"Thanks for coming guys. This is C-Lo and my little brother Zylar. C-Lo and Zy this is Blade and his brother Steel." Zay introduced us and we all dapped up.

"Follow us to the back so we can all hit this blunt and talk privately." Zay said as we all made our way to the covered benches at the back of the lot, the employees used for smoke breaks.

Once we made it to the benches Zay wasted no time pulling out three blunts and putting them in rotation. After we had all taken at least two pulls off the weed Zaylar started to talk.

"I would like to have you guys join my team and be my exclusive hittas. That means if we have beef in the streets or some niggas that need to be handled you guys will take care of it quickly and quietly. This will work differently than contract work because you guys will be on the payroll and get a check every week regardless of us having beef or not. Working for me does not mean you can't take outside work. As long as you handle any situation that arises and don't take a conflicting contract, y'all can work other jobs with no blowback from me. So, what do y'all say? Are you both interested?" Zay asked as he pulled out another blunt and lit it up.

"Wait. Are you telling us that we get paid regardless of us having to put in work or not? And we can take other contracts from outside clients as long as it doesn't interfere with our work for you and is not from a client that has beef with you?" Steel asked with an incredulous look on his face.

"That's exactly what I'm telling you. In order to keep you guys on payroll as my exclusive hittas, I have to compensate for your time even if we don't have any beef for you to handle at the time. You still need to be paid, so when some shit jumps off you just step in and handle it. That keeps my guys out of the beef in the streets so they can concentrate on making that money. In the end it's a win-win all the way round." Zay told them, surprising the hell out of me. I thought that's what we had Killian, Kahmala, Kilayla, and Khiershan for.

"Shit I'm in. Just let me know a little more about what you expect and what we need to handle right now." Blade said and turned to his brother. *"What about you Steel? You in?"*

"Hell yeah. I'm in. I just want to know when do we start?" Steel said, making us all laugh.

"First things first. The pay will be roughly $7,000 a month unless you have to travel out of town. In those cases, I will raise it up to $10,000 so you can cover your expenses. For your first job I need you both to locate and kill Stacy "Biz" Clay and Eric Taylor. We have a $500,000 bounty on both of them Niggas heads dead or alive. Preferably dead. You take them out, the million is yours on top of your base salary. Them niggas stole from me and I really am not sure how deep the betrayal goes with that situation, because I keep finding more snakes

from that old crew." Zaylar said, sounding tired and disgusted. I can't blame him with all the shit he found out today.

"*Yo Zay, what about Killian, Khiershan, Kilayla, and Kahmala? Are you cutting them loose?*" Zylar asked the question I had uppermost in my mind.

"*Hell no!*" Zay looked at Zy like he had grown a new head. "*Why the fuck would I cut loose four of the best hittas and cleaners in the business. I'm just adding Blade and Steel to the team. Their Pops Switchblade used to work for Pops, and he was the most thorough hitta in the south. Pops said no one could track and kill faster and more efficiently than Switch. If he trained his sons, I want them working for us, not against us.*" Zay told us all while lighting up a new blunt. If he keeps taken them blunts to the head that Nigga gone be fucked up by the time we leave.

"*Well, that makes sense, but you know you gotta make time for us to introduce them, so they don't bump heads out in the streets. Kahmala can be a handful. I don't want her killing off the new crew,*" Zylar said while reaching for the blunt.

"*I need to get the top members of the crew together along with Killian, Khiershan, Kilayla, and Kahmala to meet up at the Jordan Street Rec Center tonight so I can introduce them to Steel and Blade. C-Lo you and Zylar call everybody and let them know to be there at 8pm. Have Myron get Shanna to cater a meal for 20 people. Tell him to do the pick-up and use her delivery truck. We want this all to be legit so we can welcome Blade and Steel to the team properly. Any questions?*" Zay asked and we all conversed about the changes until Zaylar told them to come on, let's go inside to fill out their paperwork. Everybody that works for us is on payroll at one of the businesses so that Myron can funnel the drug money through each business and clean it properly. That Nigga has degrees in both business and finance, so he set it up, so that Zaylar cleans the dirty money as soon as we make it.

We entered the building and headed over to Mr. Smith's office so he could get Steel and Blade started on their paperwork. Just as we were about to knock, I saw Shamena opening up the door while looking down at the paperwork in her hands. She started forward and walked right into Blade. "*Axel is that you?*" She said with tears in her eyes.

"*Shamena!*" Blade said while hugging her tightly.

"Shamena!" Steel said and he joined Blade surrounding Shamena in a hug while she cried.

What the fuck is going on. Both of them Niggas were hugging my girl and looking her over carefully. My first thought was one of jealous possession and I reached to separate them. Before I could touch them, Blade broke off from the embrace and pulled out his phone. *"Pops, we found Shamena. We're at "Zan's Exotic Cars" on Bert Kouns in the Auto Mall. Come quick Pops and tell Aunt Andria."* Blade hung up the phone and stepped back over to Shamena and Steel to talk.

I calmed down a bit after learning these were her people, but I still found it hard to accept them touching on my woman.

Peeping the situation, Zaylar told them to move around to Myron's office and for Mr. Smith to get two hire packages and send them over along with Myron.

Shamena broke off from Blade and Steel and walked into my arms crying. *"Don't cry, Beast. This is a good thing, right?"* I asked her as I rubbed her back and guided her over to Myron's office.

I was happy that my arms were the ones she sought for comfort. It went a long way in helping me to accept the casual touches. Going off their reactions to each other I'm guessing these are the relatives that she mentioned last night.

Because of the commotion we had attracted the attention of everybody on the sales floor and her girls all came rushing up ready for war.

Ray was the first to reach us and wasted no time checking on Sha. *"What's wrong Shamena? Are you okay? Why are you crying?"* She fired off question after question in rapid succession and looking around the room mean muggin' everybody.

"I'm okay Ray. Better than okay actually." Shamena smiled as she sat in the chair in front of Myron's desk while everybody piled into the office.

"What's going on then? Why are you crying." The one called Deana asked looking from person to person for answers just as hostile as Ray.

"Hold on guys. Give me a second. Cree can you have everybody, but you, my girls, and cousins step out for a minute. This is kind of private and we have a lot of people in here." Sha told me while looking around the office.

Sure enough, when I looked around damn near every employee off the sales floor had migrated to Myron's office and the hallway right outside of it peeping inside.

"Okay guys clear out. Shamena and the girls will be back in a couple of minutes," I told them, noticing the wide variety of concern and worry on the employee's faces.

In just the couple of hours Shamena and the girls have been here. They have already made an impact on the staff.

Once everybody filed out Shamena stood and walked over to that Nigga Blade. *"This is my cousin Axel and his brother Adam on my daddy's side. Their father and mine were brothers. I haven't seen them since I was 8 years old when mom moved us into the projects."* Shamena finished while giving both of them Niggas a tight hug while sporting a huge grin. I'm still not cool with the touching, but the familiar connection somewhat soothes my anger.

"That's wonderful Shamena. I'm so happy for you." Ray told her while she and the other girls rushed her and gave her hugs while grinning and talking a mile a minute.

Shamena pulled away from the girls and asked her cousins. *"What are you guys doing here? Did you all come to purchase a car?"* She asked while looking back and forth between the two.

I saw the instant Blade misunderstood Sha's presence at the dealership. Both he and Steele had veins popping in their necks and along their temples. I couldn't explain with Sha and the girls here, but I'll clear it up once they are out of earshot.

"No. We will be working here starting today." Blade told her while cutting his eyes over at me.

I had already peeped what this Nigga was thinking, by the vein popping. Now these niggas are standing here with their nostrils flaring, breathing all hard like they are scaring me, or they are gone whoop my ass. Not happening.

Shamena frowned, looking at them in confusion. *"Oh, well. I can help you both with your paperwork. Give me your social security cards and driver's licenses so I can make copies. Here are the hire packages. Fill out all the basic information. Mr. Smith or Myron will have to do the job description and pay. I'll be right back."*

Shamena changed gears getting back to work. They both pulled out the items and handed them over to Shamena and she left out followed by the girls.

Blade and Steel both rounded on me when the door closed behind the girls. *"Hey, slow y'all roll. Shamena is my girl and I'd never have her tied up in anything illegal. This is just where you will be getting paid from. Neither one of you will have any affiliation with this business, nor any of the others. This business is completely legit and Shamena just started working here a couple hours ago. I know you guys are just looking out for her, but I got her,"* I told them Niggas giving then the same level of aggression they are giving me. Ain't no hoe in my blood and it's whatever.

Both of them Niggas immediately relaxed and rubbed the backs of their necks in unison. The shit was so comical I damn near burst out laughing but controlled myself due to the seriousness of the situation.

"Look you guys go ahead and get started on the paperwork. Y'all are gonna have to hook up with Shamena after she gets off work later," I said and headed out as Shamena stepped back in followed by an older dude that looked like the older version of Blade and Steel.

I left them in the office and went to talk to Zaylar. I found all of them Niggas talking to Mr. Smith about how well the girls were doing. I just stood back and listened as he described how fast they caught on and how energetic and hardworking they seemed. Zaylar caught my eye and sent everybody back to work as he, Myron, and Zylar approached me with a speculative look.

I don't know why they are looking at me like I can shed some light on all the wild shit that's been happening, because I can't. I guess things are happening the way they should. Shamena told me her mother took her away from her father's family when she was eight. Being that she seems to only abuse her mentally and physically makes no sense. The Lord must have decided to make things right.

"This shit is crazy Bruh. In fact, everything since Zylar found Ray two days ago has been crazy," Zaylar spoke, looking like he could not quite believe what had just happened.

"No shit Sherlock. I'm still struggling with the fact that all y'all have hooked up with one of Ray's girls, and now Shamena turns out to be some kin to the

Niggas you plan to put on payroll Zay. It's a sign and I for one am paying close attention," Zylar said and walked off to go and talk to Ray.

Zaylar waited for Johnya to finish talking to one of the salesmen about some paperwork and pulled her out front. I guess he's finally about to show her the new car he bought her. That reminds me that I need to find something nice for Shamena. I want her to be able to get around wherever she needs to go in her own ride.

With that in mind I found Mr. Smith in his office and went over the list of midsize SUVs we have on hand. We were able to find her, the 2012 Acura MDX fully loaded for $55,000 with black-on-black interior and chrome wheels. I did a transfer to pay cash for the vehicle and had Mr. Smith pull Shamena's hire packet to put it in her name. Then we linked everything, and I called my insurance company to add her and the car to my policy. That done, I went inside to get Myron to make sure we had everything set up for tonight's meeting with the crew.

CHAPTER FIFTEEN
Raylexia Gavion

Today has been eventful in more ways than one. I am happy Shamena finally has some family that seems to love and support her, because her mother is a cold piece of work. The shit she has been doing to Shamena makes no sense, especially since it seems she's had family willing to take her in all this time. My mom has always been an absent parent, but I never got the impression that she didn't love us or that she hated us in some way. I just feel like she had us before she was ready, and she refused to stop living the way she wanted just to take care of us. I can't be mad at her, because she could have had an abortion instead, but she never did. For that I will be forever grateful. Shaking off that train of thought, I gathered the rest of my paperwork and moved it to the file cabinet. I looked at the clock to see it's time to get off, glad the workday is finally over, and we can all head home.

Just as I shut down the computer at my desk Zyler walks into the office looking all yummy in a pair of Ralph Lauren brown polo jeans with the matching sweater and jacket. He had brown Timbs on his feet and his bust down Iced Out Gold Rolex around his wrist. Around his neck he wore his Cuban link chain with the dog tags now containing Zan, me, and his information. I swear, Zylar is the preppiest thug I ever met. He's too hood to be a square, and too preppy to be a gangsta.

"Are you almost ready to head out Ray?" He asked as he leaned in for a kiss making my kitty thump.

"Mumm" I moan and rub my fingers across his braids as he gripped my ass while lifting me up to grind on his erection. My legs automatically went around his waist to hook behind his back as I grinded hard on his erection.

"Yes. I'm ready. I just shut everything down so I can head out." I spoke between kisses making sure to grind extra hard and give him more tongue.

"Mr. Smith and Myron gave us all off tomorrow so Mr. Gains can hire additional security guards and install the new cameras. I'm glad we don't have to come in tomorrow because we set up that shopping trip to the mall with all the girls at 12pm. I would have hated to have to cancel because of work," I told him as he sat me back down on my feet breathing hard and sporting a huge erection that got my mouth watering. I reached up and wiped my lip gloss off his mouth as he adjusted his erection in his jeans. I damn near pulled him into the restroom for a quickie.

"That's good but check it. Zaylar called for a meeting with the crew tonight and I have to go. Can you hang over at the girl's apartment until I finish so we can all go home together? It shouldn't take long, maybe an hour or so." Zylar asked as he helped me gather my things to head out of the office. I thought about it. I didn't want to get in the habit of keeping the kids out too late, but since it's the weekend it should be okay.

"Sure. We'll stay since the kids don't have school tomorrow, but from now on after I get off work, I have to head straight home to get them ready for bed. With us having the 30min drive home they won't be able to settle down for bed until after nine. That's two hours later than they do now. I don't want to disrupt their schedule any more than we have to if possible," I told him as we headed out front where the rest of the girls were waiting.

"That's cool," he said and loaded my bags in the back of my SUV, gave me a hard kiss on the lips and walked off to where Zaylar and C-Lo were standing watching the girls as they checked out the two vehicles. Zylar walked over to them and they got in their rides and pulled off with their security following close behind.

I made my way over to the girls who were looking over Shamena and Johnya's new rides. We all checked out both vehicles and then loaded up to head to the apartment. Deana drove the Expedition with Winkie riding shotgun.

It took us 20 mins to get to the apartments and head inside. Mrs. Chance had Tylan and Zander asleep in their Pak-in-plays in the living room, with Reign and Rod watching their movie of choice and eating popcorn. Each of the girls spoke to Mrs. Chance and went off to their bedrooms to drop off their bags, shower, and change clothes.

I made my way over to Mrs. Chance, Reign, and Rod to give them the rundown of the new job. After I satisfied their curiosity, Reign and Rod went back to the movie, but Mrs. Chance watched me with a worried expression. In the time that I stayed with her, she learned to gauge my moods and expressions, so she knows I have something on my mind.

I thought about it for a moment and then asked, *"come on in the kitchen so we can talk Mrs. Anna, so we don't disturb their movie,"* Mrs. Chance and I headed to the kitchen to get bottled water out of the fridge to drink. Once we settled at the barstools, I took a deep breath and began.

"I feel that things are moving fast and I'm afraid my friends may get caught up in the fast money and lifestyles that Zy's friends can provide them with and lose themselves," I told Mrs. Chance and waited for her opinion. It's hard to explain, but I can talk to her about anything and I feel no judgment. She always gives me sound advice and allows me to reason out my thoughts on my own.

"Why? What has happened? Because from what little you have told me about your friends, they all are very sensible. They don't sound like the types to get caught up in material things." Mrs. Chance reasoned. I nodded in agreement.

"It's not that I think they will get caught up in the material things but the fast living and forget our goals of bettering ourselves so that we can all be self-sufficient. I know that Zylar is generous with his money, he always has been where I am concerned. If not for the money he kept supplying me with before mom moved us, we would have been put out the second month after we moved. His willingness to share his money is not the issue," I told Mrs. Chance trying to put my feelings into words. I rubbed the back of my neck and took a deep breath.

"Take your time and explain what you mean, because this seems to be about a lot more than money." Mrs. Chance told me with an even deeper look of concern.

Taking my time to gather my thoughts properly I opened up and told Mrs. Chance my true concern. *"Mrs. Chance Zylar likes to do a lot of things that I don't really enjoy, and he wants me to be with him while he's doing them.*

I have never really had time for the school dances, games, movies, and events that the other kids at school participated in because of having to take care of my siblings. Now that I have some time and the means to indulge in those activities, I don't find them enjoyable. I don't want to come off as being mean or difficult, but do I really have to change who I am to be with someone?" I asked, frustrated.

"No, you don't have to change who you are and it's best if you have a serious heart to heart talk with Zylar about this before it becomes a problem. If a man wants to change you, he's not really interested in you, but remaking you into who he wants you to be. Don't let anyone change who you are, not to say that you can't compromise, because you can. Just keep in mind that there is a difference between compromising and settling. You compromising and doing things he enjoys occasionally is fine, but you have to set boundaries and stick to them. Otherwise, you'll just be settling, and you're not weak willed or weak minded enough to go along with that. What else because there has to be more for you to be this out of sorts." Mrs. Chance told me while giving me a hard stare.

"Well, I have been telling the girls about some of the things that you talk to me about, and I would really appreciate it if you would share some of your knowledge with them just as you have with me. You have taught me so much in a short period of time and I feel I'm better for it. All of them have mothers that love and look out for them except for Shamena. Me and her are basically in the same boat with the parental abuse and neglect, just in different forms," I told Mrs. Chance hoping she'll be willing to school my girls along with me.

"I don't mind sharing my knowledge with the girls, but as you say they have mothers of their own. What if they have a problem with me talking to their daughters about life experiences? I don't want to come between them and their parents." Mrs. Chance told me while she went to straightening up the kitchen. I could tell she was preparing to get ready to leave. This is as good a time as any to find out if she's willing to move into the guesthouse and stay there.

"Mrs. Anna, have you had time to think about moving into the guesthouse? I know it's a lot to ask, but I'll feel better having you there with us. You're the first real parental unit me, Rod, and Reign have had since Grandma Etta passed and I want to keep you close. I know we can talk on the phone, and I can call you about anything, but having you stay just a pool length away sounds even better.

What do you say, Mrs Anna? Move in and be our mom," I told her and she burst into tears.

"I would love to move in to be closer to you guys. I hated for you all to leave when you got emancipated, but I understood your need to be self-sufficient on your own. After having endured all that, you have while living with your mother, I knew nothing other than doing it on your own would have settled your mind and spirit. Now that I know you'll be okay, can I start to mother you the way I'd like?" Mrs. Chance asked me with a wide grin and tears running down her face.

She never had kids because her husband didn't want any. Then after she was past her prime and no longer at any age where it is safe to give birth to a healthy baby, he started cheating and asked for a divorce. That left Mrs Chance devastated and childless.

"Yes, Mam, we would love for you to mother us as you like. When will you be moving in? I can get Zylar to set it up, you just give me the day and time. And thanks for this Mrs. Anna, me and the kids miss you when you're not around," I told her as I rushed around the bar to give her a tight hug.

Just as we finished our private moment the girls all came into the kitchen and got bottled water while discussing the events of the day. When Johnya asked me if I thought she was moving too fast with Zaylar and I deferred to Mrs. Chance it opened the dialogue for her to converse with them on a more intimate level. They all seemed to be interested in what Mrs. Chance had to say and everybody dove right in and asked all types of questions. The most intimate came from Deana and Winkie who wanted to know what was too soon to give a man your body? We all turned to Mrs. Chance to listen to her answer.

"Girls there is no time limit on when you decide to be intimate with your partner. The key is respect. A man that truly cares for you will love you if you have sex with him the first day you meet or a year later. In most cases you will feel when the time is right. There's this overwhelming urge to be one, a throbbing in your core, heart palpitations, wet palms, shortness of breath, but most of all you just know it's the right time." Mrs. Chance told them while giving them an assessing glance.

Johnya was the first to open up about her experience after giving Mrs. Chance some background on her and Ty's relationship. *"I didn't feel anything like that my first time, but with Zaylar I felt like I would go crazy if I didn't get him inside me as soon as possible. It was completely different from with Tyrone, because all I felt then was fear, pain and shame. The experience was totally different too. With Tyrone I felt used, and with Zaylar I felt like he was worshiping me mind, body, and soul. Why were the feelings so different?"* She asked Mrs. Chance.

"The first reason they were different is that you had no business with Tyrone to begin with. He was a sexual predator, who preys on young girls with impressionable minds. He thought that he could mold you and shape you to do anything he wanted, and you probably would have if not for your parents and friends. With Zaylar the attraction was mutual and pure. Despite your age difference he shows you respect and caring. When a man really has feelings for you the respect is automatic and shows in all aspects of his interactions with you. That's why the feelings were so different, because they originated from two totally different places. One came from a place of love tinged in security and safety. The other came from uncertainty and danger. Even if you didn't know that what was happening was wrong, on some unconscious level your internal warning system knew. Somewhat like when you teach young children about stranger danger. It's the same concept." Mrs. Chance told Johnya while looking around to include the rest of us. I'm so happy she told my girl that, because I have long told Johnya that I felt something was off with Tyrone. When we finally found out his true age after she had Tylan it was too late. I'm just happy my girl is free of that perverted snake.

"That makes so much sense. I thought that the feelings I was having when I met him at the park were strange, but after listening to you explain why I was having them. I know now that it was my body's way of trying to warn me to get away from him." Johnya told Mrs. Chance with a faraway look on her face.

"Remember Johnya, you did nothing wrong here. The blame is totally on the adult in the situation. You were the victim here and you have nothing whatsoever to feel ashamed about." Mrs Chance stood up and walked around the bar and gave Johnya a hug.

I could tell my friend needed that hug. It felt good to see Mrs Chance getting along with my friends. From the care and attention, she is showing Johnya, I know she is helping her with some of the guilt Johnya has been carrying around all this time. They separated and Johnya pulled herself together and sat back down on the stool. She looked as if a weight had been lifted from her shoulders. Mrs Chance made her way back to her stool and took a seat. She took a deep breath and looked up at us.

"You girls also have to remember that in a new relationship, there is the thrill of getting to know each other and a wide variety of feelings, but you can't let that prevent you from achieving your goals. Remember whatever they give you is secondary to what you can provide for yourself. If he gives you money, bank everything not needed to sustain your current needs and always plan for a rainy day. Let him take care of you but be prepared to take care of yourself no matter what. You can let him lead and be the man of the relationship but protect yourself while you're at it. Do you all understand what I mean?" Mrs. Chance asked us while looking at us with a determined gaze. I knew this was an important topic for her, because she was totally dependent on her husband and he left her with nothing. Unable to even support herself.

Deana was the first to reply. *"I think what you're telling us is, even with the guys giving us money and buying us things, we should always be in the position to be able to provide it for ourselves. Let them lead us but be able to lead on our own if necessary."*

"Yes, and make sure you save for a rainy day. His money is his money, and your money is your money. Always keep your own bank account that you control, and never get comfortable enough to sit back and not have your own income coming in. That way leads to disaster and co-dependency. If they control your money, they control the way you move. Not to say the guys will use their money as a way to control your moves, but having your own money removes the option." Mrs. Chance told us, and I could see all the girls shaking their heads in agreement.

"Do you girls have any more questions for me? Because if not I am going to get ready to head out since I'll be moving over the weekend." Mrs. Chance told us as she stood and headed to the living room to grab her bags.

Me and the girls followed her to the living room to find Reign and Rod laid out on the sectional asleep in front of the TV. We all grabbed Mrs. Chance's bags and walked her down to her car. As we loaded her bags in the trunk, I could see Buck and Grey stop Maine from approaching us from the other side of the parking lot. Mrs. Chance told me to call the police and let them handle it, and that's exactly what I did.

Mrs. Chance stayed there with me and waited for the police to arrive. When I explained the situation and showed them a copy of the restraining order I got this morning, they read him his rights and took him to jail. Buck called Zylar to let him know what happened and he said he was about 5 min away. When Zylar and the guys arrived, Buck gave them the full rundown of what happened and had someone follow Mrs. Chance home. Zylar had C-Lo set up the movers and packers to help Mrs. Chance move in tomorrow morning at 8am. We all stood outside talking about what happened for another 20 min before me and Zylar loaded up the kids and headed home.

CHAPTER SIXTEEN
Raylexia Gavion

January 21, 2012

At 9:30am Zylar got a call from the gate to come down and get Mrs. Chance setup with her code and the movers and packers made quick work of getting her settled into the Guesthouse out back. The place was really nice having three bedrooms and four and a half baths, two living areas, a wide spacious kitchen with center island and a connected bar area. The house was fully stocked and furnished similar to the main house. Mrs. Chance just had to put her own personal touch on it, and she'd be all set.

Me, Reign and Rod were helping Mrs. Chance get settled when Mrs. Della showed up with brunch and I introduced the two. They made fast friends and decided they'd keep the kids while I went to the mall with the girls and kicked me out. Not having anything else to do at home I dressed for the mall and headed over to the apartment to chill with the girls. I made it to the apartment a little before 11am and a shirtless Zaylar answered the door holding a grinning Tylan.

"What's up Ray? Ma called and told me to bring Tylan over to your place. They are having a movie and snack day with Grandma or something. So Johnya will be out after she gets him dressed so we can head out." Zaylar told me as he let me in and made his way back to Johnya's room.

"Well, hello to you too, brother-in-law." I laughed and made myself at home on the sectional.

After he walked out the living room I thought about how similar he and Zylar were. At 24, Zaylar is the older version, to Zylar's 18-year-old, ruggedly handsome frame. Standing a commanding 6'3", Zaylar towers over most people with an imposing presence. His body is sculpted with more muscle mass than Zylar who stands at an 6'even. Also, Zaylar's skin is a rich peanut butter shade, a tone deeper than Zylar's, and he has expertly inked tattoos that are tastefully sprawled across his upper body. Next, Zaylar's eyes mirror marble gray, contrasting with Zylar's gunmetal gray gaze, and while Zylar rocks long, braided black hair, Zaylar sports a crisp Caesar cut with deep waves. Both brothers share the distinctive traits of bowed legs and a mustache-goatee combo, though Zaylar's facial hair is notably thicker than Zylars. Each of them carries a unique swagger that sets them apart from most other men.

I had been sitting for about 15 min when a fully dressed Tylan, Zaylar, and Johnya came from the back. Zaylar kissed Johnya on the lips, waved bye to me, scooped Tylan up, and headed out the door. I just smiled in amusement because Zaylar went from a bachelor to family man overnight.

"Hey girl. How are you doing this morning?" I asked Johnya and I could see the happiness and fear all over her face.

"I'm scared Ray. Zaylar has come into my life and his mom wants to spend time with my son and get to know him. I have never had anyone besides my parents and you guys to help me with him. With Zaylar he now has a new grandma as Zaylar calls her, but what if we don't work out and my son is getting close to these people?" Johnya asked me in a full-blown panic.

I sighed mad at Tyrone's snake ass. He fucked my girl up to the point where she is scared to open up and accept genuine love and affection.

"This is a good thing Johnya. Just see how it goes first before you start to panic. Tyrone has never really been a part of Tylan's life so you have no real experience with how a man would treat his son. Zaylar has taken on the role of his father since you guys are together, and this is how a man takes care and acts with his child. Zaylar is showing you that he is willing to step up to the plate and be a real father to Tylan. Not just a man to you. This lets you know he's not just committed to you Johnya, but to being a father to Tylan as well. Relax and let the relationship develop naturally. If things change and there is a problem, you'll know and make adjustments as you go," I told her and she seemed to calm down a little.

Shamena, Winkie, and Deana all came out the back smiling and walking funny. They were all glowing and it looked good on them. Even Johnya had a glow to her and a smile shining out past the fear. We all decided to ride together so we could talk about what happened last night, so we all loaded up in my Escalade. I wasted no time asking them about their new walk and everybody took turns explaining their first time or new experience with their men until we pulled up to the mall. Judging from the number of cars parked in the lot, The Pierre Bossier Mall was packed.

I parked close to the exit near Dillard's and we all got out. I wasn't planning to buy anything except for Rod's Jordans, but I planned to thoroughly enjoy the experience of watching my girls shop.

Shamena decided to share the money on the gift cards with the other girls, so we decided to hit Dillard's first where they all bought several pairs of jeans and shirts that were reasonably priced. To my surprise Johnya pulled out Zaylar's black card to pay for her items, and Shamena, Deana and Winkie all had over $2000 in cash to spend. We made our way over to Footlocker to get Rod's Jordans when I got a call from Kahmala. I told her to meet us at Footlocker where I introduced her to the other girls. While talking she told us about meeting Adam last night and they were now a couple. After that Shamena started calling her cuz-in-law and we all teased her because she kept a resting bitch face on no matter her mood.

The other girls started to show up one after the other and we all decided to meet in the food court where we introduced the rest of the girls and Josie to Kahmala. Things were going well, and we were having a ball until a group of over eight girls walked up and started talking crazy to Shanna, Awaii, Sonya, and Felisha. Not knowing what was going on me, Kahmala, Josie, and the girls stood back to peep the situation.

"I see you scary bitches hang out together when we're not around. Couldn't pay you hoes to come turn-up at the club, but y'all all together in the mall." Some light skinned chick with a baby doll face yelled at Shanna.

"Chandra who I hang out with in or out of the club has nothing to do with you, and scary ain't never been me. I just don't fuck with you or the birdbrained bitches that you socialize with. Why would I come down off my throne to deal with a peasant?" Shanna replied, making all of us laugh.

So, this was the infamous Chandra. I had to give it to her. The girl was bad standing at a little over 5'6" with a honey butter complexion, wide hips, thick thighs, large breasts and dressed in Prada from head to toe. Her heart shaped childlike facial features would have been endearing if she weren't so toxic. Her innocent appearance is overshadowed by the putrid nonsense comin' out her mouth. Her behavior is totally unacceptable. I could tell, she's trying too hard.

"Bitch, are you trying to be funny?" Chandra asked after seeing everybody laughing at her.

"No, I'm just trying to figure out what would make you think it was a good idea to approach me in the mall. I don't fuck with you, never have, so why would you even stop to speak to me about anything? Just because my man deals with someone you know, doesn't mean we are okay like that. Get your friends and get the fuck out of my face before we have a problem." Shanna told her while taking up a fighting stance.

I immediately peeped out that Chandra was all talk. She backed down from Shanna and started talking to Awaii, which produced the same response. Her friends all stood back to watch but none of them made any moves to come to Chandra's defense. That let me know right there that Chandra didn't have any friends, just hoes she socialized with riding her coattail.

When they walked off Kahmala told us she had to go to work and would catch up with us later. She walked off in the direction that Chandra and her friends went, making me remember she was supposed to handle Chandra and Derricka. I watched as she trailed them through the mall until they were no longer in sight. The whole little incident was anti-climatic. I was all worked up ready for some action, and Chandra's worthless attempt at checking Shanna and Awaii was so feeble it made me mad. She must not be from the hood, because hood girls come with mad shit talk and lethal hands to back it up.

After that little scene we hit a couple more stores and Shanna suggested we hit up her sports bar to have a bite to eat. We all gathered up our bags, loaded up the SUV and followed Shanna to the same shopping center where we were going to open the shop.

Upon entering the restaurant, I could already tell something was wrong. There were several groups of customers standing by the hostess desk and six seating areas that needed to be cleaned. Shanna took off for the back end of the bar and returned wearing an apron with two other men in aprons that started busting and cleaning the tables. Seeing that they were obviously shorthanded today the girls and I walked over to Shanna and volunteered to help bust the tables while she got the customers seated.

It took us no time to get the tables cleaned and Shanna, Felisha, Josie, Awaii, and Sonya seated the customers and took their drink orders. Once we got the dining area cleaned it was easy to clear the tables as each set of customers left after their meals. Two hours later, around 5:30pm the crowd began to thin out and we were all able to take a break. We all took seats at the bar and ordered soft drinks.

"Thank you, guys, for helping me out today. I really appreciate it." Shanna told us while sipping on her drink.

"We didn't mind, shit I haven't had that much fun working since I got hired at Price-Lo. I'd rather bust tables than to stand in the same place all day working the checkout line," I told her as I took a drink of my coke.

It was fun and the time flew by so fast, I had no idea I'd been working for two hours. What I really took note of is that Shanna has a steady customer flow. If business is like this or better Shanna will make a killing. I also like the laid back, chill vibe I get from the place. I could definitely see myself bringing the kids here to eat.

Shanna's place was set up like the classic sports bar with a central bar surrounded by high stools, with additional seating in booths or at tables strategically placed for the optimal view of the TV's. The lighting in the bar is soft and subdued, ensuring that the TV screens are the focal points of each customer. The bar area is well-stocked with a variety of hard liquors and beers, from the popular domestic brands to craft brews that she imported. The best feature of her bar is her menu full of Cajun, seafood, soul food, and hearty comfort food including wings, burgers and fries, and nachos. The perfect food for game day.

"I had fun too. I haven't worked waiting tables since college and I can see it's still fast paced and exciting. Nothing can compare to the lunch rush." Josie added, smiling from ear to ear.

"What happened Shanna? I know you would not have been at the mall with us while they are short staffed here." Shamena asked while giving Shanna the side eye.

I shook my head at Shamena with her no filter having ass. But that's my girl. You can't help but to love her, blunt to her core ass. *"Really Sha?"* I squawked.

"What? I just asked what you're thinking." Sha shrugged.

"It's okay, Ray," Shanna cut in. *"And no, Shamena. Of course, I wouldn't have been shopping at the mall while my restaurant is short-handed. I let my mom help with the schedule for this week and she didn't schedule for the extra volume we have on the weekend. Tonight, everything should be fine since the evening shift has already started to come in, but I won't be letting her handle the schedule anymore."* She shook her head in obvious frustration. *"I need to hire a manager, but it's hard to find good quality managers that you can trust in a black owned business."* Shanna explained.

"How much are you paying? My mom is a manager on the boat, and she's been trying to leave since they started taking her vacation time if she doesn't use it within the year. She said every time she puts in for her vacation it's been getting denied with the excuse, they are short staffed and can't afford to let her have the time off," Winkie revealed.

Mrs Sandra is a wonderful woman and she works all the time. If she can get on here, I would definitely become a regular customer here. She can cook her ass off, no one makes peach cobbler and apple pie the way she does.

"Girl, give me your mom's information so I can give her a call now. As long as it's reasonable, I'll match what she makes. Having a reliable manager will free up my time to work on expanding." Shanna told Winkie as they both walked off to the back towards her office.

Me and the other girls ordered a bite to eat and talked amongst ourselves getting better acquainted. We all liked the atmosphere at the bar and decided to meet up here after work on Saturdays going forward.

Mrs. Sandra showed up after interviewing with Shanna on the phone, filled out her paperwork and walked around the restaurant pointing out things to Shanna that needed to be changed. I noticed the time and let the girls know I needed to be heading in to get the kids. We all hugged Mrs. Sandra bye, told the other girls we'd give them a call and headed back to the girl's apartment.

CHAPTER SEVENTEEN
Raylexia Gavion

February 3, 2012

This is my birthday weekend and Zylar wants to throw a big party at their strip club to celebrate. I keep telling him I'd be more comfortable if we just have a small get together with our friends at the house, but he refuses to listen. It's like the more I compromise with him about the party situation, the farther he tries to push the boundaries. Since he's hard of hearing I arranged for Mrs. Della and Mrs. Chance to set up something for me and the girls at Mrs. Della's old house. We all decided to have a small get-together for us all together since all our birthdays fall in February. We are all staying the night and having a slumber party with the catering provided by Shanna. I don't know what Zylar is doing, and I no longer give a fuck. Things have been tense in our household over the last week and I'm over it. I refused to keep having the same conversation with him over and over again, so I decided to do my own thing.

We had an intimate dinner at Copelands last night and Zylar gave me a charm bracelet with my siblings and Zanders birthstones in it, and a pear shaped engagement/promise ring for my birthday. I almost didn't accept the ring until he said it was a promise, we'd be together in the future. I'm not even sure that we'll make it past next month, let alone end up together in the future. Although it was my birthday Zylar went to the club with his friends after we arrived home from dinner and stayed out until well past 3am. What the hell kind of birthday celebration is that? No birthday dick, head, conversation, nothing. Then I'm the one being unreasonable because I have an attitude and refuse to go along with his bullshit. Zylar seems to have conveniently forgotten that we have responsibilities, and we can't just run the streets and do whatever the hell we want just because Mrs. Chance lives in the guesthouse and can watch the kids. He wants to stay out til all times of the night and expects to drag me along with him. I don't care how many times I explain that with the kids, my job and school, that's not something I'm willing to do for him and nobody else. Zander, Reign and Rod are my responsibility and I refuse to let him or anybody else cause me to neglect my duty to them. I can understand he's young and wants to party, but with the added responsibilities we have partying every night is just not possible. Either Zylar needs to grow the hell up or find a different girl to be with. I refuse to let Mrs. Chance take on raising my son and siblings just to cater to Zylar's selfish ass.

"Ray, what the hell do you mean you're not going to the party I set up for you at the club tonight?" Zylar asked as I got Zander ready to take him and the kids to the guesthouse with Mrs. Chance.

He'd been standing there mean mugging me since I started getting dressed earlier. I don't know who he thinks he's scaring but it ain't me. It's crazy that what popped in my head is that dry ass dinner we had for my birthday. All his so called promises that he was gonna change and do better. Yeah, right. When pigs take flight round this bitch.

"I meant exactly what the fuck I said. I'm not going. I have been telling you all week that I don't want a party at the club. That's not how I want to celebrate. I only tolerate the club and gatherings as it is. What would make you think I would want to celebrate my birthday surrounded by mutherfuckers I don't know, or care to know. I want to chill, walk around in my pajamas, joke and have fun with my friends. It's my birthday so I should be able to celebrate how I see fit. The shit you set-up at the club is for your benefit, not mine," I spazzed while he stood there looking at me crazy.

"So, you just weren't gonna tell me you were doing something else while I got all this shit setup at the club?" He asked me, angrily.

I sighed, feeling mentally drained, *"Zylar, I did tell you, but I've come to realize that you tend to only hear what the hell you wanna hear. I said I didn't want a party at the club when you told me about it last week. I told you that I wanna chill at the house with our friends, but no. You wanna stunt for the folks at the club, cut up, get drunk and act a fool. That's not fun for me. You set up this elaborate party and invited people I don't know. You did that shit for you, because all of my girls are kickin' it with me tonight. I told them and you I'd rather have something lowkey with the people I care about, but no. You had to do something that I would get no pleasure from. So, is it really for me, or you?"* I asked him and I waited while he stood there staring at me.

"Nothing to say?" I chuckled, *"thought so."* I shook my head at him, and once I had Zander's bag ready, I headed out the room to get Reign and Rod so we could leave.

AFTER MY ARGUMENT WITH Zylar, I now regret my decision to take him back without demanding proof of his change. We've only been back together for two weeks, and he's already on that same old bullshit. Now I know he was just placating me until I moved in with him, only to show his true colors afterward. Zylar is still selfish, always wanting to get his way, so I guess it's time for me to show his hard-headed ass that I'm not the one to play with. Like Shamena said, *"that dick must be something serious,"* because I'm feeling dick silly right now for giving in and believing his lies again. If it weren't for the fact that I feel totally safe in that big-ass house, I would have moved us all back in with Mrs. Chance, until I could secure another place for us. The only good thing to come from this stupid move is that I've been reunited with my girls and even helped them get their own place. These thoughts raced through my mind as I pulled up to the apartment wearing my silk two piece pajamas and knocked on the door.

Deana answered the door wearing a thick plaid flannel pajama set, her attention glued to her phone, oblivious to my distressed expression as she continued texting. Feeling like shit, I doubted even a slumber party could lift my spirits now. Everything felt so damn depressing. I composed myself and walked over to the sectional, determined not to let Zylar ruin my weekend or my time with my girls. I sat down, turning just in time to see Deana still glued to her phone screen.

"Ray, I'm glad you're here," Deana said, eyes still on her phone. *"Day Day asked me to ask you if you'd be willing to do the halftime shows for his football tournament. He'll pay $1500 a show, which means $300 each for us, plus we get to enjoy the game for free. We haven't done any shows or taken any gigs since*

you've been gone, so we'd need to come up with some new routines if you're in. Oh, and I forgot to mention— Day Day's out of the service for good."

"What?" I thought, my mind reeling as I squeezed my legs together, feeling a sudden throb at the mention of Daylon's nickname. It had been over a year since I last saw him, and damn, I missed him like crazy. Daylon was the kind of man you could talk to about anything—he always listened and never judged. Breaking ties with him cut deep, but I had to do it to keep things smooth with Zylar and to protect my own peace of mind. Ever since the chaos after our last game, I've been scared to even acknowledge my feelings for Daylon. His tour in the Navy made it easier to hide from him and from these tangled emotions I've been fighting to suppress.

With him being older and knowing all my struggles, I couldn't shake the fear that he saw me as just a charity case—someone who needed saving. How could we build something real from that?

"I don't know if it's a good idea for me to deal with Daylon on any level, Deana, especially knowing how he feels about me, and with me being with Zylar. That's just asking for trouble. So, my answer is no. I'm not interested," I told her, just as Shamena walked in wearing a thick linen wool one piece pajama set, carrying her overnight bag. I tried to ignore how just hearing Daylon's name made my body react.

"What are you guys talking about?" Shamena asked, settling into the sectional next to me. I could tell by the way she was eyeing me that she sensed something was off. If Deana weren't so wrapped up in her phone, she'd probably notice too.

"Ray here was just hearing about Day Day's request for us to perform at his football tournament halftimes on the upcoming Sundays," Deana explained, her eyes still glued to her screen.

"Girl, what the hell is so important on that phone that you can't put it down?" I snapped at Deana, desperate to shift the focus away from anything to do with Daylon. The way he still affected me scared the shit out of me. He'd asked me to respect his space, and I intended to keep doing just that. It's bad enough things between Zylar and me are on shaky ground. If I started seeing Daylon regularly, I'm not sure I could keep hiding my feelings from myself.

"I'm talking to Kayden. He told me earlier he was gonna take Brea to see her mom, and he's still over there. That was at 2 PM and now it's 7:30 PM. I could understand if he dropped her off and went back to pick her up, but just sitting up at her house for five hours is a no-go for me. He says he doesn't trust her enough to leave her alone with Brea, so he has to stay the whole time because she's got supervised visitation twice a month," Deana explained, punching in a final message before shutting off her phone.

I shook my head, me and Shamena exchanging a look. K-Boy is either still fucking his baby mama, or he is dedicated as hell to his daughter spending quality time with her mom. Either way it's a sticky situation and I want no parts.

Besides I didn't know what to say, because I'm with Deana on this. What kind of supervised visit lasts five hours? When Johnya and Tyrone had visitations set up for Tylan, they were only an hour. I can't fathom what they'd arrange for five hours. I know my girl is hip to the game, so I don't need to speak about it.

"So, what do you say? You wanna do the halftime show for Day Day?" Shamena asked, shifting the topic, because neither one of us wanted to dwell on the fucked-up games Kayden was tryin' to play.

"Like I told Deana, I don't think it's a good idea for me to be around Daylon like that, knowing how he feels about me. He's got genuine affection for me, and I'd feel like I was playing with his feelings if I was in his space for too long. Daylon and his brothers are savages out here, and I don't need those kinds of problems in my life. Zylar is already a big enough headache. Besides, if I start dancing for Daylon, y'all know that boy gets all possessive and shit. It never used to worry me before I started seeing Zylar, because I thought it was just brotherly love," I sighed, my thoughts spiraling.

That episode still scares me. The intensity, passion, and raw need in Daylon's eyes were breathtaking. Knowing a man desires me to that degree is arousing, almost mind-blowing. As I thought about it, I subtly adjusted my position and crossed my legs, trying to apply pressure where the throbbing intensified.

"That all changed for me after the last game we played in the summer Spar Tournament. Y'all know Daylon can be scary as hell, but I've never been afraid of him, not once. That day, though, he scared the shit out of me, and it was for

a totally unexpected reason. And trust me, Zylar is not gonna be cool with that," I told them just as Johnya and Winkie walked in with their overnight bags. Johnya wearing a cashmere two piece and Winkie wearing a satin onesie.

"Y'all ready to go?" Johnya asked as she plopped down next to Deana on the far side of the sectional, followed by Winkie.

"I just told Ray about Day Day wanting us to dance at his tournament, and she's worried about him and Zylar bumping heads," Deana chimed in as we all settled onto the sectional.

"Not just that. Ray was dropping some new tea," Shameena hinted. *"Spill."*
Before I got the chance to say anything, Johnya cut in.

"Well, I agree with Ray. If she starts dancing for Day Day again, that's gonna cause problems between her and Zylar and might send Day Day the wrong message. The only reason she didn't have issues before is that Ray is a homebody, and nobody on our side of town really knows about her thing with Zylar. When Ray disappeared, Day Day went just as crazy as Zylar looking for her. I thought it was better not to mention him since Ray has never really been into him like that," Johnya spoke up causing me to look at her crazy. *"Did she being one of my closest friends really not know that I care for Daylon?"*

"What the hell do you mean he went crazy looking for me when we moved? I haven't talked to Daylon since about a month after I started seeing Zylar," I shot back. my mind swirling with confusion.

"It's true, Ray. Outside of us, no one knew you had a boyfriend, and whenever Zylar came over, you two always stayed indoors. So, nobody on our side knows you're with someone but the five of us. Day Day lost his mind when he came home and found out you moved away without leaving an address or a way to contact you," Winkie added, leaning in as if she was disclosing a top secret. *"Plus, with him having to leave for his last tour not knowing where you were, he was livid. I heard he beat up some dudes and damn near went to jail over it."*

"And there's more," Deana interjected, her voice dropping to a whisper. *"The night before he left for the tour, Day Day was asking around, looking for any clue about where you might have gone. He's been holding onto something for you, something he never got the chance to give you before everything went down."*

I was stupefied. I couldn't for the life of me guess what Daylon could be holding onto for me.

"What? This is crazy. I had no idea all of that happened, but you guys, Daylon knows I have a man because I told him myself a month after me and Zylar made things official. I stopped dealing with him after that because he damn near tried to rape me but couldn't go through with it. He said he's not that type of guy and if he has to take it, he doesn't need it. He was really hurt, and that's why I don't go to The Hill, The Bottom, or The Middle anymore, so I won't run into him. Daylon knows I can't dance for him and why. He asked me to respect his mind and space, and that's exactly what I've been doing by staying away from the places I know he'll be," I spilled everything, and they all shot me a 'bitch, what?' look.

"What the fuck, Ray? Why didn't you tell us about this?" Shamena exploded, upset.

"I didn't tell you guys because I didn't want your relationship with Daylon to change because of what he almost did to me. He loves me, guys, and I have genuine affection for him too, but in the way of a big brother or cousin. He helped me keep food on the table and extra money when shit was tight, and I'll never forget that. But I'll also never forget that he cared enough for me to have almost taken it too far. So, I'll never put myself in that position again. Besides, I'm still with Zylar, so going around him like that would still be a violation of his space," I explained, trying to shake off the memories of Daylon touching my body and stirring feelings that reached deep into my soul.

Zylar has never evoked those feelings and sensations in me. To this day, he has never touched me with that level of reverence and care. That says a lot when he's the only man I've ever been with, and he doesn't make me feel anything even close to it. The level and depth of their feelings for me are different, and I can feel and tell the difference.

"Damn that explains so much. I used to wonder why we stopped making the extra money for performing at the tournaments and why you stopped playing ball after you got with Zylar. It was because you were trying to avoid Day Day," Winkie said while looking at me with an understanding expression.

"Deana how did Daylon know I'm back around?" I asked her because I make sure not to frequent any of the places where I could run into Daylon.

"He told me that Slim did some work on his Old School Cutlass and happened to mention that he saw you when they came to check out Winkie's new place." I had no idea how to respond to that. Although I'm not afraid of

Daylon, I also have no desire to push the boundaries of his will power. Not to mention the fact that he had me all hot and bothered from just touching and kissing on me. Which confused and scared the shit out of me.

"Well guys now that you all know what happened, please don't treat Daylon any differently than you always have. He's a really good guy, just not the right guy for me, maybe," I told them as I stood up and headed for the front door.

I have no idea how to explain my constant arousal for Daylon. Is it lust or love? I can't decide which because it so overwhelms me to the point where I want to find Daylon. Pin him down to a bed and explore every inch of that 6'3" well defined, thickly muscled, perfectly proportioned caramel colored body.

"Let's go ladies. Shanna should be arriving with the food in another hour. I wanna make sure we set the bedrooms up for us all to spend the night. There are 11 of us and we have 5 bedrooms and 6 bathrooms to split between us so we all should be comfortable. Mrs. Della stocked the fridge so we can cook a big breakfast before we go home tomorrow," I told them and we all grabbed our coats and exited the apartment after setting the alarm and locking the door.

Zylar Crewens

February 3, 2012

I can't believe Ray's ungrateful ass let me setup all this shit for her birthday and she was not even planning on telling me she's not going. Now I have to call and cancel all the shit I had arranged. I ranted as I dialed Nayara. She's this pretty yellow bone that's been trying to get me to dick her down since Ray went missing. We used her to plan the special events at the club, so she planned the shit I had set up for Ray tonight.

"Yo, Naya cancel the shit we had planned for tonight. Make sure to remove all the happy birthday banners and balloons. Let DJ Flay know to cancel his announcements and just roll like normal for a Friday night. Me and the fellows should be fallin' through there around 12 am." I rattled off as soon as she answered the phone.

"Okay Boss, will do." She answered and I ended the call.

Since it was only a little after 8pm I decided to take a shower and get some sleep before I hit the club tonight. I had just come out of the bathroom when I heard noise coming from down the hall. Throwing on some boxers, gym shorts, and a t-shirt, I made my way down the hall to see what the hell was going on. Approaching Rod's room, I heard his call of duty game and thought he must have forgotten to turn it off and that was the sound. Imagine my surprise to find that nigga posted up on his couch in front of the TV talking shit into his mic.

I went in and took a seat next to Rod and grabbed a controller and headset. *"What's good My G I thought you were out there with Mrs. Chance for the night?"* I asked him as I waited for the new round to start so I could join the mission.

To my surprise and shock, Rod shut the game off and turned to face me, aggression radiating off him in waves. *"Zylar, why did you come to bother us if you knew you didn't want to be with us? We were fine. Ray had a job. We have food, clothes, and even money saved. Ray was taking good care of us without you, and we were good. She never told me why y'all broke up, or even that y'all did, but I know you did something Ray couldn't accept. So why come back around if you know you don't really wanna be here with us?"* Rod's words threw me for a loop. He's only 12, so him checking me and talking like a grown man shocked me, but it was the truth in his words that hit harder.

"Why would you think I don't want to be here with Ray and you guys? I love Ray and Zander more than anything, and I care about you and Reign too. What gives you the impression I don't want to be here?" I asked Rod, concerned that if he felt this way, maybe Ray did as well.

Rod let off a sarcastic laugh and shot back. *"How many days have you actually stayed home and just chilled with us since we moved into this house? How many of Zander's diapers have you changed at night, or how many bottles have you fixed? Did you know Ray switched to online classes so she doesn't have to go to school anymore, reducing the chance of running into Maine until after the court case? Do you even know that Ray works from 8 am to 5 pm Monday through Friday and takes Saturdays and Sundays off so she can take Reign to see her dad on Sundays? You have no clue because you're too busy running the streets and partying to care. You don't live here with us; this is just where you sleep occasionally. So, I ask you again. Why did you come around and disrupt our lives, making changes when you know you don't really want to be here with us?"* Rod pressed, leaving me speechless.

What the fuck could I say to him when I had no clue about none of the shit he just said. Maybe I'm not ready for all this after all. I just know I want to be with Ray and Zan, but am I really ready for the level of responsibility we have right now. Rod seemed to take my silence as his answer and put his headset back on, restarted the game, and went back to playing. I got up and made my way over to our bedroom and stretched out across the bed with all the shit that Rod just told me on my mind.

Raylexia Gavion

S o far, the party is in full swing, and we have a really chilled vibe going on. Shanna provided us with the perfect finger food and snack selection that we can hold in our hands while dancing. Since we have been here, we have come up with four different dance routines and I asked Sonya to take my spot, so the girls can make that money and attend games. So far, she has the routines down but she's not as limber as me and she stands out to anyone that's familiar with us as a group. I told her I'd work with her up until the game so she can get more comfortable with the moves and we set up a schedule to meet at the girl's apartment 3 times a week up until the first game.

"Let's take a break. I'm exhausted." Johnya said and plopped down on the couch drinking her bottled water.

"It looks good Sonya. With a little more practice, you'll fit in perfectly," I told her. Glad she agreed to dance with the girls so they wouldn't have to miss the tournament.

"Girl, I'm glad to help. I just didn't know so much work was involved in dancing. Keeping up with the counts and where I need to be at each count is the hard part. It's not just dancing but thinking as well. I have a newfound respect for the school dance lines because they have three or more new routines every game. I'd be stressed, the hell out trying to keep up with all that." Sonya said, making everybody laugh.

"Girl, most of those girls work that hard because they have scholarships to the college of their choice to participate in dance already lined up. Believe me when I say they have good reason to put in hard work when you get four years of college plus room and board paid for to shake your ass on the field for two hours a game. When I was dancing that was my main goal but having to get my siblings after school killed all that. If not for my ACT scores and TOPS scholarships I'd be shit out of luck right now. Since I stayed in town and got the Pell Grant my

271

tuition is paid for. Most of the high cost of college is for books, food, room and board," I told them while taking a drink of my own water.

"That's true. I am still paying back my student loans and having to take two extra years of college for my degree in criminal justice didn't help. I'm just glad I passed the Bar Exam the first time around, because there was no way I would have been able to come up with the money to stay in school another semester to retake the exam next go round." Josie told us as she sipped her frozen daiquiri. Her and a couple of the other girls made them some fruity drinks that contain alcohol.

"I really appreciate you guys coming to celebrate with me tonight because I needed a break from all the bullshit going on right now. School is fine but juggling work and the kids get hard after a while. Mrs. Chance was happy to give me a break tonight," I told them and Johnya nodded in agreement.

"If the girls and Zaylar weren't there to help me with Tylan I think I'd go crazy. Every now and then I just wanna have some me time to just take a bath, soak and relax." Johnya said causing me to think about Zylar's selfish ass.

Since we moved into the new house, he hasn't helped with anything to do with the kids. He's always in the streets handling business or at the club. It makes me wonder why the hell did he even bother to find me in the first place. He leads a totally separate life from me and the kids. If not for seeing his clothes in the dirty clothes hamper, I'd think I lived in that big ass house alone with just the kids.

"Ray, where the hell did you go girl?" Shamena asked me with a look of concern that was mirrored by the rest of the girls in the room.

"Girl, I'm just thinking about my current situation and where I wanna be," I told them and everybody seemed to get lost in their own thoughts just as we all heard multiple gunshots coming from close by outside.

Everyone dived on the floor with their hands covering their heads except for Kahmala and her sister Kilayla. They made their way to the side exit while Kahmala barked orders to our security into her phone. I don't know Kilayla well but she seems to be just as deadly as Kahmala.

A short while after they both went outside the gunshots stopped and we could hear tires screeching down the street.

"Is everyone okay?" I asked the girls as we all stood up to check on each other.

Josie was on her phone calling Nico and Johnya was ranting to Zaylar. Shamena's phone started ringing followed by the rest of our phones. I pulled my phone out and answered for Grey, my head of security. *"Hello? Yes, we're all good. Did you catch the guys doing the shooting?"*

"John and Lake are tailing them right now. We were able to stop them before they got too close to the house, so the bullets only hit our cars and some of Mrs. C's fence trim. Since you guys are good, let me call and check-in with Zylar. Are you going to stay the night, or will you be heading home?" Grey asked.

"I think we're going to pack up and head home. No sense in tempting fate. I don't want anybody getting hurt and we have no idea if they'll come back," I told Grey and went to let the girls know to pack up so we could leave.

We were gathering our belongings when Deana, Johnya, Winkie, and Shamena walked over to check if I was okay.

"You good Ray? The party is ending abruptly. Do you wanna all go to your place and continue?" Deana asked.

"No, you guys. I'm over it. I was trying to get into the grove, but I'm not really in the mood to socialize. I have too much on my mind right now to even enjoy everyone's company. So, it's best if everyone heads to their own place." I told them and they left me to finish packing up. We would just have to come over tomorrow and clean out the fridge. Once the guys gave us the okay. We all loaded up and headed in separate directions.

CHAPTER EIGHTEEN
Stacy "Biz" Clay

February 3, 2012

"I can't believe them lil niggas fucked the shit up. Now we have to get rid of them niggas and lay low out of town. There is no way Stone gone let this shit ride." I yelled at Eric and that nigga Tyrone. All this time we been tryin' to catch them niggas slippin so we can take that Nigga Stone out and take over this shit. We were able to take out Big Z, but Stone seems to have a fuckin' guardian angel looking out for him. This shit should've been ours long ago, but them lil niggas hit Big Z before he hooked up with Zaylar to pick up the drop. I know people think I'm grimy for fuckin' over my boy after all he's done for me, but I want to be the King of Louisiana and I'll get there by hook or crook.

"Nigga fuck you. I told you we should have never gone up against that man in the first place. Zaylar broke bread with us and paid us well, but that was never good enough for you. You wanna be the Nigga in charge so bad you fell to see we had it made. Zaylar practically let you, me, and Red run this shit with him as equals, but you to busy tryin' to fuck him over to realize you were one of the Nigga's in charge. It's bad enough you set Red up to get caught with a kilo in his car. Then you go and pull this shit. What the hell were you thinking. Stone has hittas on his team that stay on go, and you recruiting niggas that's trigger happy with no pedigree behind them to take out savages. It's bad enough I can't show my face around town are visit any of my people because I joined you on this dummy mission. We stole over 5 million dollars from that man. You know he's out for blood now. Deuce has disappeared so we no longer have eyes on Zaylar anymore. Not that the nigga was of any use anyway since he knows nothing about the new setup. All the traps have been moved and he has a whole *new crew that's loyal to him. Now you shot up his mother's house. You act like you wanna see that Nigga Stone. Ain't no tellin what that man gone do when he finds out you went at his Momma. You forgetting we got family that live all over this bitch with no protection?"* Eric ranted letting me know he's frustrated with the situation. If he wasn't my Bitch, I'd have offed his ass by now.

Tyrone didn't say anything. He rode with us to the warehouse where the young hittas stripped the van, set it on fire, broke the weapons down and tossed them inside. When they finished, I sent a bullet through the heart and dome of each one of them and set the bodies on fire alongside the van. There could be nothing to tie us to this fuckup. With this move I'm sure we just woke up that Nigga Stone. Zaylar was chill as fuck, but he didn't play about his mother.

When we pulled up to the meeting spot to talk to Zaylar's aunt and uncle, their daughter Stephanie ran over and jumped in that Nigga Tyrone's arms. I still can't believe they came up with this whole elaborate scheme to get Stephanie into Mrs. C's house, but for some reason it all backfired on them. That Nigga whipped Stephanie's ass and Mrs. C still wouldn't let her stay with her.

"What the fuck happened? Did you take out Della?" Zaylar's Uncle Willum asked while standing next to his wife Joyce who is Big Z's baby sister. These folk are fucked up for real. Willum approached me six years ago with a plan to take Big Z out so we could run the streets together. He doesn't want to be involved with the drug game, just reap the benefits and rewards. I've been paying this bitch ass nigga over $500k a year and I feel its time to cut them off. I don't trust the muthafuckas anyway. Any muthafucka that's grimy enough to plot and kill their own brother for money can't be trusted and I'm tired of carrying their deadweight.

"No, we didn't get close enough to the house to take her out. They had security guarding the property both in and outside her gate. It seems as though after the incident with Stephanie they are on high alert," I told them while Eric just stood off to the side looking pissed.

"So, what's next? Since you are no longer working for Zaylar you haven't had access to any money of late and we've damn near used up all the cash we got to keep the business running. I need more cash and quick." Willum told me like it's my job to support him and his gambling habit.

"Nigga you would have money and plenty of it, if you stayed your ass off them boats and kept Joyce out the mall. I'm taking all the risk and you reaping all the rewards, so I think it's time for me to cut the extra baggage," I said as I pulled my gun from behind my back with my silencer attached, sending a bullet through Willum's heart and head as Eric sent one through Tyrone's head and heart. Stephanie and Joyce started crying and running for the exit as me and Eric sent bullets through their heads spraying brain matter all across the floors and walls. Imagine our surprise when we heard clappin coming from the back of the warehouse and them Niggas Stone, Zylar, Nico, C-Lo, K-O, K-Boy, Myron, Jayce, Lance, Kam, Jamie, Kahmala, Khiershan, Kilayla, and Killian all stepped out from the shadows of the warehouse. I damn near lost my bowels as I saw Switchblade and his son's Blade and Steel come out from the other side with some wicked looking blades in their hands.

Switchblade was the hitta Big Z had on his payroll and he was vicious. We were lucky he never connected us to the guys that killed Big Z, because he killed them after he tortured them to death. They were all found with no skin, guts, or head. I made sure to commission some niggas from out of town and gave them a false name, so no one could trace it back to me. Now staring at him holding that big ass knife, I'm willing to beg for mercy.

"Stone man don't let them Niggas torture us like this. Please. I'm begging you. Please use the gun." I begged and pleaded, but Stone ignored me as his eyes turned black.

"Question Stacy. You too Eric. Why'd y'all plot and have my father killed? After he brought y'all into the business, taught y'all all about the game along with me. His sole purpose was so y'all and Red could be my right and left hand, and so we would be unstoppable in the game. He said we could move from state to state and be the biggest kingpins in America. His goal was always for us to run this shit together. So, what made you bitch ass Niggas believe it was okay to violate his trust in this way? Not only did you plot and kill my Pops and set Red up to go to jail, but you sent Niggas to kill Ma. You killed a man that thought of you both like sons and betrayed a Nigga that would have given his life for y'all, but y'all really fucked up when y'all tried to take out my Ma. For that you will pay in blood." Stone spewed crudely as he walked over and grabbed the hunting knife from Switch and approached Eric.

"You let this Nigga lead you to ruin. Now you have no one but yourself to blame for the loss of your family. I'm going to make sure I have your entire bloodline wiped from existence. Don't worry, Stacy's family will be joining yours. Maybe the next muthafuckas that want to bite the hand that feeds them will think twice before fuckin' with me and mines. Y'all both must have forgotten. My Muthafuckin' Name Is Stone!" With that Stone carved out every one of Eric's organs with him screaming after he skinned his ass alive. I begged and pleaded but my cries failed on deaf ears because Stone skinned me until I passed out and everything went black.

Zaylar "Stone" Crewens

I can't believe the Niggas I called family and broke bread with killed my Pops and set my boy Red up. This shit has to be a bad dream. I thought as I finished removing the rest of Stacy's bitch ass organs. Everybody in the warehouse was looking at me cautiously like I was going to spazz out, but I'm good. I just need to get this shit cleaned up and send Steel, Blade, Killian, and Kahmala to kill everyone in them Nigga's family. No one is to be spared all the way down to the pets. I want to make an example so the next muthafucka will think twice before fuckin' with me.

"Kilayla you and Khiershan clean-up these rotten muthafuckas and dispose of the bodies so they will be found. I want my Grandparents to at least be able to bury these grimy muthafuckas and not be worrying about them if they go missing. Blade, Steel, Kahmala, and Killian I want everyone in Stacy and Eric's family dead. Pets included," I told them as I wiped down Switchblade's knife and handed it back to him, hilt out careful not to touch the blade.

"On it." was all Killian said as he pulled out his burner phone and called for the meat wagon. Their family owned a funeral home so we could make them disappear easily, but I wanted them to be found, so that called for a little extra work.

Nico walked up to me and held my head in both of his palms, putting our foreheads together. *"Let that shit go Zay. Go home to your lady and let her soothe the hurt away. We always knew that in order for Pops to get taken out the way it happened. There had to be help from the inside. Then when Red got caught with that kilo in his ride, we knew it had to be a set-up, because Big Z made sure you all never drove your personal vehicles when y'all were riding dirty. I just never expected it was family and Stacy's bitch ass that was behind the shit. You took care of that. Now let that shit go. Don't give them bitches another minute of your time."*

I took a deep breath and let go of the guilt that was riding my back. Like Nico said, *"them bitches didn't deserve another minute of my time."*

Zylar walked up and him, me, and Nico all hugged it out and took a deep breath and just like that. We let it go.

"We gon be good. We all have good women at home to help us remember and forget the bullshit. Let's get out of here." Nico said and we all broke off headed out of the warehouse as the cleaning crew came in and got started.

"AHHH! I'M ABOUT TO Cumm!" Johnya moaned into the pillow as I continued to beat her pussy up from the back. It's been hours since we left the warehouse and I brought Johnya to my house. Time, we entered the door and set the alarm, I pinned her up against the wall, tearing her pussy out the frame. Johnya is the perfect woman for me. She is sweet and quiet, but in bed she's all fire. We have tried every position and she's willing to learn and try whatever.

"Wait, Zay. Hold on, Ahhh!" She cried out as I worked her g-spot over and over without letting up. She has cum so many times that I can barely hear her voice from her screaming out her release.

"Come on baby. I'm not nearly done yet. Look at my pussy squirting out all over my dick. She's talking to me calling my name. Say my name baby. Whose pussy is this Johnya? Tell me whose is it?" I asked, never letting up on my strokes.

"Yours Zaylar. It's all yours. I promise to never give it away. It's all yours baby. Take your pussy. Zay. AHHH, AHHH, AAHHHHH!" Johnya screamed as she came and passed out pussy gripping down on my dick, dragging my nut out from my toes. My back bowed and I roared like a wild animal. I fell to the side trying not to smash Johnya while catching my breath. Making love to Johnya gets better each time. I thought as I got out of bed and went to the bathroom to get cleaned up. After I got washed up I brought a towel out and washed between Johnya's legs and bottom. She didn't stir as I got back in bed and laid her across my chest. I know I was a bit rough with her tonight, but she took everything I had to give and begged for more. This girl is really and truly my soul mate.

281

Zylar Crewens

It was late when I finally decided to make my way home. Half past 3am and my mind is still clouded. I drove around all night trying to come to grips with what all had happened. The events from tonight and the revelations that were revealed have me doing some deep reflection. I opened the door to the house, locked it and set the alarm. As I made my way down to the sitting area with the bar. I spotted Ray lounging on the wrap around sofa under a blanket. She sat up when I walked through the door and took a seat at the bottom of the sofa she was laying on.

"We need to talk?" We both said in unison.

"You first," she said and looked at me waiting for me to start.

I really didn't know where to begin, so I just told her how I felt, *"Ray, I love you and Zan with all my heart and I care about Reign and Rod, but I'm not sure if I'm ready for the level of responsibility involved in taking care of them on a daily basis."*

After thinking about all that Rod revealed last night, I now know that I am nowhere near ready for the level of responsibility that comes with being Ray's man. I love her and my son, but I'm way too young to be living like an old man.

"So, what exactly are you saying?" Ray asked and I was afraid to answer. Knowing this would change everything. She sat forward and looked at me intensely. I could see the raw emotions spread across her face.

"I'm not ready for all this, so I think it's best if I moved out. So I'ma get an apartment for me and we can just co-parent Zander. This house, the cars and all are in your name so you're all set. I just realized I'm only 18 and the level of responsibility that comes with being with you is too much for me," I told her and she just nodded her head.

I swallowed the spit trapped in my mouth and tried to lift my tongue. Then my mouth suddenly went dry, and my head started spinning. I damn near felt dizzy.

Raylexia didn't say anything. She just stared at me for a while and then looked away. She just stared blankly at the bookshelves along the wall behind me. After a while she stood up and looked me directly in the eyes.

"You're sure this is what you want to do? Because once we're done and you walk out that door. There will be no coming back from that. You cheated on me once and I gave you another chance. Since we moved into this house you haven't put forth any effort to be a part of this family or to help us grow as a couple. The streets and clubbing seem to be more important to you than being a part of this family. I didn't think that you could be as cruel as you were today, but you coming up in here saying the shit that you just did without even once asking me if I was good after your mom's place got shot up is telling. You don't give a lovely fuck about me or my wellbeing. We can co-parent and I'll set it up so Mrs. Della can pick Zan up for the visits. I don't wanna be around you for a while. Make arrangements to pick up your stuff before Monday, because I plan to change the locks." Was all Ray said as she picked up her blanket and the baby monitor and left me standing there with a lump stuck in my throat.

When she walked out of the room, I kept thinking I'd just made the biggest mistake of my life.

I DECIDED TO GRAB SOMETHING to wear for tomorrow and headed over to my Ma's place. Letting myself in, I locked the door and reset her alarm. I was headed to her guestroom off the foyer when I heard movement from behind me. I turned to see Ma coming from the kitchen with a water bottle in her hand. *"Hey Ma. What are you doing up so late?"*

"What am I doing up so late? What're you doing in my house? Why are you not home?" She asked as she took notice of the duffle bag I was carrying.

"What's happened Zylar?" Ma asked as she followed me to the guest room where I dropped my bag on the bed and ran my hands through my braids.

"Everything Ma. I didn't know it would be so hard living with someone else and raising kids. Ray never wants to go out and just have fun, Zander is up all times of night needing a diaper change or bottle, and Reign and Rod need constant supervision. It's all just too much, and I can't do it. I love Ray and Zan, but I can't live with them full time. I feel like I'm suffocating," I told Ma.

This was the first time I really explained to anyone how being with Raylexia makes me feel. It's suffocating me slowly to the point where I feel like I'm dying a slow death.

"What do you mean you can't live with them fulltime? What did you do Zylar?" Ma asked me, looking hurt.

I know how much she has come to care about Raylexia, but I am her son and I have to do what's best for me. Trying to stay and make things work with Ray under these circumstances would only end up hurting us both.

"I told Ray that we could co-parent Zander, and I am getting my own place. We have completely different tastes, likes, and dislikes, and all Ray wants to do is stay cooped up in the house all the time. She doesn't enjoy any of the things that I like to do. So, I decided to end things. This way we can at least be friends," I told my Ma who was looking at me funny.

"Okay. What about Zander? How do you plan to help raise him if you're not there? Wait a minute. You said maybe you can still be friends and you're moving out. So does this mean you're no longer a couple?" Ma asked me, sounding all upset.

"Ma I'm not ready for all that responsibility. I plan to provide for Zander and see him often, but I don't want to be in a relationship right now. I'm too young to be tied down," I told her and Ma just walked away.

I know she's disappointed in me, but I would rather us separate now as friends. Then to stay together and become enemies.

Nicclo "Nico" Lorion

"*Nico are you alright?*" Josie asked me as she took the shot glass from my hand and placed it on the coffee table.

"*I'm good Jos. We just learned some foul shit tonight and I'm worried about Zay and Zy. Them Nigga's be trying to act all tough but I know they are hurting inside. Especially Zay. Them Niggas that pulled this shit were his friends. I know he has to be thinking if he wasn't friends with them Niggas, they wouldn't have gotten a chance to hurt Pops. That's where he would be wrong. Grimy muthafuckas like that always find a way to do dirt,*" I told her as I started to undress her.

Josie has been with me since my freshman year of college and I love her more with each passing day. She knows the struggle I have with my father's family and the bullshit behind the succession law. My father is the heir to the Lorion Family and I am his one and only heir. He knows I have no intention of taking over the family, but his family is another story. Having this shit come up with Zay and Zy just made me think about my own fucked up family situation.

The fact that Zy and Zay's aunt actually setup her big brother to die over his money is crazy. Big Z did more than enough for his whole family. While he was alive, he helped them start their own businesses and to purchase their own homes. At every turn he stayed helping them out in some way or another. His little sister Joyce being one of the ones to benefit the most. I just can't understand it.

"*How was the sleepover before the shooting?*" I asked her to change the subject. If I keep thinking about the shit I might just end up putting a hit out on the rest of that fucked up family of theirs.

"*I had fun. Ray and her friends are really talented and smart. They made three new dance routines in just a couple of hours and Ray can sing her ass off.*"

We all got a chance to hear her sing and that girl has some lungs. Shit she's good enough to do it professionally," she told me, sounding animated. It was good to see her smiling and enjoying herself out with friends. Her job is so demanding she rarely has time for anything else.

"You sound like her personal cheering squad." I laughed as I continued to undress her. She was wearing a two pieced silk pajama set that she purchased solely for the slumber party. It did nothing to hide her shapely body underneath.

"Not so much her cheering squad as I can appreciate how talented and down to earth she is. She's also really smart. Did you know she has a double major in business and accounting?" Josie asked me once I finally got her out the rest of her clothes.

"No, I didn't know that. Zylar hasn't told me much about her and what I do know. I found out from the private investigator I hired for Ma. She hasn't had it easy and her Mom's a piece of work," I told her as I slipped a finger inside her folds while massaging her clit. She opened her legs wider giving me full access.

She reached over and undid my belt and unzipped my pants letting them fall to the floor along with my boxers. I stepped out of them as she wrapped her hand around my dick and spread the precum that leaked from the tip over the head all the while massaging my balls with her other hand. All conversation ceased as she went to her knees and took the tip in her mouth. She licked my slit and nibbled on the tip before swallowing my dick whole. All 11 inches slid down her throat as she gagged and swallowed. Josie sucked so hard I rose up on my tiptoes as my seed erupted down her throat. Josie swallowed them all and continued to suck and massage my dick and balls until I was hard again and throbbing.

I grabbed her up and she wrapped her legs around my back as she slid down on my dick as far as she could go. I looked up to see her face contort in pain as she held still trying to adjust to my size. Once I felt her pussy muscles start to relax, I eased in giving her the rest. *"You okay baby?"* I asked, giving her time to adjust once more. Josie nodded and began to slowly ride my dick. Seeing she was good I took over hitting her with long deep strokes making her legs shake and pussy leak like a faucet. I sat back on the couch and Josie spun around and started riding me reverse cowgirl with her leg spread in a split. She reached down to the floor and started bouncing in place on my dick. On each downward stroke I could feel her bumping her g-spot making her shriek in pleasure.

Not to be out done I grabbed her by the hips and placed her on the rug in front of the fireplace as I went in deep from the back. Each time I hit bottom she screamed for more. *"That's it Nico deeper baby! Fuck me harder! OOohhh!"* Josie loved this position because I could go as deep as I wanted and she begged for more. With every stroke her pussy sounded like stirring macaroni. My baby got that gushi.

Cree "C-Lo" Logan

After we finished handling the business with Stacy and Eric, I decided to pick Shamena up and take her home with me tonight. The fact that the Niggas shot up Mrs. C's old crib where the girls were, was an eye opener for me. I really love this girl. The thought of something happening to her made me sick to my stomach, and I have only ever felt this way when I was afraid for my Ma. There was no way I could close my eyes tonight without having her in my arms, and I plan on making her scream my name all night long.

When we made it to my place I drove in and parked in the garage. Once the garage door was shut, I exited the car to open the door for Sha to get out and enter the house through the garage entry door. I was so eager to get inside of Shamena, I damn nearly forgot to set the alarm. Once I finished putting the code in, I grabbed Shamena around the waist and lifted her onto the kitchen island in the center of the floor. I made short work of removing her clothes and attacked her pussy, licking her folds and swallowing her clit. Shamena screamed and started to shake as I switched between licking and sucking and tapping on her clit with my tongue and ball. I made sure to rub the ball underneath the hood stimulating her clit. She came screaming and I licked and slurped up all her juices then started all over again. By the time I released her pussy she was sobbing for me to stop because her sex was so sensitive. That's when I got up, dropped my pants and boxers, and slipped into her wet folds. Her pussy gripped my dick so hard the piercing shut sparks through my dick. I had to concentrate to keep from busting prematurely. Once I counted to ten twice, I threw her legs over my shoulders and went to work. We fucked all over the house christening every room.

"Are you okay, Cree?" Shamena asked me after we both showered and were laying in my bed. *"I enjoyed everything we did, and you made sure to*

pleasure me, but you seem off. I can't describe it but tonight just seemed different somehow. Can you tell me what's wrong?"

"I just realized that I love you and I don't want to lose you. When I got the call from security letting me know about the shooting, I damn near panicked until they let me know everyone was fine and no one was hurt. I haven't been scared like that since back when my dad would beat my Ma. You have come to be a very important part of my life in a very short period of time, so I was trying to assure myself that you were good." I explained and she gave me a shy smile that turned into the cutest little giggle.

"I don't know how alright I am after the hurting you put on my body. I can still feel you deep inside me now. I love to walk around after we have made love. I feel you intimately for hours. It's a wonderful feeling," she told me and kissed me deeply. *"I love you too, by the way."* She whispered in my ear while settling down with her head on my chest and her body wrapped around mine. In no time we were both fast asleep.

Karel "K-O" O'gan

The shit that Stacy and Eric did to Zaylar and Red was grimy as hell. I grew up with them just like Zylar so them Niggas have always been around to some degree, but to find out they have been plotting on Zaylar and his family is unbelievable. The shit just brings to mind that you never really know what a person will do for greed. I thought before shaking my head to clear the shit from my mind. I picked up Shayla and brought her to my crib because I didn't want to be alone, and I wanted to reassure myself that she's good after the shooting.

"This place is beautiful Karel, but don't you think it's a bit much for you alone?" Shayla asked as she walked through my 4 bedroom 5 and a half bath home in the subdivision where Mrs. C's old house is. Me, C-Lo, and Myron got homes for ourselves and our parents in the same area. In fact my parents' home is down the street from the home C-Lo got for his Ma.

"No. I think I can grow into the house and this is the perfect place to raise a family. Whenever you're ready to give me some babies." I answered, causing her to smile wide.

"I'll give you all the babies you can handle once I finish with school. I want to decorate homes and businesses so I plan to study interior design and decoration with a minor in business when I go to college. Since I was already accepted at the University Of Shreveport, I'm just waiting to graduate so I can apply for the summer session. Me and all the girls plan to take the full load each semester so we can finish early," she told me, all animated.

"We have time so I can wait until after you have finished school, but in the meantime let's practice," I told her as I started removing her clothes.

"Yes. We need lots of practice," she said and dropped to her knees to release my dick from my pants. After she freed my member, she tongue kissed the head and nibbled on my slit. Running her tongue down the underside of my

dick she swallowed as much as she could take while sucking hard. From base to tip she used her hands and mouth to suck my dick and massage my balls. I felt that tingling at the base of my spine letting me know I am about to cum. For Shayla to have been a virgin she has some killer head skills. Just the thought of me being the only man she's ever been with feels me with pride. I plan to do everything within my power to keep it that way.

Myron Dax

When I got the call that the party had been shot up my heart dropped to my shoe. I never wanted the street life that I am involved in to affect Shanna in any way, but I see now that was just wishful thinking on my part. The bullshit with Eric and Stacy proves to me that snakes come in all forms and to keep her safe she has to be more aware. That's why as soon as we left the warehouse, I picked up Shanna and brought her back to my crib. I couldn't lay down to rest tonight without telling her enough to keep her safe and make sure she's more aware. After we got to my house, I set the alarm and pulled her into the living room and took a seat on the oversized sofa.

"What's wrong baby? Are you alright?" Shanna asked me and I truly didn't know where to begin explaining all this bullshit. Taking a deep breath. I released it and told her everything I was involved in and how I need her to be careful and more aware of her surroundings. To my shock and surprise, she told me she was aware of what I had been doing for some time, and that my boys talk a lot so the secret has been out.

"Why have you never asked me about what I did or let on that you knew what I did?" I asked, wondering why she was so calm about the situation.

"My for the most part you have kept your dealings in the street away from me, but you do realize that with friends like Jayce and Jamie that use being dope boys as a pickup line y'all secret is no longer a secret right? But to be honest it didn't really bother me, because you put my safety first and never really complained that I didn't want to hang out with you and your boys. So, your other life didn't really intrude on mine. Besides, with the amount of money you started to make I knew it wasn't from legitimate means," she said as she started to undress.

"So you're okay with me being in the drug game?" I asked as I watched her reveal each part of her delicious body.

"I wouldn't say I'm okay with you being in the dope game, but I'm not going to leave you because you are. As long as you continue to keep me safe and put my wants and desires first. I'm rockin 'as long as you're rollin," she told me as she stepped out of her panties.

At that point I forgot everything we were talking about and reached over to grab a handful of her delectable ass. Wrapping my other hand around the back of her neck I smashed my lips with hers and pushed my tongue into her mouth in a brutal kiss. Releasing her lips I licked down her neck until I reached her sensitive spot between collar bone and neck taking a bite then I licked at it with my tongue causing her to shiver in delight. I kissed my way down to her breast before taking her nipple between my teeth and biting gently. She gasped and moaned as I played with her nipples back and forth until she screamed out her first orgasm.

Making quick work of discarding my clothes, I slipped on a condom and slid into the hilt. Shanna's pussy clamped down on my dick like a vice, damn near making me cum prematurely. I held still for a full minute until her pussy muscles started massaging my dick. I started a slow grind that turned into deep penetrating strokes. Shanna took all nine and a half inches while throwing her hips back in a circular motion. We made love all night and slept right there on the living room floor.

Kayden "K-Boy" Blake

I can't believe I let this bitch get me caught up again. I only went to Shaye's house for our regular visit. I should have known she was up to no good when she answered the door wearing a tank top and booty shorts with half her ass hanging out. I had no plans on fuckin' the bitch, but it's just something about that girl I can't resist. We fucked and I fell asleep and she let me sleep for hours. I only woke up when my phone started ringing and I checked the caller id to see it was Deana calling me. That didn't bother me in the least. It was the fact that the time on the caller id read 7:30 pm. I damn near broke my leg jumping out the bed so fast to put on my clothes and tripped over my shoes landing wrong on the floor. I looked up to see Shaye giving me an evil smirk, making me wanna punch this hoe in the face.

"Why the fuck did you let me fall asleep Shaye? You know damn well I don't fuck with you like this. When you started neglecting my daughter, I lost all respect and love I had for you. I can't believe I fell for this bullshit again." I ranted as I quickly got dressed and grabbed Brea headed for my car. While sitting in my truck. I texted Deana back.

Me: Still at Shaye house with Brea, I'll call you as soon as I leave.

My Girl: What type of visit are you having that lasts for 5 hours? Do you take me for a dummy?

Me: No girl I'm telling you we're leaving now. I have to be here for Shaye's visits with Brea because I don't trust Shaye to be alone with Brea and the courts ordered supervised visitation.

My Girl: No, you stay and continue to enjoy your visit. While you're at it. Lose My Number.

That was Deana's last reply and when I tried to text or call her back the call kept going straight to voicemail letting me know she blocked my number.

"Fuck. fuck, fuckkkk!" Was all I could say as I beat up my steering wheel, causing Brea to wake up in the back seat screaming.

"Sorry baby girl, everythings okay. Go back to sleep. Daddy is headed home so you can get in your bed," I told Brea as I started the truck and headed home. I couldn't put my finger on it, but something was telling me that Deana was done with me for good and I felt sick to my stomach.

WHEN WE ALL GOT THE call about Zylar's Ma's house getting shot up, I just knew it was my chance to talk to Deana. To my shock and surprise, she still refused to take my calls. I called her from my burner phones and she hung up as soon as she realized it was me. I was just trying to check and make sure all was good with her but she didn't give me a chance to say anything. We all headed over to the location the security team gave us for them fuck niggas Stacy and Eric just to find them meeting with Zylar's aunt and uncle on his father's side. I can't believe them niggas was working with Big Z's own sister and her husband to take him out. Then we finally learned how Red came up with the drugs in his car. We all knew it was a set up, we just didn't know who did the shit. Even worse, they were trying to kill Zy's Mom too. That's some straight up grimy shit for real for real. The kicker came with watching Zay play doctor as he skinned and cut out all them niggas organs. That shit was chillin because Zay didn't show a lick of emotion while he did that shit. I bet them niggas wished they wouldn't have fucked with that nigga Stone.

Once I made it back in from the warehouse I decided to try Deana one last time. I called her from another burner phone and she answered on the third ring.

"Hello?" She answered sounding asleep'

"Sorry I woke you, but I really needed to make sure you were good after everything that happened tonight," I told her and heard her sigh on the other end.

"I'm good, Kayden, but thank you for your concern." Was her soft reply.

"Can we talk about earlier? Can I explain my side?" I asked while holding my breath waiting for her reply.

"One question. Did you fuck her?" She asked and I dropped my head. Why was that her first question?

"Yes, but I didn't plan it. She just knows how to push my buttons," I told her, refusing to lie about what I have done. Lies lead to more lies and I don't want a relationship built on lies. I made a mistake and I own that mistake, but I won't lie to her to keep her either. I'd rather she hears the truth from me than anyone else.

"I'm glad you're a man about yours and you owned up to it, but there's nowhere for us to go from here. If you being around her caused you to fuck her, you must have unresolved issues that still exist between you. I just wish I hadn't given you something so precious to me, and you turned out not to be who I thought you were. My first lesson with love was a hard lesson, but as my mother keeps telling me you live, and you learn. My heart will hurt for a little while, then I'll shake back." Was all she said to me as I heard the dial tone.

"Fuck man. I think I just lost my one," I said to myself as I went to take a shower before bed.

CHAPTER NINETEEN
Raylexia Gavion

February 21, 2012

I went for my scheduled doctor's appointment with my OB/GYN Dr Dixon to get my birth control shot in good spirits. Rod tried out and made the junior varsity basketball team at his middle school Hyde Middle. He not only made the team but was placed as the starting point guard for the opening game. Which made him very proud. We were told by many people that since he was trying out in his last year of middle school, he may not make the cut, but since he played so well the coach made an exception in his case. I'm happy for him because it was a boost to his ego and kept his mind off the fact that Zylar moved out two and a half weeks ago. I keep telling him that it wasn't his fault and that Zylar just wasn't ready to be a full-time parent or boyfriend. He wants to date other girls and not have to deal with the responsibility of being a full-time parent. Basically, he's not ready to grow up.

It hurts me to admit that he came back into my life only to leave when things got to be a little too real for him. He left and it's as if we never existed as a couple in the first place, but I'm not mad at him in the least. I was actually going to break things off with him, but I decided to let him have his say first. Since he broke up with me, I can move on with my life without having to worry about him being an issue. Mrs. Della picks up Zander every Friday and he stays with her until Sunday to visit with Zylar. Since he has been gone, he's put $7000 into my bank account and buys Zander shoes and clothes, so I have no complaints in regard to financial support. The fact that he folded in a little over two weeks, let's me know he's not the person I want with me to brave the storms coming in my future. If he can't handle our basic day to day stresses, I know he would fold under real pressure and leave me struggling if shit gets real.

Reign is excited that her dad is scheduled to be released in the next three weeks. I told her that once he gets settled, she can stay with him on the weekends.

C-Lo introduced Shayla, Deana, and Johnya's parents to Myron and he is helping them all get qualified for some foreclosed properties over where Mrs. Della's old house is located. Since Myron has his own mortgage company called Dax Home Mortgage, he is handling the sale of the properties and the home loans. That way they didn't have to have perfect credit, just the income to secure the loan amounts required to purchase the homes. In fact, Shayla's mom, Mrs. Sandra, is trying to qualify to purchase Mrs. Della's old home.

Another good thing to come from us all linking back up is that Mrs. Della, Mrs. Chance, Mrs. Sandra, Mrs. Johnny Mae, and Mrs. Danelle have all met and become fast friends. In fact, they have ladies' night at Shanna's Sports Bar & Grill every other Friday night. On the off Friday night, they spend time with the kids out at Mrs. Della's new house in the King's Landing Gated Subdivision where Nico, Zaylar, Mrs Della, and me all have homes built out there on 5 or more acres. My home, in fact, is worth over 8 million with all the renovations and improvements Zylar has done. After Zylar and I split, Myron made me get an appraisal done of my home and the land. It came out to be a little over 8 ½ million dollars.

After some deep soul searching and Shamena being reunited with her father's family. She finally decided to pursue the steps for her to be emancipated. Josie was able to connect her with a family lawyer that got her in to see a family court judge right away. Since we all testified along with the girl's parents that Shamena's mother would put her out of the home randomly and she was not providing for her basic needs. The judge emancipated Shamena February 16, 2012, and she went down to the Social Security Office and had her benefits switched over into her name. It's crazy that Shamena found out that her father was married and she has a 16 year old brother that her mother knew about. She was a typical bitter baby mama that took out all her frustrations on Shamena.

Deana completely broke off all contact with Kayden and has just been concentrating on work and school. She said that she would use this as a learning experience and move on. I can tell that she is disappointed and a little bit sad, but after a long conversation with her mother she has bounced back like the experience never happened.

Both Winkie and Johnya are thriving in their new relationships and I'm happy for them both. Johnya deserves some peace after all the bullshit Tyrone put her through at such a young age. Good thing for her, Zaylar seems to be more than up to the challenge of erasing all the shit Tyrone fucked up. He's even helping Johnya to rebuild her confidence that Tyrone tried to break. My girl is glowing every time I see her, letting me know Zaylar is doing things right. K-O has Winkie smiling as well. After her experience with Marcus, I didn't think Winkie would give a guy a chance for years to come, but K-O sneaked in under her nose and settled down in her heart. She's nowhere near as guarded as she used to be, and she is smiling all the time. Winkie is shy and never really speaks out unless provoked, but I think K-O has got my girl covered.

I was brought out of my thoughts when the nurse called my name and escorted me to the back where she took my vital signs, weight, and height. She asked me how I was feeling and gave me a cup to get a urine sample. She then showed me what room I'd be going to once I finished up in the restroom. I went to the restroom, got the sample, wiped my bottom, washed and dried my hands and sat the specimen cup on the collection table. I then went to the examination room to wait for Dr Dixon. Ten minutes later Dr Dixon came in with my chart and gave me a small smile.

"Hey Raylexia. How have you been doing?" Dr Dixon asked me while frowning down at my chart.

"I've been good. I have no complaints," I told her and waited for her next question.

"Well, I have some bad news. You won't be able to get your birth control shot today because your test came back positive. You're pregnant," she told me, making me look at her as if she was crazy.

"What do you mean I'm pregnant? How can I be pregnant when I'm on the birth control shot? The shot was supposed to last three months. So how can I be pregnant?" I asked her damn near screaming at this point.

"Calm down Raylexia. You know that no form of birth control is 100% effective besides abstinence. Let's check and see how far along you are and discuss

your options. This is not the end of the world you know." Dr Dixon told me trying to sound positive while I'm freaking the fuck out.

"That's easy for you to say. You're not the one that's pregnant while on birth control," I told her as I felt myself start to hyperventilate.

"Breathe Raylexia and relax. No matter what you decide. Everything is gonna be alright." Dr Dixon told me as she walked over to answer the door and roll in the ultrasound machine.

She stepped out of the room to allow me time to undress and put on the hospital gown. Once I was ready, she came back in and performed the ultrasound. I was exactly four and a half weeks pregnant. Meaning I got pregnant the first time Zylar and I had sex. I can't fuckin' believe it.

I got my prescriptions for prenatal vitamins and iron along with my follow-up appointment with Dr Dixon and headed out the office. I was preoccupied with my paperwork and walked straight into the person coming through the door. Immediately my clit began to throb and my heart started to race.

"Sorry I wasn't looking where I was going. Excuse me," I said as I stepped back while lifting my head to see none other than Daylon "Day Day" Belvins himself.

TO BE CONTINUED......

NOTE TO READER

Dear Reader:

Thank you so much for choosing to read my book. I sincerely hope you enjoyed it and that it provided you with a memorable experience.

As a new author in the fiction genre, I rely on feedback from readers like you to grow and improve. If you enjoyed the novel, would you consider leaving a review? It can be as short or as detailed as you like. You can post it where you purchased the book or on any other review platforms you use.

Your support means the world to me and helps other readers discover my work. Thank you again for your time and your thoughts!

I love to hear any feedback about my book and enjoy interacting with my readers, so please feel free to email me at: rjackson318@allureproductionsllc.com authorrenessadjackson@gmail.com

If you would like to sign up for early notification of new releases, sign up here.

Thanks again!

Renessa D Jackson

WHAT'S NEXT ON
YOUR READING LIST?

If you would like to read the first chapter of the next book in the series, here is Chapter One of Luvin A Young Ratchet City Boss 2.

CHAPTER ONE
RAYLEXIA GAVION

February 21, 2012

The moment I saw him, my legs nearly gave out. The sun beaming down mixing with the cold winter air made me lite headed and I swayed on my feet, the heat rising in waves effecting my equilibrium. I should've known I'd bumped into Daylon or Zylar from the intense reaction of my body. *"Fuck,"* I whispered under my breath, the word barely detectable over the hum of traffic passing down the busy street.

"What's the matter, Lil Mama? Cat got your tongue. You look like you've seen a ghost," Daylon taunted, blocking the doorway to trap me inside. The scent of his cologne—a heady mix of sandalwood and something distinctly male—wafted over me, making my head spin.

"Hey Daylon," I managed to say, my voice shaky. Being in his presence rattled me after such a long absence. Just locking eyes with his piercing green gaze made my heart slam against my chest. Breath short, pulse wild, and now my panties soaked. This was the second time he'd affected me like this. Him and Zylar—the only two who ever lit my inner passions.

A gust of wind carried the sterile smell of disinfectant from the clinic's open door, mingling with the aroma of fresh-cut grass from the nearby park. The contrast was shrill, much like Daylon's presence in this dull setting.

"You're tough to track down. But now that you're here, you're not slipping away until we talk. I just need a minute to grab something for my Grams inside, then we're settling this. Don't go anywhere, Lil Mama. We've got unfinished business, and there's something big we need to discuss." He pressed a slow kiss to my forehead, his lips warm against my skin, before slipping inside the building.

The automatic doors whooshed closed behind him, the sound unnaturally loud in the wake of his departure.

Daylon wasn't just a pretty boy; he was a work of perfection. His body was a testament to strength, his arms muscular extensions from a heavily muscled torso, all wrapped in smooth, caramel skin. As I watched his fine self stride away, my mouth watered—it was like I was seeing him for the first time.

He wore an all-black Nike hoodie, dark brown Polo jeans, and wheat Timberlands. A platinum Jesus piece hung around his neck, catching the sunlight and throwing off dazzling reflections. It was complemented by a platinum Rolex with black diamonds on his left wrist, the watch face glinting as he moved.

He radiated power, his confidence thrumming, commanding control in any situation. It was a confidence that captivated everyone, making it clear he was the most dangerous man in any room. As he moved, I noticed all eyes on him—women with lust, men with envy. His presence alone commanded attention.

Not keen on being here when he returned, I rushed to my truck, the gravel crunching under my feet. I jumped in, the familiar creaking of the driver's seat oddly comforting. I fired up the engine, its rumble vibrating through the steering wheel and into my trembling hands. Just as I was about to pull out, a 2012 candy apple red Range Rover blocked my path, its glossy paintwork gleaming under the harsh midday sun.

Looking over, I saw Daylon's older brother, Dayvon, grinning and waving from the driver's seat. I couldn't help but wave back, breaking into giggles and shaking my head. Daylon must have told Dayvon not to let me leave.

With no other option, I killed the engine, the sudden silence broken only by the tick-tick-tick of the cooling metal. I leaned my seat back to relax and steel myself for facing Daylon. The leather seat was warm against my back, and the lingering new-car smell mixed with the faint aroma of the air freshener hanging from my rearview mirror. I hadn't laid eyes on him since that charged night back on June 18, 2010.

As I waited, the weight of the pregnancy test results heavy in my mind, I couldn't help but wonder how this encounter with Daylon would change things—and whether I should tell him about the baby.

FLASHBACK

June 18, 2010

We had just won our last game of the season. Amid the celebration, Zylar pulled me aside to congratulate me. His kiss was deep, breath-stealing, and left me flushed and wanting as he dashed off to meet K-O at the exit. Before I could catch my breath, I was jerked back, my arms clutched tightly, and dragged into the gym's storage room. Panicking, I thrashed around until the lights snapped on and strong arms wrapped around me, pinning my own to my sides.

"Calm down, Lil Mama. It's just me," Daylon's whisper sent a shiver through me, my body tensing as he eased his grip.

"Why the hell would you do that? You scared the hell out of me!" I snapped, spinning to face him while clutching at my racing heart.

"No, you tell me—why were you out there, all over another man like I wasn't even there?" Daylon's voice was low, laced with a dangerous edge that confused and alarmed me.

"Daylon, what are you talking about? Why does my kissing Zylar upset you so much?" I shot back, my mind racing to piece together his over possessiveness.

"Ray, don't play games with me. You think I'll just stand by and watch as you move on with another nigga? I told you I'd wait until you were legal before I made my move. That didn't mean I'd sit back and watch you with someone else. I'm not built like that, and you need to respect that," Daylon said, his eyes a turbulent mix of hurt and anger.

I sighed and dropped my head. This has never been an issue before, because I wasn't attracted to anybody. Now that I am, I don't know how to deal with Daylon's possessiveness.

"Daylon, I'm truly sorry, but I don't feel that way about you. You're like a brother to me, not a romantic interest. I care about you, so I'll stop coming to your games and dancing at your events. That way, you won't have to see me with him," I explained, turning to leave.

Before I could get far, Daylon grabbed me, his grip firm, and pinned my hands above my head. He kissed me roughly, stirring a storm of confusion and feelings I hadn't anticipated. It took me a moment to react. But when his hand moved aggressively, pushed into my shorts and began to rub and massage my clit, the sudden intense sensation overwhelmed me. Then he slid two of his fingers inside me moving them in and out causing me to shake and tremble from the intense sensations running through my body. The feeling was unbelievable and I felt another orgasm coming. Not understanding the feelings, he invoked and trying to make him stop, I trembled, the unexpected rush of pleasure confusing and frightening.

"Daylon, please stop! Please, don't do this!" I managed, turning my head away, to break the kiss, my voice a desperate plea as I struggled to understand the overwhelming emotions and make him stop.

He froze momentarily, then reluctantly lifted himself off me, releasing my hands and withdrawing his fingers. Collapsing to the floor, I curled into a ball, my body shaking uncontrollably. His eyes, ablaze with a fiery emerald intensity mixed with love and lust, bore into me. Deliberately, he licked my juices from his fingers, his gaze never leaving mine, each move thick with unresolved tension.

"I care about you too much to force anything, Lil Mama. If it's something I have to take, then I don't want it at all. But let's get one thing straight—you're still way too young for what I have in mind," he said, his voice rough, his hand gripping the back of his neck in a visible struggle against his own desires.

"I'll give you space but remember this: watch how you move when you're out. Respect my mind, respect the space I'm giving you," he demanded, his frustration palpable. With those final words heavy in the air, he turned and stormed out of the storage room, leaving me alone, enveloped in the echoing aftermath of our confrontation.

End of flashback

I WAS JOLTED BACK TO reality when Daylon tapped on my window. There he was—all 6 feet 3 inches, caramel skin, long lashes, and those lips that seem to promised dark nasty pleasures in kissing. His deep wavy hair was cut into a neat Caesar that screamed 'touch me.' Caught in my not-so-innocent daydream, I nearly drooled over him. When I finally met his eyes, he was smirking, as if he could read every X-rated thought I had about him. *"Damn, Raylexia. Get a grip, girl,"* I scolded myself aloud, fumbling to start the engine and roll down the window.

"So you were just gonna ghost me after I asked you to wait?" he asked, catching my sheepish look as I avoided his gaze.

"It's cool, Lil Mama, but check it—pop the door open for me. We gotta swing by my Grams' place to drop off this package," he said, circling to the passenger side with an expectant look.

Trapped by DayVon, I had no escape. I sighed dramatically, hit the unlock button, and watched him adjust the seat before sliding in.

"You know, it's weird for you to just jump up in my car without an invitation," I teased as he got settled into the seat and adjusted it again to accommodate his large frame.

He gave me a pointed look and ignored what I just said, then gave me directions to his grandmother's house, which, to my surprise, was located in the same gated community as mine. Just sitting next to him, my mind kept screaming for me to reach out and touch him. It got so bad that my fingers were tingling, and I continued to convulsively grip the steering wheel to control myself.

As we pulled up to the entry gate, the guards waved at me. I let down the window and waited for Daylon to either give me his code or buzz his Grams through the intercom for entry permission. He provided the code and instructed me on how to open the gates. Once inside, I followed his directions to his grandmother's home, located on the far side of the community near the duck pond.

The landscape on this side of the estates was breathtaking even in winter, with the frost-kissed grass now muted to a soft, yellowish green. The road is flanked on either side by an eerie yet captivating array of skeleton trees with bare branches arching overhead, forming a delicate pattern against the pale winter sky. Standing tall as silent sentinels against the harsh wind blowing outside.

In some ways, the scenery reminded me of my fucked circumstances at this moment. Leaving me feeling frustrated, conflicted, confused, bemused, and horny as hell. Just sitting here next to Daylon, smelling the light scent of his Creed cologne, makes me so hot and bothered I can hardly concentrate to drive. I can't count the number of times I have squeezed my legs shut to relieve the throbbing of my clit in my jeans.

Luckily for me, we are now approaching the gate leading to her property. We repeated the entry steps, and I drove the short distance to her house. Unlike my two-level home, hers was a sprawling one-story ranch, massive in scale. At the back, a barn with several levels towered over the property. I spotted what looked like three different sets of fenced areas stretching across the grounds. It seemed they had built a ranch right in the middle of the city.

Once parked, Daylon stepped out of the SUV and circled around to open my door. As he reached in to guide me out by my elbow, a spark zipped through me, making the fine hairs on my body stand on end. He let go of my arm as we walked, but his hand soon found a new place on my lower back, steering me up the driveway to the front entry. The touch sent electric pulses straight down to my core, stealing my breath.

I had to pause momentarily, stopping us both right at the doorstep, to steady my breathing. I took in deep breaths of the crisp and invigorating air, filled with the sharp scent of cold earth and pine wood. Each breath helping me to get my raging hormones back under control.

Once composed, Daylon knocked and rang the doorbell. Soon after, the door opened to reveal a beautiful middle-aged woman with the same piercing green eyes as Daylon, who immediately started fussing at him.

"What the hell did I tell you about playing on my door, boy? Either ring the bell or knock, don't do both like I'm not quick enough for you. You keep this up, and I'm gonna break out my strap and whip your behind. Keep playing on my door." She chided him, her eyes twinkling as her lips stretched into a big, Kool-Aid smile. Her playful threat sent me into a fit of uncontrolled giggling. The image of this barely five-foot-tall dynamo threatening to take a strap to six-foot-three Daylon was priceless—I'd pay to see that showdown.

Once I managed to compose myself, I noticed they were both looking at me, amusement in their eyes. I straightened up, wiping the smile off my face. *"Sorry, I just really needed that laugh after the kind of day I've been having. No offense intended. My name's Raylexia, by the way."* Extending my hand, I introduced myself to Daylon's grandmother, who regarded me with a mix of curiosity and warmth.

She grabbed my hand and drew me into a warm embrace. *"My name is Daylandra, and around here, we hug,"* she declared with a comforting smile. I allowed myself to relax a little into the hug, a brief respite from the turmoil swirling in my head.

When we stepped back, she looked at me with a blend of curiosity and kindness. I offered a small smile, trying to mask my inner chaos. As long as she didn't bring up anything to Daylon, I figured I'd manage.

"Grams, meet Ray, my future wife. Please make her feel welcome," Daylon announced with a proud grin, catching me completely off guard.

My head snapped up and over at him, mouth agape. I stared at him, speechless. Could it be true that all these years, when he said I'd be his once I turned eighteen, he wasn't just teasing? The thought that Daylon might have harbored deep feelings for me all this time was overwhelming.

Looking into his eyes, I saw nothing but sincere affection and intent. It dawned on me that his commitment was genuine, explaining all the times he'd gone out of his way to support me. His words left me stunned, yet a warmth began to spread through me, realizing the depth of his feelings.

His grandmother effortlessly sliced through the tension. *"Daylon, where's my prescription?"* she asked, just as I was grappling with my shock and uncertainty.

"With my own set of complications and a past lover who couldn't handle the heat, could I truly trust Daylon's intentions?" I asked myself.

Daylon reached into his jacket, retrieved a prescription bag, and handed it to her. *"Here you go, Grams. The nurse said the doctor gave you a two-month supply to last until your next appointment, and to call them if you need anything sooner."*

"Are you sure she was talking about me, or was that message meant for you?" she quipped, throwing him a playful side-eye.

STAY CONNECTED

@

Join My Email List

Stay up to date with everything happening in Renessa D. Jackson's world-including new releases, upcoming releases, sales, updates, giveaways, events, and more.

Newsletter Link

authorrenessadjackson@gmail.com

CONNECT ON SOCIAL

X
https://x.com/
Allure_Pro_LLC?t=BmAST0NE7pOAgwoMk_v6KA&s=09

Snapchat
https://www.snapchat.com/add/
allure_prollc?share_id=XZnXibghlIk&locale=en-US

Instagram
https://www.instagram.com/allure_productions_llc/

TikTok
https://www.tiktok.com/@allure_productions_llc?lang=en

YouTube
https://www.youtube.com/@AllureProductionsPresentsRenes

Website
https://allureproductionsllc.com/

Renessa D. Jackson Ratchet City Readers Facebook Group
https://www.facebook.com/groups/2070696710014497

ABOUT THE PUBLISHER

Allure Productions LLC is a dynamic publishing company dedicated to bringing powerful, authentic stories to life. Specializing in urban fiction and diverse narratives, we're passionate about amplifying unique voices and delivering captivating tales that resonate with readers. From raw street fiction to heartwarming romances, Allure Productions LLC strives to publish stories that inspire, entertain, and connect with audiences on a personal level. With a commitment to quality and creativity, we're building a platform where compelling stories find their way into the hands of book lovers everywhere.

ABOUT THE AUTHOR

Renessa D. Jackson, a native of Shreveport, LA, was born under the vibrant sign of Aries in April. Her temperament personifies the bright optimism and meticulous organization that her zodiac sign suggests. Her journey through life's challenges has molded her into a determined and confident leader, traits that shine through in every aspect of her personal and professional endeavors.

Renessa's love affair with reading began in her twenties, sparked by the captivating worlds of Manga and Manhwa. This initial spark soon grew into a blazing passion that now includes fanfiction, romance, and urban fiction. Today, she finds joy in exploring a wide array of genres, immersing herself in the diverse and rich narratives that books provide.

Her deep appreciation for literature seamlessly translates into her own writing. As an author, Renessa is excited to welcome readers into the vivid and dynamic stories that have been brewing in her imagination. "Luvin a Young Ratchet City Boss," her debut novel, marks the beginning of the Ratchet City Boss series, promising many more enthralling tales to come.

Contributing to her bustling life, Renessa is surrounded by a loving family, including her six children, grandchildren and host of extended family members and friends.

Renessa continues to call Shreveport home, where she is a cherished and active member of the literary community. She treasures the connections she makes with fellow authors and readers who share her passion for storytelling.

ACKNOWLEDGEMENTS

I would like to extend my heartfelt thanks to my Ratchet City Readers and everyone else who took the time to read my book and provide honest feedback and constructive tips for improvement.

Special thanks to Jonessa Johnson for enduring my wild mood swings and the numerous changes to the cover.

I am immensely grateful to Dr. Dee Davis for assisting with all the technical details that I worried about completing on time.

Shut out to Jaylen Davis for helping me with advertising on the different social media platforms. He is a lifesaver because I am lost in the social media world.

Lastly, I would like to thank my cover model and graphic designer for their patience with my steadfast resolve to remain genuine in my presentation.

9 798330 268764